RICH KID
SMART KID

Para Marisol
y
Victor

D0170361

Rich Dad Series

#1 *New York Times*, #1 *Wall Street Journal*, #1 *Business Week*, #1 *Publishers Weekly*, as well as a *San Francisco Chronicle* and *USA Today* bestseller. Also featured on the bestseller lists of *Amazon.com, Amazon.com UK and Germany, E-trade.com, Sydney Morning Herald* (Australia), *Sun Herald* (Australia), *Business Review Weekly* (Australia) *Borders Books and Music* (U.S. and Singapore), *Barnes & Noble.com.*

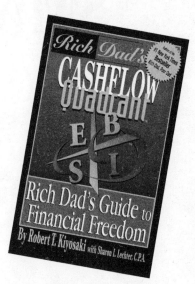

Wall Street Journal, New York Times Business and *Business Week* bestseller. Also featured on the bestseller lists of the *Sydney Morning Herald* (Australia), *Sun Herald* (Australia), *Business Review Weekly* (Australia), *Amazon.com, Barnes & Noble.com, Borders Books and Music* (U.S. and Singapore)

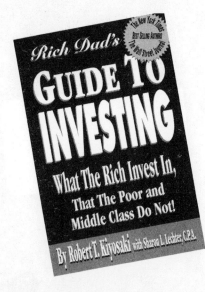

USA Today, Wall Street Journal, New York Times Business, Business Week and *Publishers Weekly* bestseller.

RICH KID SMART KID

Giving Your Child
a Financial Head Start

BY ROBERT T. KIYOSAKI

WITH Sharon L. Lechter, C.P.A.

**BUSINESS
PLUS**

NEW YORK   BOSTON

This publication is designed to provide competent and reliable information regarding the subject matter covered. However, it is sold with the understanding that the author and publisher are not engaged
in rendering legal, financial, or other professional advice. Laws and practices often vary from state to
state and if legal or other expert assistance is required, the services of a professional should be sought.
The author and publisher specifically disclaim any liability that is incurred from the use or application
of the contents of this book.

Although based on a true story, certain events in the book have been fictionalized for educational
content and impact.

Grand Central Publishing Edition

Published by Grand Central Publishing in association with CASHFLOW Technologies, Inc.

Monopoly® is a registered trademark of Hasbro, Inc.

CASHFLOW is a trademark of CASHFLOW Technologies, Inc.

 are trademarks of
CASHFLOW Technologies, Inc.

Business Plus
Hachette Book Group
237 Park Avenue
New York, NY 10017

Visit our Web sites at www.HachetteBookGroup.com and www.richdad.com.

Business Plus is an imprint of Grand Central Publishing.
The Business Plus name and logo are trademarks of Hachette Book Group, Inc.

Printed in the United States of America

First Edition: January 2001
10

LCCN: 00-109230
ISBN 978-0-446-67748-6

This book is dedicated to parents and teachers everywhere.

You have the most important job in the world
because our children are our future!

Table of Contents

Why Your Banker Does Not Ask You for Your Report Card

Education is more important today than at any other time in history. As we leave the Industrial Age behind and enter the Information Age, the value of one's education continues to increase. The question today is, Is the education you or your child receives in school adequate to meet the challenges of this brave new world we enter?

In the Industrial Age you could go to school, graduate, and start your career. You usually did not need additional education to succeed simply because things did not change that fast. In other words, the education you learned in school was all you needed for your lifetime.

As millions of baby boomers get ready to retire today, however, many are faced with the realization that they have not been adequately educated for the new world they face. For the first time in history, many well-educated people are facing the same economic difficulties that the less educated are facing. They repeatedly find themselves having to get additional education and training in order to satisfy their current job requirements.

When Do You Measure the Success of Your Education?

When do you measure the success of your education? Is it the final report card the day you graduate from school, let's say at age twenty-five, or is education's effectiveness measured when you retire, let's say at age sixty-five?

In the Sunday, July 16, 2000, issue of my local paper, the *Arizona Republic,* an article included the following statistic: "About 700,000 seniors will be cut from their Medicare Choice HMOs according to a survey released earlier this month by the American Association of Health Plans."

The article went on to state that providing health care for senior citizens was too expensive and was not profitable for insurance companies, so senior citizens are being dropped from supplemental health care protection. The health care problem for seniors will only increase, as seventy-five million baby boomers hit that age bracket in the next ten years.

Health Education and Welfare Stats

Based on a study performed by the Department of Health, Education and Welfare, of every one hundred people at age sixty-five, one is rich, four are comfortable, five are still working, fifty-six are needing government support or family support, and the rest are dead.

It is not becoming the one rich person that this book is about. It is the fifty-six who still need someone else to support them I am concerned about. I do not want you or your child to wind up in that big statistic.

People often say to me, "I won't need much money when I retire because when I retire, my living expenses go down." While it is true that your living expenses may go down after you retire, there is one thing that often goes up dramatically, and that is health care. And that is why the HMOs (health maintenance organizations) in the previous article are cutting seniors from supplemental medical coverage. Senior citizens are just too expensive to cover. In the next few years it will be clear that health care will literally be a life-and-death issue for millions of older people. Putting it bluntly, if you have money, you may live; and if you don't have money, you may die.

The question is, Did these senior citizens' education prepare them for this financial challenge at the end of their lives?

The next question is, What does the plight of these senior citizens have to do with your child's education?

There are two answers to these two questions.

Answer number one is that it is your child who will ultimately have to pay for the health care of these millions of senior citizens if they cannot pay for it themselves.

Answer number two is another question: Will your children's education prepare them to be financially secure enough not to need government financial and medical support at the end of their working days?

The Rules Have Changed

In the Industrial Age, the rules were go to school, get good grades, find a safe, secure job with benefits, and stay there all your life. After twenty years or so you retire, and the company and the government take care of you for the rest of your life.

In the Information Age, the rules have changed. The rules now are go to school, get good grades, find a job, and then retrain yourself for that job. Find a new company and a new job and retrain. Find a new company and a new job and retrain, and hope and pray you have enough money set aside to last you much longer than age sixty-five because you will live well beyond the age of sixty-five.

In the Industrial Age, the defining theory of the era was Einstein's $E = mc^2$. In the Information Age, the defining theory of the era is Moore's law, which spawned the current ideology that the amount of information doubles every eighteen months. In other words, to keep up with change, you need to virtually relearn everything every eighteen months.

In the Industrial Age, change was slower. What you went to school to learn was valuable for a longer period of time. In the Information Age, what you know becomes obsolete very quickly. What you learned is important, but not as important as how fast you can learn, change, and adapt to new information.

Both my parents grew up during the Great Depression. For them job security was everything, which is why there was always a little bit of panic in their voice when they said, "You must go to school so you can get a safe, secure job." In case you have not noticed, today jobs are plentiful. The challenge is not to get left behind because you become obsolete working at your current job.

Other subtle yet significant changes between the ages:

In the Industrial Age, the employer was responsible for your retirement plan.

In the Information Age, the employee is responsible. If you run out of money after age sixty-five, it is your problem, not the company's problem.

In the Industrial Age, you became more valuable the older you got.
In the Information Age, you become less valuable the older you get.

In the Industrial Age, people were employees for life.
In the Information Age, more people are now free agents.

In the Industrial Age, the smart kids went on to become doctors and lawyers. They made the big bucks.

In the Information Age, the people who make the big bucks are the athletes, actors, and musicians. Many of the doctors and other professional people are actually making less than they did in the Industrial Age.

In the Industrial Age, you could count on the government to bail you out if you and your family got in financial trouble.

As the Information Age begins, we hear more and more politicians promising to save Social Security and other government safety net programs. You and I are smart enough to know that when politicians begin to make promises to save something, the chances are what they are proposing to save is already gone.

When change occurs there is typically resistance. In the last few years there are many examples of people recognizing the opportunities that arise during a period of change.

1. Bill Gates became the richest man in the world because the older men at IBM failed to see the market and the rules changing. Because of these older executives' failure to see these changes, the investors in IBM literally lost billions of dollars.
2. Today we have Information Age companies, started by twenty-year-olds, buying Industrial Age corporations run by forty-five-year-olds (AOL and Time Warner are two examples).

3. Today we have twenty-year-olds becoming billionaires because forty-five-year-old executives failed to see the opportunities the twenty-year-olds saw.

4. Today we have twenty-year-old self-made billionaires who have never had a job, and at the same time we have forty-five-year-olds who are starting over, retraining for a new job.

5. It is said that in the near future, the individuals will go on-line and bid for jobs rather than apply for jobs. It is said that people who want jobs longer than a year (greater security) will have to accept less money for that security.

6. Instead of hoping to find a good job with a big company, more and more students are starting their own businesses in their dorm rooms. Harvard University even has a special office that assists students in developing their incubator businesses—touted as a way to help them build the business, but more likely intended as an incentive to keep them in school.

7. And at the same time, half of the employees of one of America's largest employers earn so little that they qualify for food stamps. What will happen to these employees when they are too old to work? Was their education adequate?

8. Home schooling is no longer a fringe form of alternative education. Today the number of kids being educated at home is increasing by 15 percent per year.

9. More and more parents are seeking other educational systems, such as the Catholic system, Waldorf, or Montessori, just to remove their children from an antiquated government-run educational system that does not cater to their child's needs. More and more parents realize that their child's early education is as important to a child's development as college is.

    Super Camp is a shorter-term, intensive learning environment utilizing the latest teaching techniques to improve test scores and increase a teen's self-confidence. It is sponsored by the Learning Forum and can be found at www.supercamp.com.

10. Simply put, the Information Age will bring economic changes that will dramatically increase the gap between the haves and have-nots. For some people, these changes will be a blessing; for others, these com-

ing changes will be a curse; and for still others, these changes will make no difference at all. As my rich dad said, "There are people who make things happen; there are people who watch things happen; and there are people who say, 'What happened?'"

Education Is More Important Than Ever Before

Education is more important than ever before because things will be changing faster than we have ever seen before. For the first time in history, those who do well in school may face the same economic challenges as those who did not do well. All of us need to pay attention when our bankers ask for our financial statements rather than our report cards. Your banker is trying to tell you something. This book is about what your children need to learn for personal and financial success in the real world.

Is the education your children are receiving today adequately preparing them for the future they face?

Is the school system catering to the special needs of your child?

What do parents do if their child dislikes school or is doing poorly in school?

Do good grades insure lifelong professional and financial success?

Does your child even need to go to a traditional brick-and-mortar school in order to receive the education he or she needs?

Whom Is This Book For?

This book is written for parents who realize that the world has changed and suspect that our current system of education may not be adequately catering to the special needs of their children. This book is written for parents who are willing to take a more active role in their child's education, rather than leave the responsibility to the school system.

It is written to assist parents in preparing for the real world . . . the world after school is over. It is written specifically for parents who:

want to give their child a financial head start in life without costing them a fortune.

want to insure that their child's natural genius and learning style are protected and their child leaves school excited about being a lifelong learner.

may have a child who does not like school or a child who is having difficulty learning in school.

All of the above.

How This Book Is Organized

This book is written in three parts.

Part I is an overview of education both academic and financial. Those who have read my other books already know that I had two father figures in my life. One man I called my rich dad was my best friend Mike's dad; and one man I called my poor dad was my real dad. The benefit I had was that both men were geniuses in their own right. The man I call my poor dad in my opinion was an academic genius and educator. After the age of nine I began having serious problems in school. I did not like what I was learning and how I was being taught. I saw no relevance between what I was being forced to learn and how I could apply it to the real world.

Part I of this book was how my smart but poor dad continued to guide me through this very difficult part of my life. If not for my smart dad, I would have dropped or flunked out of school and never would have gone on to graduate with my college degree.

Part I of this book is also about the educational process my other dad, rich dad, put me through. I would say my rich dad was a financial genius and also a great teacher. In part I of this book I explain how rich dad began preparing my young mind to think like a rich person. Between the ages of nine and twelve and because of my rich dad's guidance, I was absolutely certain that I would attain great wealth, whether or not I did well in school or got a high-paying job. By the age of twelve I knew that becoming rich had little to do with what I was learning in school. Knowing I was going to be rich, regardless of how I did in school, did create some unique attitude problems for me while I was still in school. Part II of this book is how both dads worked to keep my attitude problem in check and guided me to complete my college education.

Part II is about some simple action steps, academically and financially, parents can take to begin preparing their child for the real world. I begin part

II with a story of how I almost failed high school because of my changes in attitude about school. In part II you will begin to gain further insights into how my smart dad and rich dad kept me in school and how my rich dad used my academic failures to prepare me to become rich.

In part II my rich dad explains to me why his banker never asked him for his report card. My rich dad goes on to say, "My banker has never asked me if I had good grades. All my banker wants to see are my financial statements. The problem is, most people leave school not knowing what a financial statement is." Rich dad would also say, "Understanding how financial statements work is essential for anyone wanting to build a life of financial security." And in today's world of less and less job security, it is essential that your child have the skills to insure a life of financial security.

When you look at an overview of the current educational system, it is obvious that the system focuses on two main areas of education:

Scholastic Education: the ability to read, to write, and to do arithmetic.
Professional Education: the education to become a doctor, lawyer, plumber, secretary, or whatever you want to do to earn money once you leave school.

America and many Western nations have done an excellent job in making these two fundamental types of education available to their citizens. This education has contributed greatly to the advantage the West has in the world today. The problem is, as stated previously, the rules have changed. In the Information Age, we need more new education, not more of the same education. Each and every student now needs some of the basic education my rich dad gave me:

Financial Education: the education required to turn the money you earn from your profession into lifelong wealth and financial security. The financial education those seven hundred thousand senior citizens didn't have. The financial education that will help insure that your child does not wind up a financial failure late in life or financially destitute and alone after a life of raising a family and working hard.

The reason your banker does not want to see your report card is that he or she wants to see how smart you are after you leave school. He or she wants to see a measure of your financial intelligence, not your scholastic intelligence. Your financial statement is a much better measure of your financial intelligence than your report card.

Part II has some simple, concrete examples of things parents can do to give their child a financial head start into the real world of jobs and money.

Part III is about some of the latest technological breakthroughs in education that will enhance parents' ability to find their child's natural learning ability and natural genius. Part III is about giving your child an academic head start.

Years ago one of Albert Einstein's teachers scoffed and said, "He will never amount to anything." Many teachers thought him dull-witted because of his failure to learn by rote memorization.

A year later in his life, when Einstein was told that a prominent inventor declared that fact knowledge was vitally important, Einstein disagreed. He said, "A person does not need to go to college to learn facts. He can learn them from books. The value of a liberal arts college education is that it trains the mind to think." He also said, "Imagination is more important than knowledge."

While being questioned by a group of reporters, one asked, "What is the speed of sound?" Einstein replied, "I don't know. I don't carry information in my mind that is readily available in books."

Almost every parent I have met is certain that his or her child is smart and a genius. When that child reaches school, however, the child's natural genius is often shoved aside or takes a subordinate role to the single genius and single learning style emphasized by the educational system as the right way to learn. My smart dad and many other educators realize that the current school system does not cater to the various different geniuses that children are born with.

It is unfortunate that our current educational system is mired in controversy and old ideas. While our current system may be aware of many of these educational breakthroughs, the politics and red tape surrounding the profession of education prevent many of these new innovative ways of assessing your child's genius from becoming part of the system.

My smart dad was the head of the educational system of Hawaii. He did his best to change the system but was crushed by the system instead. He later said to me, "There are three different types of teachers and administrators in the system. There is one group that works diligently to change the system. There is another group that works diligently against any kind of change. And the third group does not care if the system changes or not. All this group wants is their job security and their paycheck. And that is why the system has remained the same for years."

In Conclusion

It was my smart dad who often said, "A child's most important teachers are his or her parents. Many parents say to their children, 'Go to school and study hard. A good education is important.' The problem is that many parents who say these words do not continue with their own education or studies." My smart dad also said, "Parents are the child's most important teachers . . . but students learn by watching more than they do by listening. Children are tuned in to watching for discrepancies between words and actions." Children love to catch parents saying one thing and doing something else. My rich dad used to say, "Your actions speak louder than your words." He also said, "If you want to be a good parent, you need to walk your talk."

If you have children, I thank you for taking an interest in a book on education and an interest in your children's education. Most parents say their child's education is important, but few pick up books on educating their children.

AUDIO DOWNLOAD

In each of our books we like to provide an audio interview as a bonus with additional insights. As a thank-you to you for reading this book, you may go to the Web site www.richdad.com/richkid and download an audio of my discussion with Kathy Kolbe called "Find Out How Your Child Learns Best . . . Because All Children Learn Differently."

Thank you for your interest in your child's financial education.

"*Money Is an Idea*"

*W*hen I was a little boy, my rich dad often said, "Money is an idea." He would go on to say, "Money can be anything you want it to be. If you say, 'I'll never be rich,' then the chances are you'll never be rich. If you say, 'I can't afford it,' then chances are you can't."

My smart dad said much the same about education.

Is it possible that every child is born with the potential to be rich and smart? There are some people who think it is possible . . . and there are others who don't. The first part of this book is dedicated to protecting that possibility for your child.

Chapter 1

All Kids Are Born Rich Kids and Smart Kids

Both my dads were great teachers. Both men were smart men. But they were not smart in the same subjects, and they did not teach the same things. Yet as different as they were, both dads believed the same things about all kids. Both dads believed that all kids are born smart and all kids are born rich. Both believed a child learns to be poor and learns to believe that he or she is less smart than other kids. Both dads were great teachers because they believed in bringing out the genius that each child is born with. In other words, they did not believe in putting knowledge *in,* they believed in bringing the child's genius *out.*

The word *education* comes from the Latin word *educare,* which means "to draw out." Unfortunately for many of us, our memories of education are long, painful sessions of cramming little bits of information into our heads, memorizing them for the test, taking the test, and then forgetting what we had just learned. Both my dads were great teachers because they rarely tried to cram their ideas into my head. They often said very little, waiting instead for me to ask when I wanted to know something. Or they *asked me* questions, seeking to find out what I knew, rather than simply *telling me* what they knew. Both my dads were great teachers, and I count them as some of the top blessings in my life.

And not to forget the moms. My mom was a great teacher and role model also. She was my teacher for unconditional love, kindness, and the importance of caring for other people. Unfortunately my mom died at the young age of forty-eight. She had been sick most of her life, battling with a heart weakened from rheumatic fever from childhood. It was her ability to be kind and loving to others in spite of her personal pain that taught me a vital lesson. Many times when I am hurt and want to lash out at others, I simply think of my mom and remember to be kinder . . . instead of angrier. And for me, that is an important lesson I need reminding of daily.

I once heard that boys marry women just like their moms, and I would say that is true for me. My wife, Kim, is also an extremely kind and loving person. I regret that Kim and my mom never got to meet each other. I think they would have been best of friends, as Kim is with her mother. I wanted to have a wife who was also my partner in business, because the happiest days of my parents' marriage were the days they worked together in the Peace Corps. I remember when President Kennedy announced the creation of the Peace Corps. Both my mom and dad were thrilled by the idea and could not wait to be a part of the organization. When my dad was offered the position as director of training for Southeast Asia, he took it and asked that my mom be the staff nurse. I believe those were the happiest two years in their marriage.

I did not know my best friend Mike's mom very well. I saw her when I was over for dinner, which was often, but I cannot say I really knew her. She spent a lot of time with her other kids, while Mike and I spent most of our time with his dad at work. Yet the times I was over at their home, Mike's mother was also very kind and attentive to what we were doing. I could tell that she was a great life partner for Mike's dad. They were affectionate, kind, and interested in whatever was going on with each other. Although a very private person, she was always interested in what Mike and I were learning at school and in the business. So although I did not know her very well, I learned from her the importance of listening to others, letting others talk, and being respectful to the ideas of others even if they clashed with your ideas. She was a great communicator in a very quiet way.

Lessons from Mom and Dad

The number of single-parent families I see today concerns me. Having both a mom and a dad as teachers was important in my development. For example, I was bigger and heavier than most kids, and my mom was always afraid that I would use my size advantage and become a bully. So she really stressed that I develop what people today would call "my feminine side." As I said, she was a very kind, loving person, and she wanted me to also be kind and loving. And I was. One day I came home from the first grade with my report card, and on it the teacher had written, "Robert needs to learn to assert himself more. He reminds me of Ferdinand the Bull [from the story about a big bull that instead of fighting the matador sat down in the ring and smelled the flowers the fans were throwing . . . coincidentally one of my mom's favorite bedtime stories for me]. All the other boys pick on him and push him around, although Robert is so much bigger than they are."

When my mom read the report card, she was thrilled. When my dad came home and read the same report card, he turned into a raging bull, and not one that smelled the flowers. "What do you mean the other boys push you around? Why do you let them push you around? Are you turning into a wimp?" he said, noticing the comment about my behavior rather than my grades. When I explained to him that I was just listening to Mom's instructions, my dad turned to my mom and said, "Little boys are bullies. Learning how to deal with bullies is important for all kids to learn. If they do not learn how to deal with bullies early in life, they often grow up allowing themselves to be bullied as adults. Learning to be kind is one way of dealing with bullies, but so is pushing back, if and when kindness does not work."

Turning to me, my dad asked, "And how do you feel when the other boys pick on you?"

Bursting into tears, I said, "I feel terrible. I feel helpless and afraid. I don't want to go to school. I want to fight back, but I also want to be a good boy and do what you and Mom want me to do. I hate being called 'fatty' and 'Dumbo' and being pushed around. What I hate most is just standing there and taking it. I do feel like I am a sissy and a wimp. Even the girls laugh at me because I just stand there and cry."

My dad turned to my mom and glared at her for a moment, letting her know that he did not like what I was learning. "So what do you want to do?" he asked.

"I'd like to hit back," I said. "I know I can beat them. They're just little punks who pick on people, and they like picking on me because I am the biggest in my class. Everyone says don't hit them because I am bigger, but I just hate standing there and taking it. I wish I could do something. They know I won't do anything, so they just keep picking on me in front of everyone else. I'd love to just grab them and punch their lights out."

"Well, don't hit them," my dad said quietly. "But you let them know in whatever way you can that you are not going to be picked on anymore. You are learning a very important lesson in self-respect right now and standing up for your rights. Just don't hit them. Use your mind to find a way to let them know that you will not be picked on anymore."

My crying stopped. I felt much better as I wiped my eyes and found some courage and self-esteem reentering my body. I was now ready to go back to school.

The next day my mom and my dad were called to my school. The teacher and the school principal were very upset. As my mom and dad entered the room, I was sitting in a chair in the corner, splattered with mud. "What happened?" my dad asked as he took his seat.

"Well, I can't say that the boys did not have it coming to them," said the teacher. "But after I wrote you the note on Robert's report card, I knew something would change."

"Did he hit them?" my dad asked with great concern.

"No, he didn't," said the principal. "I watched the whole thing. The boys began teasing him. But this time, Robert asked them to stop instead of just standing there and taking it . . . yet they continued. He patiently asked them to stop three different times, and they just taunted him more. Suddenly Robert went back into the classroom, grabbed the boys' lunch pails, and emptied them into that big mud puddle. As I rushed over from across the lawn, the boys then attacked Robert. They started hitting him, but he did not hit back."

"What did he do?" my dad asked.

"Before I could get there to break it up, Robert grabbed the two boys and pushed them into the same mud puddle. And that is how he got splattered with mud. I sent the other boys home to change their clothes because they were soaking wet."

"But I didn't hit them," I said from my corner.

My dad glared at me, put his index finger over his lips indicating that I should shut up, then turned back to the principal and teacher and said, "We will take care of this at home."

The principal and the teacher nodded their heads as the teacher said, "I'm glad I was witness to the whole event developing over the past two months. If I had not known the history leading up to the mud puddle event, I would have reprimanded only Robert. But you may rest assured that I will be having the parents and the other two boys in for counseling also. I do not condone throwing the boys and their lunches into the mud, but I hope now we will see an end to this bullying that has been going on between the boys."

The next day there was a meeting between the two boys and me. We discussed our differences and shook hands. At recess that day, other kids came up to me and shook my hand and patted me on the back. They were congratulating me for standing up to the two bullies who were also picking on them. I thanked them for their congratulations but also said to them, "You should learn to fight your own fights. If you don't, you will go through life being a coward, letting the bullies of the world push you around." My dad would have been proud hearing me repeat his original lecture to me. After that day, the first grade was much more pleasant. I had gained some valuable self-esteem, I gained respect from my class, and the prettiest girl in my class became my girlfriend. But what was more interesting was that the two bullies eventually became my friends. I learned to bring peace by being strong rather than allowing terror and fear to persist because I was weak.

Over the next week, I learned several valuable life lessons from both my mom and dad from this mud puddle incident. The mud puddle incident was a hot topic of discussion at dinner. I learned that in life there is not a right answer or a wrong answer. I learned that in life we tend to make choices, and each choice has a consequence. If we do not like our choice and consequence, then we should look for a new choice with a new consequence. From this mud puddle incident, I learned the importance of being both kind and loving from my mom and being strong and prepared to fight back from my dad. I learned that too much of one or the other, or only one and not the other, can be self-limiting. Just as too much water can drown a plant dying of thirst, we humans in our behavior can often swing too far in one direction or the other. As my dad said the night we got back from the principal's office, "Many people live in a black-and-white world or a right-and-wrong world. Many people would have advised you, 'Never push back,' and still others would have said, 'Push back.' But the key to being successful in life is this: If you must push back, you must know exactly how hard to push back. Knowing exactly how hard to push requires much more intelligence than simply saying, 'Don't push back,' or, 'Push back.'"

My dad would often say, "True intelligence is knowing what is *appropriate* rather than what is simply *right* or *wrong*." As a six-year-old boy, I learned from my mom that I needed to be kind and gentle . . . but I also learned that I could be *too* kind and gentle. From my dad I learned to be strong, but I also learned I need to be intelligent and appropriate with my strength. I have often said that a coin has two sides. I have never seen a one-sided coin. But all too often we forget that fact. We often think the side we are on is the *only* side or the right side. When we do that, we may be smart, we may know our facts, but we also may be limiting our intelligence.

One of my teachers once said, "God gave us a right foot and a left foot. God did not give us a right foot and a *wrong* foot. Humans make progress by first making a mistake to the right and then making a mistake to the left. People who think they must *always be right* are like people with only a right foot. They think they are making progress, but they usually wind up going in circles."

I think as a society we need to be more intelligent with our strengths and our weaknesses. We need to learn to operate more intelligently from our feminine side as well as our masculine side. I remember when I was angry with another guy at school back in the 1960s, we would occasionally go behind the gym and fight with our fists. After one or two punches were thrown, we would begin to wrestle and get tired, and then the fight would be over. The worst that ever happened was an occasional torn shirt or bloody nose. We often became friends after the fight was over. Today kids get angry, start thinking in the less intelligent "right and wrong" thinking, break out their guns, and shoot each other . . . and that goes for both boys and girls. We may be in the Information Age and kids may be more "worldly" than their parents, but we could all learn to be more intelligent with our information and our emotions. As I said, we need to learn from both our moms and our dads, because with so much more information, we need to become more intelligent.

This book is dedicated to parents who want to raise kids who are smarter, richer, and also more financially intelligent.

Chapter 2

Is Your Child a Genius?

"What's new?" I asked a friend I had not seen in several years. He immediately pulled out his wallet and showed me a picture of his eleven-month-old daughter. Smiling proudly, he said, "She is so smart. I cannot believe how fast she learns." For the next twenty minutes this proud dad related in exacting detail all the things his brilliant daughter was learning. Finally he realized that he had not stopped talking and said apologetically, "I'm sorry. I'm just so proud of my daughter. I am just amazed at how smart she is and how fast she learns. I'm certain she is a genius."

Is this proud boasting limited to only a few new parents? I think not. At least not in my experience. If there is one thing I have noticed from my observation of all parents, it is that they are all astounded by how fast their children learn. Every new parent I have met is sure that his or her child is the smartest in the world, maybe even a genius. And I agree with them. I think all children are born geniuses. But for many children, something happens to that genius along the way as they grow up. For some children, that genius seems to disappear, gets pushed down, or goes in other directions.

Although my wife, Kim, and I do not have children, newborn babies always fascinate me. I love looking in their eyes. When I look into their eyes, I see a most curious and inquisitive being staring back. It is easy to see that children are learning in quantum leaps. By quantum, I mean learning exponentially. Their knowledge base must be doubling each second. Everything they can soak in with their eyes is new, is a wonderment, and is being added to their databank unedited, qualified, or without much prejudice. They are soaking in this new experience called life.

Just the other day I went to another friend's home. He was in the pool with his three-year-old daughter. As I waved and walked up to the pool, he shouted, "Look at my little girl. She is going to be an Olympic swimming star." I watched this little girl bravely churning up the water, nearly drowning, but still making progress as she swam toward her proud father. I held my breath as this young girl, who had no flotation devices on and was barely getting her head up to get a breath of air, thrashed her way toward her dad, waiting in the deep end of the pool. Finally I sighed in relief as her dad put his arms around her and said, "That's my brave little swimmer. You're going to be an Olympic swimming star someday." And I think she will be.

What was amazing to me was that only a week before, this same little girl was terrified of the water. Only a week before, she was so afraid of the water, she cried when her dad carried her into the pool. Now he is calling her a future Olympic swimming star. That, to me, is the kind of quantum learning only a genius is capable of . . . and every child is born capable of learning at that level.

My Dad Believed That All Kids Are Born Geniuses

As described in an earlier book, *Rich Dad Poor Dad,* my real dad was the superintendent of education of the state of Hawaii in the late 1960s and early 1970s. He ultimately resigned from office to run for lieutenant governor of the state as a Republican, which was not the smartest of decisions. He chose to run out of moral conscience. He was very upset with the levels of corruption he found in government, and he wanted to change the educational system. He thought that he could do something to reform the system if he ran for office. Knowing that he would probably not win, he ran anyway and used his campaign to bring to light the wrongs he thought should be righted. But as we all know, the public does not always vote for the most honest and truthful candidates.

I still believe my dad was an academic genius. He was a voracious reader, a great writer, a brilliant speaker, and a great teacher. He was a top student all through school and served as a class officer. He graduated from the University of Hawaii way ahead of the rest of his class and went on to become one of the youngest school principals in Hawaii's history. He was invited to do graduate work at Stanford University, the University of Chicago, and Northwestern University. In the late 1980s he was selected by his peers as one of the top two educators in Hawaii's 150-year history of public education and awarded an honorary doctorate degree. Even though I call him my poor dad because he was always broke regardless of how much money he made, I was very proud of him. He often said, "I'm not interested in money." And he also said, "I'll never be rich." And those words became self-fulfilling prophecies.

After reading *Rich Dad Poor Dad,* many people say, "I wish I had read this book twenty years ago." Some then ask, "Why didn't you write it earlier?" My reply is, "Because I waited for my dad to pass on before writing it." I waited for five years out of respect. I know the book would have hurt him if he'd read it when alive . . . but in spirit form, I think he supports the lessons that we all can learn from his life.

In this book, *Rich Kid Smart Kid,* many of the ideas about how children learn and why all children are born smart come from my dad. The following story is about a classmate of mine who was labeled a genius early in life. It is also about how we are all geniuses in one way or another.

Does Your Child Have a High Financial IQ?

When you say someone has a high IQ, what does that mean? What does your IQ measure? Does having a high IQ guarantee that you will be successful? Does having a high IQ mean you will be rich?

When I was in the fourth grade, my teacher announced to the class, "Students, we are honored to have a genius in our midst. He is a very gifted child, and he has a very high IQ." She then went on to announce that one of my best friends, Andrew, was one of the brightest students she had ever had the privilege to teach. Up until that time, "Andy the Ant," as we all called Andrew, was just one of the kids in the class. We called him "Andy the Ant" because he was tiny and had thick glasses that made him look like a bug. Now we had to call him "Andy the Brainy Ant."

Not understanding what IQ meant, I raised my hand and asked the teacher, "What does IQ mean?"

The teacher sputtered a little and replied, "IQ means intelligence quotient." She then gave me one of those glaring looks that said silently, "Now do you know what IQ means?"

The problem was, I still had no idea what IQ meant, so I raised my hand again. The teacher did her best to ignore me, but finally she turned and said in a long-drawn-out tone, "Yes. What is your question this time?"

"Well, you said IQ stood for intelligence quotient, but what does that mean?"

Again she sputtered a little with impatience. "I told you that if you did not know the definition of something, you should look it up. Now get the dictionary and look it up for yourself."

"Okay," I said with a grin, realizing that she did not know the definition either. If she had known, she would have proudly told the entire class. We knew that when she did not know something, she would never admit it but instead tell us to look it up.

After finally locating "intelligence quotient" in the dictionary, I read the definition out loud. Quoting directly, I read, "Noun (1916): A number used to express the apparent relative intelligence of a person determined by dividing his mental age as reported on a standardized test by his chronological age and multiplying by 100." When I finished reading the definition, I looked up and said, "I still don't understand what IQ means."

Frustrated, the teacher raised her voice and said, "You don't understand because you don't want to understand. If you don't understand it, then you need to do your own research."

"But you're the one who said it was important," I shot back. "If you think it's important, at least you can tell us what it means and why it's important."

At that point Andy the Ant stood up and said, "I'll explain it to the class." He climbed out from behind his wooden desk and walked to the chalkboard at the front of the room. He then wrote on the board:

$$\frac{18 \text{ (mental age)}}{10 \text{ (chronological age)}} \times 100 = 180 \text{ IQ}$$

"So people say I am a genius because I am ten years of age but have test scores of a person who is eighteen years of age."

The class sat silently for a while to digest the information that Andy had just put on the board.

"In other words, if you don't increase your abilities to learn as you get older, then your IQ could come down," I said.

"That's how I would interpret it," said Andy. "I might be a genius today, but if I don't increase what I know, my IQ comes down with each year. At least that is what the equation represents."

"So you could be a genius today but be a dummy tomorrow," I said with a laugh.

"Very funny," said Andy. "But accurate. Yet I know I don't have to worry about you beating me."

"I'll get even after school," I shouted back. "I'll meet you on the baseball diamond and then we'll see who has the higher IQ." With that I laughed, and so did other students in the class. Andy the Ant was one of my best friends. We all knew he was smart, and we knew he would never be a great athlete. Yet even though he could not hit or catch the ball, he was still very much a part of our team. After all, that is what friends are for.

What Is Your Financial IQ?

So how do you measure people's financial IQ? Do you measure it by how big their paycheck is, their net worth, the kind of car they drive, or the size of their house?

Several years later, long after the discussion about Andy the Ant being a genius, I asked my rich dad what he thought financial IQ meant. He quickly replied, "Financial intelligence is not about how much money you make, it's about how much money you keep and how hard that money works for you."

Yet as time went on, he refined his definition of financial intelligence. He once said, "You know your financial intelligence is increasing if as you get older your money is buying you more freedom, happiness, health, and choices in life." He went on to explain that many people made more money as they got older, but their money only bought them less freedom—less freedom in the form of having bigger bills to pay. Having bigger bills meant the person had to work harder to pay them. To rich dad this was not financially intelligent. He also explained that he saw many people making a lot of money, but their money did not make them happier. To him, that was not financially intelligent. "Why work for money and be unhappy?" He said, "If you must work for money, find a way to work and be happy. That is financial intelligence."

When it came to health he would say, "Too many people work too hard for money and slowly kill themselves in the process. Why work hard sacrificing the mental and physical well-being of your family as well as yourself? That is not financially intelligent." When it came to health he also said, "There is no such thing as a sudden heart attack. Heart attacks and other diseases such as cancer take time to develop. They are caused by lack of exercise, a poor diet, and not enough joy in one's life over extended periods of time. Of the three, I think lack of joy is the greatest cause of heart attacks and disease." He said, "Too many people think about working harder rather than about how to have more fun and enjoy this great gift of life."

When it came to choices he would say this: "I know the first-class section of an airplane arrives at the same time as the economy section. That is not the issue. The issue is, Do you have the choice of flying first class or flying economy? Most people in the economy section have no choice." My rich dad went on to explain that financial intelligence gave a person more choices in life by saying, "Money is power because more money gives you more choices." But it was his lesson about happiness that he stressed more and more the older he got. As he neared the end of his life and he had more money than he had dreamed possible, he restated again and again, "Money does not make you happy. Never think that you will be happy when you get rich. If you are not happy while getting rich, chances are you will not be happy when you do get rich. So whether you are rich or poor, make sure you are happy."

Those of you who have read my other books realize that my rich dad did not measure his financial IQ in traditional financial measurements. In other words, he was never really fixated by how much money he had, or his net worth, or the size of his portfolio. If I were to define what financial intelligence bought him, it would be "freedom."

He loved having the freedom to work or to not work and the freedom to choose with whom he worked. He loved the freedom to buy whatever he wanted without worrying about the price. He loved the health, happiness, and choices he could afford because he was free. He loved the freedom and financial ability he had to donate to charity to help causes in which he believed. And instead of complaining about politicians and feeling powerless to change the system, he had politicians coming to him seeking his advice (and hoping for his campaign contributions). He loved having power over them.

"They call me, I don't call them. Every politician wants the poor person's vote, but they don't listen to the poor person. They really can't afford to . . . and that is tragic," he said.

Yet what he cherished most was the free time that money bought him. He loved having the time to watch his children grow up and to work on projects that interested him, whether or not they made money. So my rich dad measured his financial IQ in time more than money. The later years of his life were the most joyous because he spent most of his time giving his money away rather than trying to conserve and hang on to it. He seemed to have as much fun giving it away as a philanthropist as he did making it as a capitalist. He lived a rich, happy, and generous life. Most important, he had a life of boundless freedom, and that is how he measured his financial IQ.

What Is Intelligence?

It was my real dad, the head of education and gifted teacher, who ultimately became the personal tutor to "Andy the Ant." Andy was so smart that he should have been in his senior year of high school rather than the fifth grade. His mom and dad were pressured to have him skip many grades, yet they wanted him to stay with his age group. Since my real dad was also an academic genius, a person who graduated from a four-year university in two years, he understood what Andy was going through and respected his parents' wishes. In many ways he agreed with them, realizing that academic age is not as important as emotional and physical development. He agreed that Andy should mature emotionally and physically rather than go to high school or college with students twice his age. So after attending elementary school with regular kids, Andy would go to my dad, the superintendent of education, and spend the afternoons studying with him. I, on the other hand, went to my rich dad's office and began my education in financial intelligence.

I find it interesting to reflect back upon the fact that different fathers took it upon themselves to spend time teaching other parents' children. It's nice to see it still happening today as many parents volunteer their time to teach sports, arts, music, dance, crafts, business skills, and more. Ultimately, all adults are teachers in one way or another . . . and as adults we are teachers more by our actions than by our words. When our teacher announced to the class that Andy was a genius with a high IQ, in essence she also told us that the rest of us were not. I went home and asked my dad what his definition of intelligence was. His reply was simple. All he said was, "Intelligence is the ability to make finer distinctions."

I stood there for a moment, not understanding what he had said. So I waited for him to explain further, knowing that because he was a true teacher, he could not leave me standing there with a dumb expression on my face. Finally he realized that I did not understand his explanation, so he began to speak in the language of a ten-year-old. "Do you know what the word *sports* means?" my dad asked.

"Sure I do," I said. "I love sports."

"Good," he replied. "Is there a difference between football, golf, and surfing?"

"Of course there is," I said excitedly. "There are huge differences between those sports."

"Good," my father continued in his teacher mode. "Those differences are called 'distinctions.'"

"You mean distinctions are the same as differences?" I asked.

My dad nodded.

"So the more I can tell the differences between something, then the more intelligent I am?" I asked.

"That is correct," my dad answered. "So you have a much higher sports IQ than Andy . . . but Andy has a much higher academic IQ than you. What this really means is that Andy learns best by reading and you learn best by doing. So Andy has an easier time learning in the classroom and you have an easier time learning on the athletic field. Andy will learn history and science quickly and you will learn baseball and football quickly."

I stood there silently for a while. My dad, being a good teacher, let me stand there until the distinctions settled in. Finally I recovered from my trance and said, "So I learn by playing games, and Andy learns by reading."

Again my dad nodded. He paused awhile and then said, "Our school system puts great importance upon academic or scholastic intelligence. So when they say someone has a high IQ, they mean a high scholastic or academic IQ. The current IQ test measures primarily a person's verbal IQ, or their ability to read and write. So technically, a person with a high IQ is someone who learns quickly by reading. It does not measure all of a person's intelligence. So that IQ is not a measure of a person's artistic IQ, physical IQ, or even their mathematical intelligence, which are all legitimate intelligences."

Continuing on, I said, "So when my teacher says that Andy is a genius, it means that he is better at learning by reading than I am. And I am better at learning by doing."

"Yes," my dad said.

Again I stood there, thinking for a moment. Slowly I began to understand how this new bit of information applied to me. "So I need to find ways to learn things that best suit my learning style," I finally said.

My dad nodded. "You still need to learn to read, but it seems that you will learn faster by doing than by reading. In many ways, Andy has a problem in that he can read but cannot do. In some ways, he may find the real world a harder place to adapt to than you will. He will do well as long as he remains in the world of academics or science. And that is why he has a hard time on the baseball field or in talking to the rest of the kids. This is why I think it's great that you and your friends allow him to be on your sports teams. You are teaching him things that a schoolbook could never teach him . . . subjects and skills that are very important for success in the real world."

"Andy is a great friend," I said. "But he would rather read than play baseball. And I would rather play baseball than read. So it means he is smarter in the classroom because he learns better there. But that does not mean he is smarter than me. His high IQ means he is a genius at learning by reading. So I need to find a way to make more distinctions faster so I can learn faster . . . in a way that works best for me."

Multipy by Dividing

My educator dad smiled. "That's the attitude. Find a way to make distinctions quickly, and you will learn quickly. Always remember that nature multiplies by dividing," he said. "Just as a cell increases by splitting . . . the same is true with intelligence. The moment we split a subject into two, we have increased our intelligence. If we then split the two into two, we get four, and our intelligence is now multiplying . . . multiplying by dividing. That is called 'quantum learning,' not 'linear learning.'"

I nodded, understanding how learning could get faster once I figured out how I learned best. "When I first started playing baseball, I didn't know much," I said. "But I soon found out the difference between striking out, a home run, and an RBI. Is that what you mean by my intelligence increases by dividing or making finer distinctions?"

"That is correct," my dad replied. "And the more you play the game, the more you will keep discovering new and finer distinctions. Don't you find yourself improving as you learn more?"

"Yeah," I said. "When I first started playing baseball, I couldn't even hit the ball. Now I can bunt, drag hit, hit line drives, or go for the fence with a home run. You know that I've hit three home runs this year?" I said proudly with a grin.

"Yes, I know," my dad said. "And I'm very proud of you. And do you realize that there are many people who do not know the difference between a bunt and a home run? They have no idea what you're talking about, and they certainly aren't able to do what you're talking about."

"So my baseball IQ is really high," I said with a smile.

"Very high," said my dad. "Just as Andy's academic IQ is really high . . . but he can't hit a baseball."

"You're telling me," I said. "Andy may know the difference between a bunt and a home run, but he couldn't do either one of them if his life depended upon it."

"And that is the problem with judging a person only on their academic IQ," my educator dad said. "Often people with high academic IQs do not do well in the real world."

"Why is that?" I asked.

"That is a good question for which I really have no answer. I think it is because educators focus primarily on mental skills and not on converting mental knowledge into physical knowledge. I also think that we educators punish people for making mistakes, and if you are afraid of making mistakes, you will not want to do anything. We in education place too much emphasis on the need to be right and the fear of being wrong. It is the fear of making a mistake and then looking foolish that prevents people from taking action . . . and ultimately, we all learn via taking action. We all know we learn by making mistakes, yet in our school system we punish people for making too many of them. The world of education is filled with people who can tell you all you need to know about the game of baseball, but they cannot play baseball themselves."

"So when our teacher says Andy is a genius, does that mean he's better than me?" I asked.

"No," said my dad. "But in school, he'll have an easier time learning than you will because his reading skills are at a genius level. However, on the athletic field, you'll learn faster than he does. That is all it means."

"So having a high IQ may only mean he learns faster by reading . . . but it doesn't mean I can't learn as much as he knows," I replied, seeking greater clarity. "In other words, I can learn something if I want to learn it. Isn't that true?"

"That's it," said my dad. "Education is attitude . . . and if you have that kind of positive attitude toward learning, you will do well. But if you have a loser's attitude, or a defeated attitude toward learning, then you will never learn anything."

I pulled my baseball magazine out of my back pocket. It was worn and tattered. "I love to read this magazine. I can tell you the scores, batting averages, and salaries of all the players. But when I read this magazine in the classroom, my teacher takes the magazine away."

"As she should," my dad said. "But she should have encouraged you to read it after school."

I nodded. I finally understood why Andy had a higher IQ. But most important, I learned how I learned best. That day I learned that I learn best by doing first and then reading about it. For example, with baseball, the more I played the game, the more I wanted to read about it. But if I did not play the game, I had no interest in reading about it. It was a way of learning that worked best for me. It was a way I would learn for the rest of my life. If I tried something first and then found it interesting, I would be more excited about reading about it. But if I could not be involved physically first, or could only read about something, I was rarely interested and hence did not want to read about it. Being only ten years old, I had learned enough for the day. My attention span had been exhausted. Clutching my baseball glove and bat, I headed out the door to go make finer distinctions about the game of baseball. I had some baseball IQ to improve, and practice was the best way for me to do that. Besides, I knew that if I didn't keep practicing, Andy the Ant might replace me on the team.

That one explanation from my educator dad was the primary reason I finished high school and went on to survive a very tough federal military academy with a rigorous academic curriculum. Because of this explanation I knew that although I did not have a high academic IQ, it did not mean I was not smart. It merely meant I had to find a way of learning that worked best for me. Without this valuable knowledge, I might have dropped out of high school long before graduating. Personally I found school too slow, boring, and uninteresting. I was not interested in most of the subjects I was required to study, but I found a way to learn those subjects and pass the tests. What kept me going was the knowledge that once I left school with my college degree, my real education would begin.

How Many Different Geniuses Are There?

In the early 1980s a man named Howard Gardner wrote a book entitled *Frames of Mind*. In his book he identified seven different geniuses or intelligences. They are as follows:

1. *Verbal-linguistic:* This is the genius that our educational system currently uses to measure a person's IQ. It is a person's native ability to read and write words. It is a very important intelligence because it's one of the primary ways humans gather and share information. Journalists, writers, attorneys, and teachers are often blessed with this genius.

2. *Numerical:* This is the genius that deals with data measured in numbers. Obviously a mathematician would be blessed with this genius. A formally trained engineer would need to be good at both verbal-linguistic and numerical genius.

3. *Spatial:* This is the genius many creative people—artists and designers—have. An architect would have to be good at all three of these first geniuses, because the profession would require words, numbers, and creative design.

4. *Physical:* This is the genius that many great athletes and dancers are blessed with. There are also many people who do not do well in school who are gifted physically. These are often people who learn by doing, what is often called "hands on" learning. Many times people with this genius gravitate toward mechanics or the building trades. They probably love wood shop or cooking classes. In other words, they are geniuses by seeing, touching, and doing things. A

person who designs racing cars would need to possess all of the first four geniuses.

5. *Intrapersonal:* This is the genius often called "emotional intelligence." It's what we say to ourselves, for example, when we are fearful or angry. Frequently, people are unsuccessful at something not from a lack of mental knowledge, but because they are afraid to fail. For example, I know many smart people with good grades who are less successful than they could be simply because they live in terror of making a mistake or failing. Many times people do not make money simply because they fear losing money more than they could enjoy making money.

There is a book written by Daniel Goleman entitled *Emotional Intelligence* that I recommend people read if they are ready to make significant changes in their lives. In it Goleman quotes the sixteenth-century humanist Erasmus of Rotterdam, who states that emotional thinking can be twenty-four times more powerful than rational thinking. In other words, the ratio looks like this:

$$24 : 1$$
emotional brain : rational brain

I am quite certain most of us have experienced the power of our emotional brains over our rational brains, particularly when we are more fearful than logical or when we say something we know we should never have said.

I agree with Goleman that intrapersonal intelligence is the most important of all the geniuses. I say that because intrapersonal genius is our control over what we say to ourselves. It's me talking to myself and you talking to yourself.

6. *Interpersonal:* This is the genius found in people who can talk easily with others. People with this genius are often charismatic communicators, great singers, preachers, politicians, actors, salespeople, and speakers.

7. *Environmental:* This is the genius that emanates from humans to the things around them. There are people who are naturally gifted in dealing with such things as trees, plants, fish, the ocean, animals, and the land. This is the genius that great farmers, animal trainers, oceanographers, and park rangers possess.

Since the distinction among these different geniuses was made, over thirty other geniuses have been identified . . . so our intelligence about the subject of genius continues to increase because we keep making finer distinctions.

People Who Fail in School

People who do not do well in school, even if they try very hard, often do not have a strong verbal-linguistic genius. These people do not learn by sitting still, listening to lectures, or by reading. They learn, or are gifted, in other areas.

My real dad was definitely gifted verbal-linguistically, which is why he read well, wrote well, and had a high IQ. He was also a great communicator, which meant he was also strong in interpersonal genius.

My rich dad, on the other hand, was gifted in the genius that is second on the list . . . the mathematical genius. He was below average in verbal-linguistic skills, which is why I think he never went back to school. He was a poor writer and a poor reader. Yet he was a very good speaker, and his interpersonal skills were excellent. He had hundreds of employees who loved working for him. He also was not afraid of taking risks, which meant his intrapersonal genius was very strong. In other words, he had the ability to pay strong attention to numerical details combined with an ability to take investment risks, and he was also able to build companies that people loved to work for.

My real dad was strong in most geniuses, but his fear of losing money was his weakness. When he tried to start his own business and it ran out of money, he panicked and went back to working at a job. One thing a great entrepreneur must have, especially when starting to build a business without money, is intrapersonal genius.

The person who falls and stands up again is calling on intrapersonal genius, or emotional intelligence. People often call that genius "tenacity" or "determination." When people do things they are terrified of doing, they are calling on their intrapersonal genius. People call it "guts" or "courage." When a person makes a mistake and has the intrapersonal genius to admit it and apologize, that genius is often called "humility."

Why Some People Are More Successful Than Others

When I study the life of Tiger Woods, it is easy to understand why he is such a superstar. In order to be a great student, to be accepted to Stanford University, to be possibly the best golfer who ever lived, and to be such an influential media star, he has to be a genius in all of the seven geniuses listed. As any golfer will tell you, the game of golf requires tremendous physical genius, but more important, it takes tremendous intrapersonal genius. That is why so many people say golf is a game that is played inside of you. When you watch Tiger on television, you know why he gets paid the big dollars for endorsing products. He is paid a lot because he is a great communicator, which means his interpersonal genius is very strong. He is very charismatic and convincing as a media star. He is a hero to millions of people throughout the world, which is why companies love to have him endorse their products.

In the late 1930s the Carnegie Institute did a study on successful people that showed that technical expertise constituted less than 15 percent of the reason for their success. In other words, some doctors are more successful than others not necessarily because of what school they went to or how smart they are. All of us know of people who did very well in school, and are very smart, yet do not do well in the real world. When you look at the seven different geniuses, some of the other reasons for a person's success and lack of success can be identified. In other words, you can make further distinctions, the foundation of intelligence.

The Carnegie Institute study reported that a full 85 percent of a person's success in life was due to "skill in human engineering." The ability to communicate and get along with people was much more important that technical expertise.

Highlighting the point made by Carnegie was a study conducted by the U.S. Census Bureau of Hiring, Training and Management. Three thousand employers were asked, "What are the two top skills you look for when hiring people?" The top six skills were:

1. good attitude.
2. good communication skills.
3. previous work experience.
4. what a previous employer had said about the employee.
5. how much training the employee had.
6. how many years of schooling the employee had completed.

Once again, attitude and communication skills ranked higher than technical competence in determining successful employment.

Find Your Genius and Become a Genius

My dad, the head of education, knew that I would not do well in school. He knew that sitting in a room, listening to lectures, reading books, and studying subjects without any physical mass to them was not my best way of learning. In fact, he often said, "I doubt any of my kids will do well in school." He knew that all kids do not learn in the same ways. One of my sisters is a great artist, brilliant in color and design. Today she works as a commercial artist. My other sister is a nun and is very much in tune with the environment. She loves being in harmony with all of God's creatures and creations. My brother is a very physical learner. He loves doing and learning with his hands. Give him a screwdriver and he wants to fix things. He is also a great communicator, which is why he loves talking to people and helping them to help others. This is why I think he loves working at the Blood Bank. He loves to calm nervous people and ask them to donate blood to help others. I would say that I have good intrapersonal skills, which allows me to overcome personal fear and take action. It is why I love being an entrepreneur and an investor or why I enjoyed being a marine and flying a helicopter gunship in Vietnam. I have learned to take my fear and convert it into excitement.

My dad was smart enough to encourage his kids to find their own genius and their own ways of learning. He knew each of his kids was different, had different geniuses, and learned differently . . . although we were all from the same parents. When he found out I was really interested in money and capitalism, subjects in which he had no interest, he encouraged me to seek teachers who could teach me those subjects. That is why, at the age of nine, I began to learn from my rich dad. Although my real dad respected my rich dad, they did not see eye to eye on many subjects. My dad, being a great educator, knew that if a child was interested in a subject, that child had a better chance of discovering his or her native geniuses. He allowed me to study subjects of my interest even though he did not particularly like the subject. And when I did not get good grades in school, he did not become upset, even though he was the head of the educational system. He knew that even though school was important, it was not the place where I would discover my genius. He knew if children studied what they were interested in, they would find their geniuses and succeed. He knew his kids were smart. He told us we were smart, even though we often had poor grades in school. Being a great teacher, he knew that the true definition of education was to draw out your genius, not just cram information in.

Protecting Your Child's Genius

My dad was adamant about protecting the genius of all children. He knew that the school system recognized primarily one genius, the verbal-linguistic. He also knew that a child's individual genius could be crushed in school, especially if the child was weak in the genius from which IQ is recognized. He was concerned about me because I was a very active child and hated slow, boring subjects. He knew I had a short attention span and would have trouble in school. For those reasons he encouraged me to play sports and study with my rich dad. He wanted me to stay very active and study a subject I was interested in, to make sure that my self-esteem, which is linked directly to genius, remained intact. He did the same for my brothers and sisters.

Today I would be labeled as having attention deficit disorder, or ADD, and would probably be drugged to keep me in my seat and force me to study subjects I was not interested in. When people ask me what ADD is or wonder if they have it, I tell them that many of us have it. If we did not have it, there would be only one television channel and we would all sit there and watch it mindlessly. Today ADD could also be known as "channel surfing." When we get bored, we simply push the button and look for something of interest. Unfortunately our kids do not have that luxury in school.

The Tortoise and the Hare

My dad loved the classic fable of the tortoise and the hare. He used to say to his kids, "There are kids in school who are smarter than you in some ways. But always remember the story of the tortoise and the hare." He would go on to say, "There are kids who are faster learners than you. But that does not mean they are ahead of you. If you will study at your own pace and keep on learning, you will pass people who learn quickly but then stop learning." He would also say, "Just because a child has good grades in school does not mean that child will do well in life. Remember, your true education begins once you leave school." That was my dad's way of encouraging his children to become lifetime learners, as he was.

Your IQ Can Go Down

It is obvious to me that life is a lifelong learning experience. Just as the tortoise lay down and went to sleep, many people will lie down and go to sleep after leaving school. In today's rapidly changing world, that kind of behavior can be expensive. Reexamine the definition of IQ:

$$\frac{\text{Mental age}}{\text{Chronological age}} \times 100 = \text{IQ}$$

By definition, your IQ technically goes down with each year your age goes up. That is why my dad's story of the tortoise and the hare is true. When you go to a high school reunion, you can often spot the rabbits who fell asleep at the side of the road. Many times they were the students voted "Most Likely to Succeed" . . . but they didn't. They forgot that life's education goes on long after school is over.

Find Your Child's Genius

"Is your child a genius?" I think so, and I hope you do, too. In fact, your child probably has multiple geniuses. The problem is, our current educational system recognizes only one genius. If your child's genius is not the genius the system recognizes, your child may learn to feel stupid in school rather than smart. Worst of all, your child's genius may be ignored or may be damaged in the system. I know that many kids are made to feel less smart because they are compared with other kids. Instead of recognizing a child for his or her unique genius, all children are held to one IQ standard. Kids leave school feeling they are not smart. Children who leave school mentally and emotionally believing that they are not as smart as other kids leave school with a tremendous handicap in life. It is vitally important for parents to identify the child's native geniuses early in life, encourage those geniuses to grow strong, and protect those geniuses from a "single genius" educational system. As my dad said to his kids, "Our school system is designed to teach some kids, but unfortunately it is not designed to teach *all* kids."

When people ask me if I think all kids are smart, I reply, "I have never seen a baby who was not curious and excited about learning. I have never seen a baby who had to be told to learn to talk or to walk. I have never seen a baby who fell while learning to walk, refuse to get up again, and say, while lying facedown on the floor, 'I failed again. I guess I'll never learn to walk.' I have only seen babies stand and fall, stand and fall, stand and fall, and then finally stand and begin to walk and later run. Babies are newborn creatures that are naturally excited about learning. On the other hand, I have met a number of kids who are bored in school, or who leave school angry, or leave feeling like failures, or leave vowing never to go back to school again."

Obviously for these kids something happened to their natural love of learning between birth and the end of school. My dad would say, "A parent's most important job is to keep their children's geniuses and their love of learning alive, especially if the children do not like school." If he had not done that for me, I would have left school long before graduating. Much of this book is about how my smart dad kept my love of learning alive. I stayed in school, even though I hated it. He kept my love of learning alive by encouraging me to develop my geniuses, even though I was not an academic genius in school.

Chapter 3

Give Your Children Power—Before You Give Them Money

One day my classmate Richie invited me to spend the weekend at his family's beach house. I was thrilled. Richie was one of the coolest kids in school, and everyone wanted to be his friend. Now I had been invited to the ultimate, his beach house, located in a private estate about thirty miles from my home.

My mom helped me pack my bag and thanked Richie's mom and dad when they came to pick me up. I had a fabulous time. Richie had his own boat and many other neat toys. We played from morning until night. By the time his parents dropped me off back at home, I was sunburned, exhausted, and thrilled.

For the next few days all I talked about at home and at school was my weekend at the beach house. I talked about the fun, the toys, the boat, the good food, and the beautiful beach house. By Wednesday my family was tired of hearing about my weekend at the beach. On Thursday night I asked my mom and dad if we could buy a beach house near Richie's beach house. With that, my dad exploded. He had heard enough.

"For four days now, all this family has heard about is your weekend at Richie's beach house. I'm tired of hearing about it. Now you want us to buy a beach house. That is the last straw. What do you think I'm made of . . . money? The reason we don't buy a fancy beach house is because I can't afford it. I can barely pay the bills and keep food on this table. I break my back working all day, I come home to bills I can't pay, and now you want me to buy us a beach house. Buy you a boat. Well, I can't afford it. I am not rich like Richie's parents. I put food in your stomach and clothes on your back, and I can barely afford that. If you want to live like Richie, then why don't you move in with them?"

Later that night my mom came to my room and quietly closed the door behind her. In her hand she had a stack of envelopes. Sitting at the side of my bed, she said, "Your dad is under a lot of stress financially."

I lay there in the darkened room, my body churning with emotional turmoil, looking up at my mom. Being only nine years old, I was sad, shaken, angry, and disappointed. I hadn't meant to upset my dad. I knew we were in tough economic times. I just wanted to share with the family a little happiness and a picture of the good life . . . a life that money could buy . . . a life that maybe we could aspire to.

My mom began showing me the bills, many with numbers typed in red. "We are overdrawn at the bank, and we have all these bills yet to pay. Some of these bills are two months overdue."

"I know, Mom. I know," I said. "I didn't want to upset him. I just wanted to bring some fun and happiness to our family. I just wanted to share with the family what a life with money could be like."

My mom stroked my forehead and pushed my hair back. "I know you meant well. I know that things have not been too happy in our family lately. But right now we are in financial trouble. We are not rich people and probably never will be."

"Why?" I asked, nearly pleading for some sort of explanation.

"We just have too many bills, and your dad does not make that much money. On top of that his mother, your grandmother, just asked if we could send money to help them out. Your dad just got that letter today, and he's worried because they're also having a tough time. We just can't afford the things that Richie's parents can afford."

"But why?" I asked.

"I don't know why," my mom said. "I just know that we can't afford what they can afford. We aren't rich people like they are. Now close your eyes and get some sleep. You have school in the morning, and you need to have a good education if you want to be successful in life. If you get a good education, then maybe you can be rich like Richie's parents."

"But Dad has a good education. You have a good education," I shot back. "So why aren't we rich? All we have is a lot of bills. I don't understand," I said quietly. "I don't understand."

"Never mind, son. Don't worry about money. Your dad and I will handle our money problems. You have school in the morning, so you need to get a good night's sleep."

In the late 1950s my dad had to drop out of his graduate degree program at the University of Hawaii because he had too many bills to pay. He had planned on staying in school and getting his doctorate in education. But with a wife and four kids, the bills piled up. Then my mom got sick, I got sick, my two sisters got sick, and my brother fell from a wall and needed to be hospitalized. The only one not in the hospital or needing medical attention was my dad. He left the graduate program, moved the family to another island, and began working as the assistant to the superintendent of education for the island of Hawaii. He would eventually take over that position and then move back to Honolulu to become superintendent of education for the entire state of Hawaii.

That was the reason we as a family had so many bills to pay. It took us years to pay them off, but soon after paying off one set of bills, we would find ourselves owing money for something else that put our family back in debt.

By the time I was nine years old and met classmates like Richie, I knew there was a big difference between my family and many of my classmates' families. In *Rich Dad Poor Dad* I described how by a fluke of boundary lines, I attended the rich kids' elementary school instead of the poor and middle-class kids' elementary school. Having rich friends while being in a family with excessive debt, at the tender age of nine, became a turning point in the direction of my life.

Doesn't It Take Money to Make Money?

One of the most common questions I am asked is, "Doesn't it take money to make money?"

My answer is, "No, it does not." I then go on to say, "Money comes from your ideas simply because money is just an idea."

Another question I am asked is, "How do I invest if I don't have any money to invest? How can I invest when I can't even afford to pay my bills?"

My reply is, "The first thing I would recommend is to stop saying, 'I can't afford it.'"

I know that for many people my answers are unsatisfactory, since many times people are looking for immediate answers on how to get a few dollars quickly so they can invest and get ahead in life. I want people to know that they have the power and the ability to have all the money they want . . . if they want it. And that power is not found in money. The power is not found outside of them. The power is found in their ideas. It has nothing to do with money. It has to do with power . . . the power of their ideas. The good news is that it doesn't take money . . . all it takes is the willingness to change a few ideas. Change a few ideas and you can gain power over money, rather than allowing money to have power over you.

My rich dad often said, "Poor people are poor simply because they have poor ideas." He also said, "Most poor people learn their ideas about money and life from their parents. Since we teach nothing about money in school, the ideas of money are handed down from parent to child, for generations."

In *Rich Dad Poor Dad*, rich dad's lesson number one was, "The rich don't work for money." My rich dad taught me to have money work for me. Although I did not understand why Richie's family was richer than our family when I was nine, years later I did understand why. Richie's family knew how to have money work for them, and they taught that knowledge to their kids. Richie is still a very rich man and getting richer. Today, whenever we see each other we are still the best of friends, and when we meet it is the same friendship we had over forty years ago. Five years may pass between meetings, yet every time we meet it is as if we saw each other only yesterday. I now understand why his family was richer than my family; I see him passing that knowledge on to his children. But it is more than just the "how to" of money that I see Richie passing on. I see him passing on the power over money. And it is this power over money that makes people rich . . . not money alone. It is this power over money that I want this book to pass on to you so you can pass it on to your children.

In *Rich Dad Poor Dad*, the story of my rich dad taking my ten cents an hour away from me drew quite a reaction from our readers. In other words, he had me work for him for free. A friend who is a medical doctor called me up after reading the book and said, "When I read that your rich dad made you stack canned goods in his store for free, my blood boiled. I understand what your message is, but I don't agree. That was cruel. You have to pay people. You can't expect someone to work for free, especially when someone else is making money."

Rich People Don't Need Money

When my rich dad took my ten cents an hour away, he was taking the money away so I could find my power over money. He wanted me to know that I could make money without money. He wanted me to find the power to *create* money rather than learn to *work* for money. Rich dad said, "If you do not need money, you will make a lot of money. People who need money never really become rich. It is that neediness that robs you of your power. You must work hard and learn to never need money."

Although he gave his other kids an allowance, he did not give his son Mike an allowance, and he did not pay us for working for him. He said, "By giving a child an allowance, you teach that child to work for money rather than learn to create money."

Now I am *not saying* that you should have your kids work for free. And I am not saying to *not* give your child an allowance. I would not be foolish enough to tell you what to tell your own child, since every child is different and every situation is different. What I am saying is that money comes from ideas, and if you truly want to give your child a financial head start in life, I would be very vigilant over your ideas and your child's ideas. There is an overused saying that goes "A journey of a thousand miles begins with a single step." A more accurate saying would be "A journey of a thousand miles begins with *the idea* to make the journey." When it comes to money, many people start their life's journey with poor ideas or ideas that limit them later in life.

When Do You Teach a Child About Money?

I am often asked, "At what age should I start teaching my child about money?"

My answer is, "When your child becomes interested in money." Then I say, "I have a friend with a five-year-old son. If I were to hold up a five-dollar bill or a twenty-dollar bill and ask the child, 'Which one do you want?' which one will the child go for?" The person who asks me the question often says without hesitation, "The twenty-dollar bill." I reply, "Exactly, even a five-year-old child already understands the difference between a five- and a twenty-dollar bill."

My rich dad took the ten cents an hour away because I asked him to teach me to be rich. He did not do it just to teach me something about money. I asked to learn to be rich. I did not just want to learn about money—and there is a difference. If the child does not necessarily want to learn to be rich, then obviously the lessons should be different. One of the reasons rich dad did give his other children an allowance was that his children were not interested in getting rich, so he taught them different lessons about money. Although the lessons were different, he still taught them to have the power over money rather than to spend a life in need of money. As rich dad said, "The more you need money, the less power you have."

The Ages Between Nine and Fifteen

Different educational psychologists have told me that the ages between nine and fifteen are crucial in a child's development. This is not an exact science, and different experts will say different things. I am not an expert in child development, so take what I say as a general guideline rather than the words of professional experience. One expert I talked to said that at approximately the age of nine, children begin to break away from their parents' identity and seek their own. I know that it was true for me because at the age of nine I began to work with my rich dad. I wanted to break away from my parents' reality of the world, so I needed a new identity.

Another expert has said that between these ages, children develop what they call their "winning formula." This expert described the winning formula as the child's idea on how he or she will best survive and win. I knew by age nine that school was not a part of my winning formula, especially after my friend Andy was labeled a genius and I wasn't. I thought that I had a better chance of being a sports star or being rich than an academic like Andy and my dad. In other words, if a child thinks that he or she is good in school, his or her winning formula may be to stay in school and graduate with honors. If the child is not doing well in school, or does not like school, the child may seek a different formula.

This expert also had a few other notable points on winning formulas. This expert said that conflicts between parent and child begin when the child's winning formula for success is not the same as the parents'. The expert also said that family problems begin when the parents begin to impose their winning formula on the child without first respecting the child's formula. A parent needs to listen closely for the child's winning formula.

There will be a little more on the importance of a child's winning formula later in the book. But before we continue with giving your child power over money, there is something worth mentioning for adults.

This expert also said that many adults get into trouble later in life when they realize that the winning formulas they came up with as kids are no longer winning for them. Many adults then seek job or career changes. Some continue to try to make the formula work even after they realize it is not working. Still others go into a depression, thinking they have failed in life, rather than realize it was a winning formula that had stopped winning. In other words, people are generally happy if they are happy with their winning formula. People become unhappy with life if they are tired of their formula, or the formula is no longer winning, or they realize that their formula is not getting them where they want to go.

Al Bundy's Winning Formula

For an example of people living with winning formulas that are no longer working, take a look at the television sitcom *Married with Children*. At first I hated the program; I refused to watch it. But now I realize that I may have hated the program because it hit close to home. For those who may not be familiar with the program, Al Bundy, the star of the show, is an ex–high school football star. His claim to fame was scoring four touchdowns for Polk High School. His wife won in school by using sex as a big part of her winning formula. Because he was the football star, she granted him sex and became pregnant. They were married and had kids . . . hence the name *Married with Children*. Twenty years later he's a shoe salesman living in the memory of his four touchdowns. He still thinks, acts, and talks about things he did when he was a football star. His wife sits at home, watching TV and still dressing like the sexy young thing she was in high school. Their two children are following in their parents' footsteps. I can see the humor in the show, because I can recognize the Al Bundy inside of me. I find myself living in the glory of my past on the football field and in the Marine Corps. Being able to laugh at the program and my own life, I can see many people who are Al and Peg Bundy in real life. That television comedy is an example of winning formulas that stopped winning.

Winning Formulas with Power

When it comes to money, many people develop a winning formula without any power. In other words, people often set up a losing formula for money because they have no power. As strange as it may seem, they set up a formula that loses them money because that is the only formula they know.

For example, I recently met a person who is stuck in a career he now hates. He runs a car dealership for his dad. He makes a good income, but he is unhappy. He hates being his dad's employee, and he hates being known as the boss's son. Yet he stays there. When I asked him why he stays there, his only reply is, "Well, I didn't think I could build this Ford dealership on my own. So I thought I'd best stick it out until the old man retires. Besides, I'm making too much money." His formula is to win with money, but he loses finding out how powerful he could be if he broke free from security.

Another example of a losing winning formula is a friend's wife who stays at a job she loves but where she is not getting ahead financially. Instead of changing her formula by learning some new skills, she takes on odd jobs over the weekends and then complains that she does not have enough time with her kids. Obviously her formula is "Work hard at what I love, and endure."

Finding the Power to Create a Winning Formula That Wins

One of the most important things a parent can do is to help their child create winning formulas that win. And it is very important that a parent be aware of how to do this without interfering with the child's own development.

Recently a well-known pastor called me and asked if I would speak at his church. My record for church attendance is spotty at best. My family went to the Methodist church, but at the age of ten I began looking at other churches. I did this because I was studying the U.S. Constitution and became interested in the idea of the separation of the church and state and the freedom of religious choice. So at school I would ask my classmates what church they attended, and I would invite myself along. This did not make my mom too happy, yet I did remind her that the Constitution allowed me the freedom of religious choice. For a few years I enjoyed the experience of going to the different churches that my different classmates attended. I went to very ornate churches, simple churches, churches in people's homes, and even a church that was no more than four poles, a tin roof, and no walls. It was quite an experience sitting in church and getting soaked by the driving rain. I definitely felt the spirit that day.

I also made it a point to visit the houses of worship of many different denominations: Lutheran, Baptist, Buddhist, Jewish, Catholic, Pentecostal, Muslim, and Hindu. I would have gone to more, but the town I lived in was small and I soon ran out of different churches to attend. I enjoyed my experience, but by the time I turned fifteen my interest in attending church waned and I went less and less frequently.

So when Pastor Tom Anderson asked me to be a guest speaker at his church, I was both flattered and ashamed of my attendance record. When I told him that there were people far more qualified to speak to his church, he said, "I'm not asking you to deliver a message on religion. I am asking you to share your lessons on money."

When he said that, I rocked back in my chair and chuckled. Not believing what I was hearing, I said, "You want me to go to your church and talk about money?"

"Yes," he replied with a quizzical grin. "What is so strange about my request?"

Again I chuckled. I had to ask the question again. "You mean you want me to go to your church, stand at the pulpit where you normally stand, and talk to your congregation about money?"

And again the pastor said, "Yes. What is strange about that?"

I sat there grinning, looking back at this famous man of God, a pastor with a twelve-thousand-member congregation, just to make sure he was certain about what he was asking me to do. "Because in church I learned that the love of money was evil. I also learned that poor people had a better chance of going to heaven than rich people. There was some lesson about a camel, a rich man, and the eye of a needle. I never really understood the lesson, but I did not like the message because I definitely had plans on becoming a rich man. That is why I find it strange that you would want me to come to your church and tell them how to become rich."

This time Pastor Tom leaned back in his chair and grinned. "Well, I do not know what churches you've been attending," he said, "but that is certainly not what I teach in this church."

"But aren't there some religious groups that teach the idea that money is evil?" I asked. "Aren't there some people who believe that poor people have a better chance of going to heaven than rich people?"

"Yes, that is true," the pastor replied. "Different churches teach different things. But that is not what I want to teach in my church. The God I know loves the rich and the poor equally."

As Pastor Tom Anderson continued with his thoughts, I reflected back upon my own experience of church and the guilt I often felt because I truly wanted to be rich. Maybe I had interpreted the church's message inaccurately. Maybe my guilt about my love of money had caused me to receive the message inaccurately. In other words, I felt guilty so I heard a message of guilt. When I shared this idea with Tom, he said something that again caused me to sit back in my seat. He said, "Sometimes an ounce of perception takes a ton of education to change."

Those words of wisdom stayed with me. I thought about what he said for a long time. The depth of thought and accuracy that is found in those words is profound. Three months later I spoke to his congregation. The privilege to speak from the pulpit was an experience that helped me change a personal ounce of perception.

An Ounce Versus a Ton

My rich dad often said, "You can never teach a poor person to be rich. You can only teach a rich person to be rich."

My poor dad often said, "I'll never be rich. I'm not interested in money." And, "I can't afford it." Maybe it was having all those medical bills to pay or struggling financially for much of his adult life that caused him to say these things. But I don't think so. I think it was his ounce of perception that helped bring on much of his financial problems.

When Sharon Lechter, my coauthor, asked me if I wanted to write this book for parents, I jumped at the opportunity. It was my meeting with Pastor Tom Anderson that caused me to become passionate about writing this book, because it is the parents who can most influence a child's perceptions on life.

As mentioned before, my wife, Kim, and I do not have children, so I dare not tell parents how to be better parents. I write about how to help mold a child's perceptions on money. The most important thing a parent can do when it comes to money is to influence the child's perception about money. I want parents to give their children the perception that the child has power over money, rather than being a slave to money. As my rich dad said, "The more you need money, the less power you have over money."

Today young people receive credit cards at very early ages. You may recall from *Rich Dad Poor Dad* that my coauthor and business partner, Sharon Lechter, joined me because her own son was trapped by credit card debt in college, in spite of the fact that she is a CPA and was teaching him what she thought were sound money management skills. Even after learning sound money management, her son was tempted and succumbed to the "thrill" of "charging it" on credit cards. Sharon realized that if her child was having trouble, millions of other kids and parents must also be getting into financial problems early in life.

You Don't Have to Be Born Poor to Become Poor

Many poor people are poor because they learn to be poor at home. People can also develop a poor perception of themselves, even though they come from rich and middle-class families. Something happens to them along the road of life, and they pick up the perception that they will always be poor. I believe that is what happened to my dad. And as Pastor Tom Anderson states, it often takes a ton of education to change that perception. In my dad's case, he kept working harder, making more money. But even a ton of money, like a ton of education, may not change that ounce of perception.

When I went bust and lost my first company, the hardest thing I had to do was preserve my perception of myself. If not for my rich dad's lessons on self-perception, I do not know if I would have recovered and gotten stronger from the experience.

I have friends today who have gone bust, and although they have recovered financially, they were left with a weakened self-perception from the experience. That is why I begin my lessons for parents with the importance of being aware of and protecting the self-perceptions of your child.

Much of this book is about teaching your children how to have a strong self-perception in order to carry them through the ups and downs of life—financially, academically, in relationships, professionally, and through the other challenges their lives will encounter. This book will help you teach your child how to recover and build a stronger financial self-perception because of the ups and downs. How to protect my self-perceptions was one of the most important lessons my two dads taught me. One dad taught me how to come out stronger academically when I was set back, and the other taught me how to become stronger financially.

Many people gain a weakened self-perception along the road of life. I can hear it in their voices when they say such things as

- I'm so deeply in debt, I can't stop working.
- I can't afford to quit.
- If I could just make a few more dollars . . .
- Life would be much easier if I didn't have kids.
- I'll never be rich.
- I can't afford to lose money.
- I'd like to start my own business, but I need the steady paycheck.
- How can I afford to invest when I can't even pay my bills?
- I'll take out a home equity loan to pay off my credit cards.
- Not everybody can be rich.
- I don't care about money. Money is not that important to me.
- If God wanted me to be rich, God would have given me the money.

As my rich dad said, "The more you need money, the less power you have." There are many people who did well in school and landed that high-paying job. But because they were not taught how to make money work for them, they worked hard for money and got into long-term debt. The more they need money and the longer they need it, the more uncertain their self-perception grows.

I have friends who are professional students. Some have been in school all their lives and still have not had a job. I have one friend who has two master's degrees and one doctorate. He does *not* have *a* ton of education. He has ten tons of education, and he still struggles professionally and financially. I suspect it is one of those ounces of perception that are still in his way.

Money Does Not Make You Rich

Many people collect money in hopes of becoming rich, while others collect college degrees and good grades, hoping to become smart. My personal battle was to overcome my poor financial perception and the perception that I was not as smart as other kids—perceptions I did not really have until I began to compare myself with other kids. In other words, I did not know I was poor until I met kids who came from families with money; and I did not know I was not too smart until I was compared against kids who had better grades.

And that is why the title of this book is *Rich Kid Smart Kid*. It is my sincere belief that all kids are born with the potential to be rich and smart . . . as long as that *perception* of themselves is reinforced and protected from the *tons* of education they will receive in school, church, business, the media, and the world itself. Life is tough enough, but it can be even tougher if your self-perception is that you're not smart and that you'll never be rich. The most important role a parent can have is to mold, nurture, and protect children's perception of themselves.

Teaching Adults to Forget What They Have Learned

As a teacher of adults, I find it easier to teach a rich person to be richer and a smart person to be smarter. It is very difficult to teach someone to be rich when all you hear is

- "But what if I lose my money?"
- "But you've got to have a safe, secure job."
- "What do you mean, work for free? You've got to pay people!"
- "Don't get into debt."
- "Be a good hardworking man/woman and save money."
- "Play it safe and don't take risks."
- "If I become rich, I'll become evil and arrogant."
- "The rich are greedy."
- "We don't discuss money at the dinner table."

- "I'm not interested in money."
- "I can't afford it."
- "It's so expensive."

Questions or statements such as these come from deep-seated core personal perceptions. I found that when I raised the price of my classes into the hundreds and thousands of dollars, many of these comments disappeared and I could get on with my content.

Never Say, "I Can't Afford It"

My rich dad was not a trained therapist, yet he was smart enough to know that money was just an idea. He forbade his son and me from saying, "I can't afford it," to help us change our perceptions of ourselves. That was why he had us say, instead, "How can I afford it?" I realize that by constantly saying, "I can't afford it," I was reinforcing the perception of myself as a poor person. By saying, "How can I afford it?" I was reinforcing the perception of myself as a rich person. I recommend not saying around your child, "I can't afford it." And when your child asks you for money, you may want to say, "Write me a list of ten different things that you can do, legally and morally, so that you can afford what you want without asking me for the money."

If you examine these two statements, you will see that "How can I afford it?" opens your mind to examining the possibilities of accumulating wealth. "I can't afford it," on the other hand, closes your mind to any possibility of attaining what you desire.

As I stated at the start of this book, the word *education* comes from the Latin *educare,* which means "to draw out." By simply being aware of our words, we can detect our self-perceptions. By changing our words, we can begin to change our self-perceptions, if we want to change them. So by simply reminding myself to say, "How can I afford it?" I was able to bring out the rich person inside me. By saying, "I can't afford it," I was reinforcing the poor person who was already there.

Life Begins with Perceptions

The other day I was being interviewed by a reporter who asked, "Tell me how you became a millionaire."

And I replied, "I built businesses and bought real estate."

The reporter then responded, "Well, not everyone can do that. I know that I can't do that. Tell me what I can do to become a millionaire."

I then replied, "Well, you can keep your job and buy real estate."

And the reporter answered, "But the real estate market is too high. I can't afford it, and I don't want to manage property. Tell me what else I can do."

I then said, "Well, the stock market is hot right now. Why don't you invest in some stocks?"

"Because the stock market is too risky. It might crash any day now. And I have a wife and kids and I have bills to pay, so I can't afford to lose money like you can," said the reporter.

Finally I realized that I was doing what my rich dad had taught me not to do. I was giving answers to someone who first needed a change in perception. So I stopped answering and began asking questions. I said, "Tell me how you can become a millionaire."

He said, "Well, I can write a book and sell a couple of million copies like you did."

"Good," I said out loud. "You are a good writer, and I think that's a very good idea."

"But what if I can't find an agent to represent my book? And what if the agent rips me off? You know, I wrote a book once, but no one wanted to read the book," replied the reporter. He was on to a new subject, but his self-perception was the same.

The most important thing a parent can start with is developing and protecting the child's self-perceptions. We all have private perceptions of other people, right or wrong. You may think the person is a jerk, or stupid, or smart, or rich. I remember when I was in high school there was a girl I thought was stuck-up and arrogant. So as much as I was attracted to her, my perception of her caused me not to ask her out. Then one day I actually talked to her and found her to be kind, warm, and friendly. After changing my perception of her, I finally asked her out. Her reply was, "Oh, I wish you had asked me out earlier. I just started dating Jerry, and he and I are going steady now." The moral of the story is, just as we have perceptions of other people, we often have perceptions of ourselves—and just as perceptions of others can be changed, so can people's perceptions of themselves.

Rich and Smart Are Only Perceptions

My real dad, the schoolteacher, told me of a famous study that was conducted in the Chicago school system some years ago. Educational researchers asked a group of schoolteachers for their help. The teachers were told that they were chosen for their superior teaching abilities. They were also told that only gifted children would be placed in their classrooms. The teachers were told that neither the children nor their parents would know of the experiment because they wanted to see how gifted children would perform if they did not know they were gifted.

As expected, the teachers reported that the children performed exceptionally well. The teachers reported that working with the children had been absolutely delightful, and they wished that they could work with such gifted children all the time.

There was a hidden agenda for the project. What the teachers did not know was that the teachers did not have exceptional teaching abilities. They were chosen at random. Also, the children were not chosen for their gifted abilities. They too were chosen at random. But because expectations were high, performance was high. Because the children and teachers were perceived as smart and exceptional, they performed exceptionally.

What does this mean? It means that your *perceptions* of your children can greatly affect the outcome of their lives. In other words, if you can see the genius in your child, you will help your child become smarter. If you see your child as rich, you will help your child become richer. And if you teach your children to have those same perceptions, they will stand a better chance of having the rest of the world see the same self-perceptions and treat them accordingly.

And to me, this is where your child's education begins. And that is why I say, "Give your children power, before you give them money." Help them develop a strong self-perception, and you help them become rich kids and smart kids. If they don't have that, then all the education or money in the world will not help them. If they have that, getting smarter and richer will only get easier.

Gifts from My Two Dads

Possibly the best gifts I have received came from my two dads in the times when I was in the most trouble. When I was flunking out of high school, my schoolteacher dad always reminded me of how smart I was. When I was losing my shirt financially, my rich dad kept reminding me that truly rich men have lost more than one business. He would also say that it was the poor people who lost the least money and lived in the most fear of losing the little they had.

So one dad encouraged me to take my academic failures and turn them into strengths. And my rich dad encouraged me to take my financial losses and turn them into financial gains. They may have taught different subjects, but in many ways both dads were saying the same thing.

It is when children see the worst in themselves that it is the parents' job to see only the best. You may notice that this works not only on little kids, but on grown-up kids also.

When things are the very worst in your child's life, you as a parent are presented with a great opportunity—the opportunity to be the best teacher and friend your child will ever have.

Chapter 4

If You Want to Be Rich, You Must Do Your Homework

Both my parents and Mike's parents continually reminded us to do our homework. Again, the difference was that they did not recommend the same type of homework.

"Have you done your homework?" my mom asked.

"I'll do it as soon as this game is over," was my reply.

"You've been playing long enough! Stop playing right now and hit the books. If you don't get good grades, you won't get into college, and then you won't get a good job," she scolded.

"Okay, okay. I'll put the game away, but after I buy one more hotel."

"Listen to your mother and put that game away now. I know you love the game, but it's time to study."

That was my dad's voice, and he did not sound happy. Knowing better than to ask for more time, I stopped immediately and began putting the game away. It hurt me to sweep up the little green houses, red hotels, and property deeds I had spent hours collecting. I was close to controlling one whole side of the board. Yet I knew my parents were right. I did have a test the next day and I had not yet begun to study.

There was a period of my life when I was utterly fascinated by the game

Monopoly®. I played it regularly from the time I was eight until I turned fourteen, which was when I started playing high school football. I suspect I would have kept playing Monopoly regularly if I could have found more kids my age to play the game. But by the time you're in high school, it's not the cool thing to do. Although I played the game less frequently, I never lost my love of it, and once I was old enough, I began playing the game in real life.

Building Blocks from My Rich Dad

After a strong and healthy self-perception, one of the most important building blocks to wealth is homework.

In my previous books I explained how I learned about money while working for my rich dad from the age of nine into my college years. In exchange for my labor, he would spend hours teaching his son and me the ins and outs of running a business as well as the skills needed to be an investor. There was many a Saturday I would have rather been surfing with my friends or playing some other sport, yet I found myself sitting in my rich dad's office, learning from a man who would one day become one of the wealthiest private citizens in Hawaii.

During one of these Saturday lessons, my rich dad asked Mike and me, "Do you know why I will always be richer than the people who work for me?"

Mike and I sat blankly for a while, searching our minds for an appropriate answer. At first it seemed like a stupid question, but knowing rich dad, we knew there was something important to learn from his question. Finally I ventured what I thought was the obvious answer. "Because you make more money than they do," I said.

"Yeah," Mike said, nodding in agreement. "After all, you own the company, and you decide how much you get paid and how much they get paid."

Rich dad rocked back in his chair, grinning. "Well, it is true that I decide how much everyone gets paid. But the truth is, I get paid less than many of the employees who work for me."

Mike and I both looked at his dad with a suspicious gaze. "If you own this business, how can other people be paid more than you?" Mike asked.

"Well, there are several reasons why," replied rich dad. "Do you want me to tell you?"

"Of course," Mike replied.

"Well, when you're starting up a business, cash is often tight, and the owner is usually the last to be paid."

"You mean the employees always get paid first?" asked Mike.

Rich dad nodded. "That is correct. And not only do they get paid first, they often get paid more than I do when I do get paid."

"But why is that?" I asked. "Why own a business if you get paid last and get paid the least?"

"Because that is what a business owner often needs to do at first if he plans to build a successful business."

"That makes no sense," I replied. "Tell me why you do it, then."

"Because employees work for money, and I work to build an asset," said rich dad.

"So as you build this business, your pay will go up?" Mike asked.

"It may and it may not. I say this because I want you to know the difference between money and an asset," rich dad continued. "I may or may not pay myself more later on, and I am not working hard for the paycheck. The reason I work hard is to build an asset that increases in value. I may someday sell this business for millions of dollars, or I may hire a president to run it for me one day, and I will go on to build another business."

"So to you building a business is building an asset. And the asset is more important to you than money," I said, doing my best to understand the distinction between money and an asset.

"That's right," said rich dad. "And the second reason I get paid less is that I already have other sources of income."

"You mean you have money from other assets?" I asked.

Again rich dad nodded. "And that is the reason I asked you boys the question in the first place. That is why I asked you why I will always be richer than my employees, regardless of who makes the most money in salary. I am doing my best to teach you a very important lesson."

"And what is the lesson?" asked Mike.

"The lesson is, you don't get rich at work. You get rich at home," said rich dad strongly, making sure we did not take his words lightly.

"I don't understand," I commented. "What do you mean, you get rich at home?"

"Well, it's at work where you *earn* your money. And it is at home where you decide what you are going to *do* with your money. And it is what you do with your money after you earn it that makes you rich or poor," replied rich dad.

"It's like homework," Mike said.

"Exactly," said rich dad. "That is exactly what I call it. I call getting rich my homework."

"But my dad brings a lot of work home," I said almost defensively. "And we're not rich."

"Well, your dad brings his work home, but he really does not do his homework," said rich dad. "Just as your mom does housework . . . that is not what I mean by homework."

"Or yardwork," I added.

Rich dad nodded. "Yes, there is a difference between yardwork, the schoolwork you bring home, and the work your dad brings home from his office, and the kind of homework I am talking about." It was then my rich dad said something to me I have never forgotten: "The primary difference between the rich, the poor, and the middle class is what they do in their spare time."

"Their spare time," I said in a questioning tone. "What do you mean, their spare time?"

Rich dad smiled at his son and me for a moment. "Where do you think this restaurant business was started?" he asked. "Do you think that this business came out of thin air?"

"No," said Mike. "You and Mom started this business at our kitchen table. That is where all your businesses have been started."

"That's correct," said rich dad. "Do you remember the first small store we started with years ago?"

Mike nodded. "Yes, I do," he said. "Those were very tough days for the family. We had so little money."

"And how many stores do we have now?" asked rich dad.

"We own five," Mike replied.

"And how many restaurants?" asked rich dad.

"We own seven," said Mike.

As I sat there listening, I began to understand a few new distinctions. "So the reason you earn less from this restaurant is that you have income from many other businesses?"

"That is partly the answer," rich dad said with a grin. "The rest of the answer is found on this Monopoly game board. Understanding the game of Monopoly is the best kind of homework you can do."

"Monopoly?" I asked with a grin. I could still hear my mom's voice telling me to put my Monopoly game away and do my homework. "What do you mean, Monopoly is homework?"

"Let me show you," said rich dad as he opened up the world's most familiar game. "What happens when you go around Go?" he asked.

"You collect two hundred dollars," I replied.

"So every time you go around Go, that is like you collecting your paycheck. Is that correct?"

"Yeah. I guess so," said Mike.

"And to win the game, what are you supposed to do?" asked rich dad.

"You're supposed to buy real estate," I said.

"That's right," said rich dad. "And buying real estate is your homework. That is what makes you rich. Not your paycheck."

Mike and I sat there in silence for a long period of time. Finally I ventured a question to rich dad. "So are you saying a big paycheck does not make you rich?"

"That's correct," said rich dad. "A paycheck does not make you rich. It is what you do with that paycheck that makes a person rich, poor, or middle-class."

"I don't understand," I said. "My dad is always saying that if he got a bigger pay raise, we would be rich."

"And that is what most people think," said rich dad. "But the reality is that the more money most people make, the further in debt they get. So they have to work harder."

"And why is that?" I asked.

"It's because of what they do at home. It's what they do in their spare time," said rich dad. "Most people have a poor plan or a poor formula for their money after they make it."

"So where does a person find a good formula for wealth?" Mike asked.

"Well, one of the better formulas for wealth is found right here on the Monopoly board," rich dad said, pointing to the game board.

"What formula?" I asked.

"Well, how do you win the game?" asked rich dad.

"You buy several pieces of real estate, then you begin putting houses on them," Mike answered.

"How many houses?" asked rich dad.

"Four," I said. "Four green houses."

"Good," said rich dad. "And after you have those four green houses, then what do you do?"

"You turn those four green houses in and buy a red hotel," I said.

"And that is one of the formulas for great wealth," said rich dad. "Right here on the game board of Monopoly, you have one of the best formulas for wealth in the world. It is a formula that many people have followed to become richer beyond their wildest dreams."

"You're kidding me," I said with a bit of disbelief. "It can't be that simple."

"It's that simple," rich dad confirmed. "For years I have taken the money I have earned in my business and simply bought real estate. Then what I do is live off the income from my real estate and continue to build my businesses. The more money I make from my business, the more money I invest in real estate. That is the formula of great wealth for many people."

"So if it is so simple, why don't more people do it?" asked Mike.

"Because they don't do their homework," said rich dad.

"Is it the only formula for wealth?" I asked.

"No," said rich dad. "But it is a very sound plan that has worked for many wealthy people for centuries. It worked for kings and queens of old, and it still works today. The difference is that today you don't have to be nobility to own real estate."

"So you have been playing the game of Monopoly in real life?" asked Mike.

Rich dad nodded. "Years ago, when I was a kid playing Monopoly, I decided that my plan for great wealth was to build businesses and then have my businesses buy my real estate. And that is all I have been doing. Even when we had very little money, I was still going home and looking for real estate."

"Does it have to be real estate?" I asked.

"No," said rich dad. "But when you get older and begin to understand the power of corporations and tax law, you will understand why real estate is one of the best investments."

"What else can you invest in?" asked Mike.

"Many people like stocks and bonds," said rich dad.

"Do you have stocks and bonds?" I asked.

"Of course," said rich dad. "But I still have more real estate."

"Why?" I asked.

"Well, it's because my banker will give me a loan to buy real estate, but he frowns on giving me a loan to buy stocks. So I can leverage my money better with real estate, and the tax laws favor real estate. But we're getting off the point."

"And what is the point?" I asked.

"The point is, you get rich at home, not at work," said rich dad. "I really want you to understand that. I don't care if you buy real estate or stocks or bonds or build a business. I do care that you understand that most people do not get rich at work. You get rich at home by doing your homework."

"I got the lesson," I said. "So when you finish working here at the restaurant, where do you go next?"

"Glad you asked," said rich dad. "Come on. Let's get in my car and take a ride. I'll show you where I go after work is done."

A few minutes later we arrived at a large tract of land with row after row of houses on the land. "This is twenty acres of prime real estate," rich dad said as he pointed to the land.

"Prime real estate?" I said cynically. I may have been only twelve years old, but I knew a low-rent neighborhood when I saw one. "This place looks terrible."

"Well, let me explain something to you," said rich dad. "Think of these houses as those green houses on the Monopoly board. Can you see that?"

Mike and I nodded slowly, doing our best to stretch our imaginations. The houses were not the neat clean green houses on the Monopoly board. "So where is the big red hotel?" we asked almost simultaneously.

"It's coming," said rich dad. "It's coming. But it's not going to be a red hotel. Over the next few years our little town will grow out in this direction. The city has announced plans to locate the new airport on the other side of this property."

"So these houses and land will be between the town and the airport?" I asked.

"You got it," said rich dad. "Then, when the time is right, I will tear down all these rental houses and convert this land into a light industrial park. And then I will control one of the most valuable pieces of land in this town."

"Then what will you do?" Mike asked.

"I will follow the same formula," said rich dad. "I'll buy more green houses and when the time is right turn them into red hotels, or light industrial parks, or apartment houses, or whatever the city needs at that time. I'm not a very smart man, but I know how to follow a successful plan. I work hard, and I do my homework."

When Mike and I were twelve years old, rich dad had begun his move to become one of the richest men in Hawaii. Not only had he already purchased this piece of industrial land, he had also purchased a piece of prime beachfront property, utilizing the same formula. At the age of thirty-four he was making his move from being an obscure businessman to becoming a powerful, rich businessman. He had been doing his homework.

In *Rich Dad Poor Dad*, rich dad's lesson number one was that the rich did not work for money. Instead the rich focused on having their money work for them. I also wrote about Ray Kroc, the founder of McDonald's, who said, "I'm not in the hamburger business. My business is real estate." As a young boy, I will always remember the impact of comparing the lesson from the game board of Monopoly to the lesson in real life with my rich dad and many other very wealthy individuals. Their wealth was really gained in what rich dad called "doing their homework." For me, the idea that wealth was gained at home and not at work was a powerful lesson from my rich dad. My real dad brought a lot of work home, but he did very little homework.

Once I returned from Vietnam in 1973, I immediately signed up for a real estate investment course I saw advertised on television. The course cost $385. That single course has made my wife and me millionaires, and the income from the real estate we bought using the formula taught by that course has bought us our freedom.

My wife and I never need to work again, owing to the passive income from real estate coming in from our real estate investments. So that $385 course has paid me back in something far more important than money. The information gained from that course has bought my wife and me something far more important than job security. It has bought us financial security and financial freedom. We worked hard at work, and we also did our homework.

As my rich dad said while playing Monopoly with Mike and me, "You don't get rich at work, you get rich at home."

The Motley Fools Are No Fools

In my opinion, one of the best books on investing is written by two brothers who call themselves the Motley Fools. Their book *The Motley Fool Invest-*

ment Guide has been on the best-seller lists for years.

Recently on their Web site they had this to say about the use of games as teaching tools:

> . . . in addition to their fun and the social interaction they promote, good games make you smarter. Good games force you to think, to plan, to risk, sometimes just to guess or hope . . . but always—and ay, here's the rub—the results, your destiny, are tied up in those thoughts and actions. The act of acting and winning, or failing and learning, is an act that emerges naturally from the playing of games. One of our Foolish leitmotifs, personal responsibility, is taught and illustrated beautifully by games.

Games Require More Than One Genius

The school system focuses primarily on the genius of verbal-linguistics. Earlier I discussed the challenges a child may have if his or her genius is not the genius of verbal-linguistics, the genius that IQ is traditionally measured from. In school I was not good in reading, writing, listening, and taking tests on my own. Just sitting in a classroom was painful. Being hyperactive even today, I learn best by calling on the geniuses found in physical, interpersonal, intrapersonal, spatial, and mathematical learning. In other words, I learn best by involving more than one genius. I learn best by doing, talking, working in groups, cooperating, competing, and having fun. While I can read and write, they are the most painful ways for me to absorb and disseminate information. That was why school was painful and why I loved games as a kid and why I still love them today as an adult. More than one genius is required to learn and to win a game. Games are often better teachers than a teacher standing in front of a classroom, lecturing.

I hated sitting in the confined space of a classroom. I still to this day refuse to sit in an office. I often hear people say, "Someday I'll have the corner office with windows on two sides." I never wanted to sit in an office. I have owned office buildings, but I do not have an office. If I have to have a meeting, I use the company's conference room or go to a restaurant. I hated being confined as a kid, and I hate being confined today. The best way to keep me seated in a confined space is to play a game, and today I go to work and continue to play games—but this time it is the game of Monopoly played with real money. I play because that is how I learn best.

When my real dad saw my love of games and sports, he realized that I learned best by doing rather than by listening. He knew that I would not do well in a true academic college. Realizing that I was an active learner, he began encouraging me to choose a school that taught students by doing rather than by listening. That is why I applied for and received congressional nominations to the U.S. Naval Academy and the U.S. Merchant Marine Academy. I applied to schools that would send me to sea on board ships to study all over the world. I learned to be a ship's officer by being on a ship. After graduation, I went into the Marine Corps to learn to fly, and I loved it. I loved learning on board a ship, and I loved learning inside an airplane.

I was able to tolerate the required confined classroom work because it led to the real-life learning of sailing and flying. I studied in the classroom because I wanted to learn, and when I wanted to learn, I would study harder, I was not bored, I felt smarter, and I got better grades. Better grades meant I could do more exciting things like sailing or flying to Tahiti, Japan, Alaska, Australia, New Zealand, Europe, South America, Africa, and, of course, Vietnam.

If my real dad had not explained the different styles of learning to me, I might have dropped out of school. I would probably have chosen a normal classroom-type school, gotten bored, partied too much, and stopped attending classes. I hate being confined, I hate being bored and lectured to, and I hate studying subjects that I cannot see, touch, and feel. My dad was a verbal-linguistic genius, yet he was smart enough to know that his kids were not. The reason he rarely criticized us for not doing well in school, even though he was the head of education, was because he knew that his four children learned in different ways. Instead of criticizing us for not having good grades, he encouraged us to find the ways that we naturally learned best.

My real dad also understood that I needed an incentive, a reward, at the end of my studies. He knew I was belligerent and rebellious enough not to simply follow his orders of "Go to school." I needed a reason. He was smart enough to know that saying to me, "Go to school, get good grades so you can get a good job and sit in an office," was not going to motivate me to love school. He knew that I needed to study what I wanted to study, learn in the ways I learned best, and that I had to have an exciting reward at the end of my studies. He helped me understand this about myself. Although he did not like the idea of my playing Monopoly for hours with my rich dad, he was a smart enough teacher to know that I was playing for the rewards I could get from the game. He knew I could see my future. That was why he said, "Go to school and see the world. You can play Monopoly all over the world. I can't afford to send you all over the world, but if you get into a school that lets you study all over the world, you'll enjoy your education."

My dad did not realize that this idea would stick in my head, but it did. To him, traveling the world to play Monopoly did not make sense. Yet once he saw me light up at the idea of traveling the world to study, he began to encourage me. He found something that interested me. He even began to like the idea of my playing Monopoly, although he could not comprehend the idea of investing in real estate all over the world because it was not in his reality; but he could see it becoming a part of my reality. Since I already had a Monopoly board, he began to bring home more books about going to sea and traveling the world.

So in the end even my schoolteacher dad did not mind my playing Monopoly. He could see that not only was it fun, but I was interested in it. He was able to marry a game with subjects I wanted to study. He found the reward I would study hard for—and that reward was to travel the world and play Monopoly in real life. He felt it was a childish and immature reality, yet it was a reality I could get excited about. Somehow my dad knew that when I played Monopoly I could see my future at the end of the game. He could not see it, but he knew I could see it . . . and he used what I could see or was beginning to see as the incentive to keep me in school and study hard. Today I travel the world and play Monopoly with real money. Although my reading and writing skills are not strong, I read and write because my schoolteacher dad was smart enough to find subjects I was interested in rather than force me to read and write about subjects I had no interest in.

The Winning Formula

One of the most important things I learned from Monopoly was my winning formula. I knew that all I had to do was buy four green houses and convert them into a red hotel. I did not know how specifically I was going to do it, but I knew I could do it . . . at least that was my perception of myself at the time. In other words, between the ages of nine and fifteen, I learned that I was not an academic genius as my friend Andy the Ant was. When I found the formula on the game board of Monopoly, and then went and actually could see, touch, and feel my rich dad's green houses, I found the winning formula for me. I knew that my poor dad's formula of study hard and work hard for job security and sit all day in an office was not for me. So that was the good news. But as I said, each coin has two sides. The bad news was that by the time I was fifteen, the threat of, "If you don't study hard, get good grades, and get a good job, you won't be successful," had little impact on my motivation to study subjects I did not want to study.

When I look at the falling test scores of kids today, I believe the same lack of reason or motivation that affected me is affecting kids today. Kids aren't stupid. In fact, kids know far more about real life than many adults. One of the reasons the school system is having a difficult time teaching them is that no one has given them the exciting reason to study hard and stay in school. I think many kids would be more interested in studying if they started playing Monopoly in the first grade and then were asked which of them wanted to join the "Who Wants to Be a Millionaire When You Graduate?" curriculum. If a child really wanted to be a millionaire, you could still feed them the same curriculum I had as a kid. The child might really be willing to study it, because the reward at the end was exciting and worth studying for.

So the good news was that by playing Monopoly, I found my winning formula. I could see my future at the end of the game. Once I knew I could make it, I wanted to become a millionaire. To me that was exciting, and I was willing to study to achieve that. But more than becoming rich, I could see that my future would be financially secure and financially free at the end of the game. I did not have the self-perception that I needed a secure job or a company or the government to take care of me. At the age of fifteen, I knew I was going to be rich. I did not just think it, I knew it. When I knew that, my self-perception soared. I knew that even if I did not have good grades, go to a good school, or have a good job, I was still going to be rich.

The bad news was that I grew more restless. If not for my schoolteacher dad and my rich dad encouraging me to stay in school and get my college degree, I might have left school early. I am very grateful for the wisdom of my schoolteacher dad, my rich dad, and a few high school teachers guiding me, rather than scolding me, through that very difficult time of my life. With their help, I found a way to want to stay in school and be a good student. They helped me find out how I learned best rather than forcing me to study in the way that the school system wanted me to learn.

My schoolteacher dad could see that I learned best by doing rather than by reading and listening. He kindled my dreams of traveling the world and married those dreams with the game of Monopoly. Knowing that, he found ways to encourage me to stay in school and helped me find a school that best suited my learning style. He was not concerned about my grades or about my attending a prestigious school of higher intellectual learning. He was concerned with my staying in school, getting a college degree, and, most important, continuing to learn. In other words, my real dad had done his homework.

My rich dad taught me different things from the game of Monopoly. He taught me one of the winning formulas of the rich. He changed my perception of myself by teaching me that I could win at the game of life even if I did not do well in school or have a high-paying job. He showed me his winning formula, a winning formula that I adopted for my life. In other words, my rich dad had also done his homework. As he often said, "You do not get rich at work. You get rich by doing your homework."

Teaching Rich and Smart Kids

In early 2000 I was asked by one of the leading network marketing companies to teach what they called "the next generation" about investing. Curious as to what the next generation was, I was told that they were the kids whose parents were successful in the network marketing business. When I asked why these "kids" needed to learn about investing, the reply was, "Because most of these young people will be inheriting million-dollar, and in some cases billion-dollar, businesses. We have been teaching them the business skills, and now we need you to teach them investing skills." With that answer, I knew why I was being asked to speak to them.

I spent two days in a ski resort talking to seventy-five young people, ages running from fifteen to thirty-five, about the importance of investing. It was nice because there were no questions such as "Where do I get the money to invest?" As my rich dad said, "There are only two kinds of money problems. One problem is not enough money, and the other problem is too much money." And these young people had the second problem.

On the second day of the course, I could not help but notice how different these young people were. They were unlike many of the young people I had met previously. Even the teenagers could hold a conversation about money, business, and investing that was adult to adult, not teenager to adult. I was old enough to be their father, and I often felt as though I were talking to a peer across a boardroom table. I then realized that these young people had grown up in the business, and many of them were managing cash flows and investment portfolios much larger than mine. It was a humbling experience for me, yet as wealthy as these young people already were, there was not the jerky arrogance, cockiness, or aloofness that I occasionally find in some young people. I realized that many of these young people grew up at home with their parents and their parents' business. Not only were they comfortable with adults, they were comfortable with speaking to adults about money and business. I had previously seen some of these young people, some only fourteen years old, stand up on stage in front of forty thousand people and deliver a speech that inspired the entire room. I was thirty-seven before I ever stood up and gave a speech, and it was a boring speech at that.

As I was driven down the mountain back to the airport, I realized that my best friend, Mike, and I had been given much the same experience. I also realized that he studied much harder at college because his reward at the end of his studies at business school was taking over a multimillion-dollar business. I realized that I was also a beneficiary of a parent who worked from home and had the time to teach his son and me life skills that could transfer to real life.

When I speak to people considering a home-based business—anything from a network marketing business to a franchise to something they're starting on their own—I comment on the young people I met up on that mountain. A home-based business can provide benefits far beyond the additional source of income and tax breaks, and some of those benefits are immeasurable and priceless. For some people with children, a home-based business is their way of doing their homework and teaching their kids to do the same. As my rich dad said, "You don't get rich at work. You get rich at home." And that may include a richness that is far beyond money.

Throughout history, some of the richest people became rich by starting at home. Henry Ford started in his garage. Hewlett-Packard was founded in a garage. Michael Dell started in his dorm room. Colonel Sanders did not become rich until after a freeway was built over his restaurant and he was forced out of business. So my rich dad's advice that you don't get rich at work has worked for many very rich people.

As a side note, the board game CASHFLOW 101™ was created on my dining table. *Rich Dad Poor Dad,* which has sold over two million copies to date, was originally written in our cabin in the mountains. CASHFLOW Technologies, Inc., with the Web site richdad.com, is a multimillion-dollar business that ships and licenses rich dad educational products all over the world—and it was started in a spare bedroom in Sharon Lechter's home. The business that started on our kitchen table, then moved to Sharon's home, is now in an office building and even rents office space to other businesses. I still do not have an office, because even today I dislike being confined to a small space. I operate with the same winning formula I learned with the help of my two dads—to travel the world and play Monopoly with real money. In other words, I am still doing my homework.

Chapter 5

How Many Winning Formulas Will Your Child Need?

In looking back at the lives of my rich dad and my poor dad, I have come to realize that one was more successful than the other simply because one had more *winning formulas*.

A friend of mine recently called asking me for some advice. Adrian worked for a large corporation for many years until she was downsized in the early 1990s. Undaunted and always wanting to start her own business, Adrian bought a travel agency franchise with her savings and severance pay from her old company. Just as she got a handle on the business, the airlines began cutting the commissions they paid on the tickets that travel agents sold. Suddenly, instead of getting an $800 commission on a ticket, the airlines paid her a flat rate of less than $100 and even down to $50. She is now faced with closing down her travel agency, but this time she is out of savings and will not receive a severance package from her own company. Her franchise is up for sale, but its value has been greatly diminished by the decreased revenue from the airlines.

I believe one of the reasons Adrian is struggling later in life is that she did not have enough winning formulas to prepare her for the length of her life. Adrian is not the only person I know who is struggling because she is short on winning formulas. There are many people who did well in school but did not leave with enough winning formulas to do well in life. The following chapter is written for parents to prepare their children with enough winning formulas to win at the game of life.

Your Child Needs a Minimum of Three Winning Formulas

There are three primary winning formulas a child needs to learn for professional and financial success later in life:

A winning *learning* formula
A winning *professional* formula
A winning *financial* formula

Finding Your Child's Winning Formula for Learning

My friend Adrian did well in school because she was a fast learner and enjoyed school. Adrian found reading, writing, and arithmetic easy. Adrian sailed through college and received a bachelor of arts degree. Because Adrian did well in school, she liked school and it was a positive experience. Since her experience of school was a positive one, I recommended that she close her travel agency and go back to school to learn a new winning professional formula. She is now back in school, at the age of fifty-three, gathering enough credits so she can apply to law school.

Adrian is an example that illustrates my dad's point on different winning learning formulas for different people. While Adrian's winning learning formula would work for her, it would probably not work for me. I did not like school, and I doubt if I will ever return to the halls of formal education as a student.

Developing a Winning Learning Formula

The years from birth to approximately age fifteen are very important; this is the time when children develop their own winning formulas for learning. If a child is happy in school, learns easily, and has good grades, the child should develop a viable winning formula for learning. But when children have difficulty learning the three Rs in school because they are not strong in the verbal-linguistic genius or for other reasons, their years in school can be painful from then on. If children have a difficult time in school during these early ages, or are made to feel not as smart as the other kids, they may begin to develop lowered self-esteem and a poor attitude toward school in general. Kids may learn to feel "stupid" and feel that they cannot survive inside the educational system. They begin to get labeled with terms intended to account for their so-called handicaps—terms such as ADD or "slow" instead of the coveted "gifted" or "bright" or "genius." As an adult I hate being called "stupid" or being made to feel inferior. How do you think a child of twelve or younger handles such labels? What is the cost, mentally, emotionally, and physically?

Academic rating systems are another reason kids begin to feel less secure academically. In a bell curve scoring system, if there are ten kids, two will be at the head of the curve, two will be at the bottom, and six will be found in the middle. In general scholastic aptitude tests I was usually rated in the top 2 percent with potential, but near the bottom 2 percent in grades. Because of this bell curve method of rating students, my schoolteacher dad often said, "The school system is not really a system of *education* as much as a system of *elimination*." His job as a parent was to keep me mentally and emotionally secure and prevent me from being eliminated from the system.

The Nine-Year Change

A leading and often controversial educator is Rudolf Steiner, whose educational philosophies are incorporated in the Waldorf schools, reportedly one of the fastest-growing systems of schools in the world today. Steiner often wrote and spoke about what he called "the nine-year change." His findings are that around the age of nine, children begin to separate from their parents' identity and seek their own. Steiner has found that this period is often very lonely for the child, a time of perceived isolation. The child begins to seek his or her own "I" and not a "we" as family. During this period, the child needs to learn practical survival skills. For this reason, children in the Waldorf system at that age are taught to plant gardens, build a shelter, bake bread, and the like. It is not that they are learning these skills as future professions; rather, they are learning these skills as a personal reassurance that they can survive on their own. The children *need* to know that they can survive during this period of seeking their own identity. If they do not develop a sense of personal security during this period, the effects can dramatically affect the children's future direction and choices in life. Obviously, how each child responds or reacts to this identity crisis is different, which is why a parent's careful observations and sensitivity are vital. A teacher with thirty kids cannot possibly be aware of each child's different choices and needs at this stage of life.

My smart dad was not aware of Rudolf Steiner's work, but he was aware of this period of development in a child's life. When he noticed that I was not doing well in school, and how being Andy the Ant's friend affected me when I was informed that Andy was a genius and I wasn't, he began to observe me and guide me a little closer. That was why he encouraged me to play sports more. He knew that Andy learned by reading and I learned by doing. He wanted me to know that I too could survive academically in my own way. He wanted me to find a way to maintain my self-confidence in school, even if it was through sports rather than academics.

Our family was also having money problems at this point in my life. I suspect that my smart dad realized how much his inability to earn enough money affected me. He knew that I often came home to find my mom crying over all the bills we had to pay. I think he knew that I would probably begin to seek a different identity from him, and I did. I began studying with my rich dad at the age of nine. In retrospect, I was looking for my own answers on how I could help out my family during this period of economic struggle. I was definitely seeking an identity that was not like my mom and dad's.

Adrian's Formula Versus My Formula

Because Adrian's experience of school was positive, it only made sense that she return to the halls of education to learn a new profession. My learning formula is different. It is the formula I learned at age nine, which is the formula to seek a mentor and learn by doing. Today I still seek mentors to learn at their feet. I seek mentors who have already done what I want to do, or I listen to audiotapes of them telling me what they did. I also read, but only as a last resort. Instead of going back to business school to learn about business, I built my own business, because I learn by doing rather than sitting in a classroom. I would seek a mentor, take action, make mistakes, and then seek books and tapes telling what I did wrong and what I could learn from my mistakes. For example, when the marketing campaign in one of my businesses began to fail, I went into a massive study and research mode to find new answers. Today I am a pretty good marketer . . . but I would not have been one if I'd just sat in a classroom, read books, and listened to teachers who might or might not have owned their own companies.

Each child will have a separate and unique winning formula for learning. It is the parent's job to observe and support the child in choosing the formula that works best for the child. If the child is not doing well in school, work closely without smothering the child and support the child in finding the ways that he or she will learn best.

If your children do well in school and love school, feel blessed. Let them excel and enjoy their experience. If they do not like school, let them know that they are still geniuses, and encourage them to find their own way of learning in a system that recognizes only one genius. If they can learn to do that, they will be gaining excellent educational survival skills for the real world, a world that requires multiple geniuses to survive. That is what my dad encouraged me to do. He encouraged me to find my own ways of learning, in spite of the fact that I hated what I was learning. It was great training for real life.

How to Become a Professional Student

I have also noticed that many times people do well in school out of their fear of not being able to survive. The children learn that getting good grades is how they can best survive. So they gain the survival skills known as "getting good grades." While this is good during their youth, problems arise when they get older and may need to leave and depend upon other survival skills . . . other survival skills necessary for the real world.

I suspect that children who learn to survive by doing well in school could easily become professional students, and some may never leave the system—some may become Ph.D.'s, seeking security via tenure. My smart dad realized that he was on this career path until his family got sick and forced him out into the real world. He said, "It is easy to stay inside the walls of education if you need the walls of education to shelter you from the real world."

Eroding Self-Perception

I have stated that debt and lack of a sense of financial security can erode a person's financial self-perception. In other words, if you have too many financial setbacks, or feel trapped by your need for job and paycheck security, your financial self-confidence can get pretty rocky. The same thing can happen to children academically, if all they are told is that they are not as smart as someone else. But for my dad's support, I would have left school early in life simply because no one likes being made to feel stupid. I knew that I was not stupid. I knew I was bored and not interested in the subjects being taught. Nonetheless, my poor grades in school still began to erode my academic self-perception. It was my smart dad who protected me during this trying period of my life. Even when I had poor grades, even failing grades, he kept reassuring me that I was smart in my own ways and that I needed to find my own ways of learning in order to survive in school. If not for his love and academic wisdom, I would surely have dropped out of school, hurt, angry, and feeling inferior to those who did well in school. In other words, if not for my smart dad, I would have left school learning the formula of a loser.

Whether or not your children are doing well in school, be observant and encourage them to find their own learning formula, because once they leave school and enter the real world, their education really begins.

Teachers Are Now Cheating

Most parents are aware that tests scores are coming down, and the pressure on educators to get those test scores up is taking its toll on teachers. The pressure on teachers to raise the test scores of their students is now causing teachers to cheat. In affluent suburban Maryland, a school principal resigned because of charges of cheating. The June 19, 2000, issue of *Newsweek* published an article entitled "When Teachers Are Cheaters":

> This spring has been a season of embarrassment for the nation's public schools. In suburban Maryland, an elementary school principal resigned last month after parents complained their children were coached to give the right answers on state tests. In Ohio, state officials are investigating charges of cheating at a Columbus elementary school that was recently praised by President Clinton for raising test scores. And in New York City, more than four dozen teachers and administrators from 30 schools stand accused of urging their students to cheat on various standardized city and state tests.
>
> It's bad enough when kids get kicked out for cheating. But as the

school year ends, an alarming number of teachers and principals face charges of fixing the numbers on high-stake tests that determine everything from whether an individual kid gets promoted to an entire district's annual budget.

The article continues:

The problem is high scores—not high standards—have become the Holy Grail.

In some parts of the country, educators get bonuses of as much as $25,000 if they raise their students' scores. In other places, school officials can lose their jobs if their students don't produce the right numbers.

And the article also states that schools are now teaching kids to take tests rather than gain a solid education. In other words, the teachers are giving the kids the answers so they can pass the tests in order to obtain higher test scores, not better-educated kids.

This sort of "teaching to the test" is a far more serious threat than outright cheating, according to some experts. Renzulli calls it the "ram, remember, regurgitate" curriculum, a new version of the three Rs. "It's nonsense content," says Linda McNeil, a professor of education at Rice University and author of *Contradictions of School Reform: The Educational Costs of Standardized Tests.* In Texas, she says, some kids spend months doing nothing but preparing for the tests. "It's like you're mentally teaching kids to hit the delete key," she says. "You're teaching them to forget. The real cheating is of a solid academic education."

So How Did the Teachers Get Caught?

Whenever I say that kids are smarter than adults, I often get this sideways glance from more intelligent adults. Yet I remember as a kid being much more tuned in to the world than my teachers or my parents gave me credit for. I knew about the first issue of *Playboy* magazine long before my mom and her friends knew about it. Today, with the Internet, kids have access to things I'm afraid to find out about. Yet we continue to treat kids like kids.

The *Newsweek* report goes on to state that the principal at the Maryland school got caught because the kids knew she was cheating. In the same issue of *Newsweek,* the following article, titled "Bitter Lessons," gave the whole story:

The kids were the heroes in the scandal. What happens when role models teach dishonesty?

The first hints of something wrong came from the kids. Whispering to one another in the hallways and on the playground, then telling their parents after school, a few fifth graders began describing the peculiar behavior of their principal, as she supervised the state assessment tests in mid-May. Some children who had already finished the test were reportedly summoned by the principal and told to "review" their answers. "You might want to look at this one again," she would say, according to the children. Other students were given an extra 20 to 45 minutes to complete the test. At one point during the social studies section of the test, she was said to have held up a map and pointed to the country the students were being quizzed about.

The kids were bothered and confused. "Some kids were saying to each other, 'I don't think she's allowed to do that,'" one fifth grader told *Newsweek*. The student, a 10-year-old boy, recounted that he was given extra time on the math test. "There was another part, on the language arts section," he continued, "where the principal helped me get the right answer. On that part I definitely thought she was cheating, but I thought if I said anything, I would get in trouble or something." The parent of another student told *The Washington Post* that her child came home and said, "Mom, I kind of thought it was cheating, but why would a principal do that?"

Not Learning to Learn

Something tragic is happening in the school systems today. On Sunday, May 7, 2000, my local newspaper, the *Arizona Republic*, ran a story with a headline that read L.A. SCHOOLS TO HOLD THOUSANDS BACK:

Los Angeles—The nation's second-largest school system backed down from plans to flunk huge numbers of students this year, but still will hold back up to 13,500 this fall when it stops automatically promoting poor-performing students to the next grade.

Los Angeles Unified School District officials originally expected to hold back as many as one-third of the system's 711,000 students, or 237,000 students, but the promotion guidelines were relaxed out of concern that mass flunkings would cripple schools.

In other words, the LA school system has failed to educate over a quarter of a million kids with the basic skills of learning. Rather than have a quarter of a million kids backing up in the system, like a drain backs up with a hairball, the system merely lowered its standards and pushes these kids out into the real world. In my opinion, it is a system that is failing, not the kids.

Why Private Schools and Home Schooling Are Increasing

Kids aren't the only ones who realize they're being cheated out of an important phase of education. For years home schooling was considered a fringe group of radical parents. Today more and more parents are taking their kids out of school and educating them at home. It has been reported that the home schooling movement increases by 15 percent per year. Many people said that children could not get a good education at home. Yet this year, the first year of the new millennium, home schoolers won the national spelling contest. Charter schools are boldly springing up, and schools that follow the Montessori and Waldorf systems are rapidly gaining in numbers. In other words, parents are taking back from the government the responsibility of educating their children.

A great resource for these parents is the Web site www.homeschool.com. Established by Rebecca Kochenderfer, this site has a wealth of information for all parents. Rebecca shares our mission to help parents better prepare their children for the world they face.

My Smart Dad's Concerns

Years ago my schoolteacher dad tried to change the system. He was aware that different children had different geniuses. He was also aware that the system was a "one size fits all" type of system, which was good for about 30 percent of the kids and horrible for all the others. He often said, "The system is worse than a dinosaur. At least dinosaurs became extinct . . . but the school system will not die. That is why it is worse than a dinosaur. The educational system is more like an alligator, a reptile that survived even after the dinosaurs died off." He went on to say, "The reason the school system does not change is that it is not a system that is designed to change. It is a system that is designed to survive."

Most of us know that the teachers are doing the best they can to educate children. The problem is, the teachers are working within a system that is designed not to change. It is a system designed for survival. It is a system that will drug kids to slow them down rather than change by speeding up. Then, after giving the drugs to the active kids, they go on to say to the same kids, "Don't do drugs." To me, that is one tough system. It is the only business I know that fails to give its customers what they want and then blames them for its failures. Instead of saying we as a system are boring, they say, "Your child has a learning deficiency." They say that rather than say, "We as a system have a teaching deficiency." As I said, it is the only business that blames the customers for its own failures.

Years ago my real dad realized that it was a system that had tremendous flaws in it. He became very disturbed when he found out that the educational system used by most English-speaking countries is an educational system that originated hundreds of years ago in Prussia. He became deeply disturbed once he realized that he was part of a system that was not designed to educate kids, but to create good soldiers and employees. One day he said to me, "The reason we have words like 'kindergarten' in our school system is that our system originated in Prussia several hundred years ago. *Kinder* is a Prussian word that means 'children,' and *garten* means 'garden.' In other words, a garden of children for the state to educate, or 'indoctrinate.' It was a system that was designed to take the responsibility of education away from the parent and educate children who would best serve the wants and needs of the state."

Where the Word Elementary *Comes From*

My smart dad also said, "The reason the early years of school are called 'elementary' is that we as educators took the *subject of interest* out of learning and broke it into elements. When you take the subject of interest out of the process of learning, education becomes boring." He went on to explain himself: "For example, if a child is interested in houses, the subject of the house is removed and broken into elements, such as math, science, writing, and art. So the students who do well in school are students who are interested in math as a subject, or writing as a subject, or science as a subject. But the student who is interested in the bigger subject, in this case the subject of a house, is often bored. His or her subject of interest has been removed, and the elements that make up the subject are all that is left to study. That is where the term *elementary school* or *elementary education* comes from, and that is why so many students find school boring. The subject of interest has been removed."

I think that these are several reasons home schooling and the number of private schools are increasing. They are taking back the power of education from the state and giving the power of education back to the parent and child.

From Samurai to Doctors to Teachers

My father's side of the family was of the warrior class, or the samurai class, during the feudal system in Japan. But soon after trade with the West was opened by Commodore Perry, the feudal system began to erode. My father's side of the family began giving up the ways of the samurai and became medical doctors instead. My father's father was supposed to become a doctor, but he ran away to Hawaii instead, so he broke the chain. Although my grandfather was not a medical doctor, it was expected that my dad would go to medical school, but he too broke the chain.

When I asked my dad why he did not become a doctor, he said, "While I was in high school, I began to wonder why so many of my classmates were suddenly missing from school. One day my friend would be there, and the next day he would be gone. I became curious and began to ask questions of the school administrators. I soon found out that the sugar and pineapple plantations had a requirement that the school system fail a minimum of 20 percent of the children of immigrants from Asia. It was the plantations' way of insuring they had a steady stream of uneducated manual laborers. My blood boiled when I found that out, and it was then that I decided to enter the field of education rather than medicine. I wanted to insure the system gave each and every child a chance for a good education. I was willing to fight big business and the government in order to insure that each child had the best education possible."

My dad fought to change the system all his life and was ultimately beaten in his attempt to change it. Near the end of his life he was recognized as one of the top two educators in Hawaii's 150-year history of public education. Although he was recognized for his courage by the people in the system, the system for the most part remains the same. As I said, it is a system designed for survival rather than change. That is not to say that the system has not done a good job for many people. It has done an excellent job for about 30 percent of the people who do well within the system. The problem is, the current system was created hundreds of years ago during the Agrarian Age, a time before cars, airplanes, radio, television, computers, and the Internet. It is a system that has failed to keep up with technological as well as sociological changes. It is a system that is stronger than a dinosaur and as tough as an alligator. That was why my dad was diligent in guiding our education at home, often saying to his kids, "Good grades are not as important as finding your genius." In other words, every child learns differently. It is up to the parent to be diligent in observing the ways in which each child learns best—and then support that child in developing his or her own winning formula for learning.

Whenever I see babies, I see young geniuses excited about learning. A few years later I sometimes see those same young geniuses bored in school, wondering why they are being forced to study things they may find irrelevant. Many students report feeling insulted because they are graded on those same subjects they have no interest in and then end up being labeled smart or not so smart. One young man said to me, "It's not that I am not smart. I'm just not interested. First tell me why I should be interested in the subject and how I can use it, then maybe I will study it."

The problem is more than bad grades. My smart dad recognized, of course, that grades can affect a student's future positively or negatively, but he was equally concerned with the effect *bad* grades can have on a student's self-perception and self-confidence. He often said, "Many kids enter school excited about learning but soon leave, having learned only to hate school." His advice was, "If a parent has one of these children who is learning to hate school, a parent's most important job at this stage of a child's life is not to make sure the child gets good grades: The parent's most important job is to make sure that the child preserves his or her God-given love of learning. Find out your children's natural genius, find out what they are interested in learning, and keep them excited about learning, even if it is not in school."

The reality is the child will have to learn much more than we ever did. If they do not, they fall behind in the next two winning formulas, which are covered in the next chapter. That is why in my opinion, developing your children's winning learning formula at home is far more important than the grades they will receive at school. As both my smart dad and my rich dad said, "Your real education begins when you leave school and enter the real world."

Chapter 6

Will Your Child Be Obsolete by Thirty?

When I was a boy, my parents' assumption was that I would graduate from school, get a job, be a loyal employee, work my way up the corporate ladder, and stay there till I retired. After I retired I would receive the gold watch and play golf at some retirement community and drive my golf cart off into the sunset.

The Older You Get, the Less Valuable You Become

The idea of one job for life is an Industrial Age idea. Since 1989, when the Berlin Wall came down and the World Wide Web went up, the world and rules of employment have changed. One of the rules that has changed is "The older you get, the more valuable you become" (to the business). That may have been true in the Industrial Age, but the rules are exactly opposite today. For many people in the Information Age, the older you get, the *less* valuable you become.

That is why a child's winning *learning* formula needs to be in place just to keep up with the changes that are coming. A child's winning learning formula must be a well-rehearsed learning formula just to keep up with the changes in his or her winning *professional* formulas. In other words, the chances are your child will probably be obsolete by thirty and need to learn a new professional formula just to keep up with professional changes demanded by the marketplace. Saying it another way, if your child has the old idea of one profession for life and is not prepared to learn and change quickly, the chances are your child will fall further behind with each passing year.

The Best Grades Don't Count

The future does not belong to the child who leaves school with the best grades. It belongs to the child with the best winning formula for learning and the freshest technical ideas. More important than learning how to take tests for good grades, a child needs to learn how to learn; learn how to change; and learn how to adapt faster than his or her classmates. Why? Because many of the skills employers and business will pay big money for in the future are not taught in school today. Just look at today's business climate. The people most in demand are people who understand the Web, a subject not taught in school only a few years ago. The people who are least in demand are people of my generation, who want large salaries but are out of touch with the Information Age.

Shortage of Workers

It seems strange to be talking about people becoming obsolete when there is a shortage of workers. I have friends who are not worried saying to me, "So what if I am older and have limited computer skills? There are plenty of jobs, and I can name my price wherever I want to work."

We have a shortage of workers simply because we are in a boom economy. There are literally billions of dollars betting on companies that will not be in business in a few years. When many of these flimsy new-technology companies begin to fold because they are out of money, the market will again be flooded with workers. And when companies begin to close, other businesses also begin to close.

Booms and Busts

To best understand this boom we are in and the shortage of jobs, it is best to look a few years back at other booms and busts.

1. In 1900 there were 485 carmakers. By 1908 only half remained. Today only 3 of the 485 are technically standing.

2. In 1983 there were approximately forty computer manufacturers in America. Today there are four.

3. In 1983 Burroughs, Coleco, Commodore, and Zenith were among the leaders in emerging computer technology. Today many young people working in the computer industry have never heard of these companies.

4. The Internet start-ups are currently pushing a lot of money into the market. But what happens when they fail to become profitable and eventually run out of money? Will we continue to have a shortage of workers and too many high-paying jobs?

5. Technology will skip continents. Almost every country I travel to today has an area it calls "Silicon Valley." Your child's competitors for a job may not even be competing for a job in this country—and they will definitely not be asking for the same salary.

At What Age Are You Too Old?

While in Australia recently, my friend Kelly Richie handed me a copy of his local newspaper, the *West Australian*. "Here," Kelly said. "This article summarizes what you have been trying to say to people for years about knowing at what age you are too old. It verifies that how old you are is now relative to your profession." Across the page of the April 8, 2000, issue of the paper ran the headline ARE YOU PAST IT? The color edition had pictures of a young graphic designer, a gymnast, a lawyer, and a model. Under the photo of each of these people representing different professions was a black caption box:

1. Graphic Designer   use by date: 30 years
2. Gymnast   use by date: 14 years
3. Lawyer   use by date: 35 years
4. Model   use by date: 25 years

In other words, in these professions, when you reach these ages, you are too old. The article began with a story of a model who is not a supermodel yet makes $2,000 a week. By age twenty-eight she is out of work. As the article further explained:

Many careers have trip wires that can derail a career at 20, 25, 30, or 40—wherever it is placed, it usually comes long before retirement age. They can be physical: models' looks fading, sporty types whose bodies won't do what they used to. They can be mental: the mathematician who makes more errors more often; the advertising or design wunderkind whose ideas are no longer quite on the money. They can be stamina-related: investment bankers and lawyers, exhausted, divorced, burnt out (or all three) by 40. It doesn't mean you'll never work in the industry again, but the opportunity to reach the top will have passed. You will become an also-ran.

The article continued:

The days when you began a career at 20 and beavered away for years, slowly rising on each rung until you finally landed somewhere near the top at age 55, are long gone. Today's truth is that if you haven't made it by 40, you never will. And in some industries, you'll know by 20 or 25 whether you need to start thinking of a fresh start in the bush with a lawn mowing business. Country towns are filled with old graphic designers doing a bit of painting, or a bit of pottery, or even running a local bakery. . . .

The manager of the careers unit at the University of Melbourne, Di Rachinger, says this modern trend for careers to peak and decline by 40 means people should always be working towards their next career and devoting some time to retraining or networking towards the new career. She says some professions, including graphic design, are seen as young and cutting edge, which necessarily excludes the over 40s.

And what happens to these older workers? The article had this to say:

But in these edgy, up-with-the-pace industries, the foot soldiers tend to be like Melissa: young, ambitious, and willing to work 12-hour days.

The best of the older workers tend to be pushed onwards and upwards into management. The rest tend to be pushed out. And crippling old foot soldiers is surprisingly easy. Last September, a national computing firm advertised for a programming troubleshooter to join them. Naturally all applications were beautifully finished with all the would-bes bringing every ounce of their whizzy desktop skills to their applications.

And, of course, they could all do the job, given half the chance. So how did the interviewers start to sort the wheat from the chaff?

Simple. "We just looked at the birth date of the applicants and divided them into the over-35's and the under-35's," our insider reports. "And chucked the over-35's in the reject pile. It's illegal, but doesn't it have a certain Darwinian simplicity?"

Survival of the fittest, failure of the oldest.

My Smart Dad's Trip Wire

For those who have read my previous books, you may already know how sensitive I am to the idea of a career "trip wire," as expressed in this article. For those who have not read my previous books, my smart dad, the head of education, hit his trip wire at the age of fifty. Here was a man with a good education, honest, hardworking, and dedicated to improving the educational system of the state of Hawaii. But at the age of fifty he was left out in the cold without a job and no real survival skills for life outside the walls of education. Although a great student in school, with a great learning formula, his *winning learning formula* was *not* able to reeducate him to survive in the real world when his *winning professional formula* failed.

Working Hard in a Dead-End Job

My friend Kelly Richie gave me the ARE YOU PAST IT? story from the *West Australian* newspaper because for years I have been saying to my classes, "Most people follow their parents' advice of 'Go to school, get good grades, and get a safe, secure job.' That is an old idea. It is an Industrial Age idea. And the problem is, most people who follow that advice wind up in a dead-end job. They may have had good grades, and they have found a safe, secure job, they may earn a lot of money, but the problem is, the job does not come with a ladder."

There are people who are working, still earning a good income, but their minds and bodies are tired, many are burned out . . . and there is no ladder to get out and over the top. Somewhere along the way they tripped the trip wire and did not know it. While they still may have their jobs, or they still have their business, nonetheless somewhere along the way, the ladder to the top disappeared. I have many friends who did well in school, went to graduate school, and attained some degree of success by forty, but then the professional magic stopped and the downhill slide began. In these cases, I believe the *winning professional formula* stopped working because the *winning learning formula* stopped also. In other words, my friends are using the same winning learning formula, and that formula is stopping the magic professionally.

Rich by Forty and Broke by Forty-Seven

I have a classmate who did very well in high school. He went to a prestigious Ivy League school on the East Coast and then returned to Hawaii. Immediately he joined his dad's country club, married a girl whose father is a member of the same club, and had kids, and now his kids go to the same private school he went to.

After working a few years, gaining a little work experience, and playing golf with the right people, he was involved in some very large real estate transactions. His smiling face was on the cover of the local business magazines, and he was hailed as one of the next generation's rising business leaders. Before the age of forty he was set for life. In the late 1980s the real estate market in Hawaii went bad when the Japanese pulled their investment money out of the state, and he lost most of his fortune. He and his wife split up because he was having an affair, and now he supports two households. He was broke by age forty-seven, with massive bills to pay.

I saw him just a few months ago. He has just turned fifty and has recovered from most of his losses and even has a new girlfriend. But as much as he says things are fine and he is doing well, I can see the fire is gone. Something has changed inside, and he is working harder than ever just to maintain his image from years past. He seems more cynical and edgy.

One night over dinner, his girlfriend was telling us about the new Internet business she was starting up. She was very excited, and it seemed the business was doing very well and receiving orders from all over the world. Suddenly my friend snapped. It seemed he had too many drinks, and the pressure from the inside was cracking his cool exterior. Obviously annoyed at his girlfriend's newfound success, or his lack of success, he said, "How can you do well? You didn't go to the right college, and you don't have a master's degree. Besides, you don't know the right people like I do."

As Kim and I drove home that night, she commented on his sudden loss of temper. "It seems he is trying to make his old formula for success work, and it doesn't seem to be working."

I nodded and reflected on what the Australian newspaper had said about tripping a trip wire. I thought about the young person saying that he divided the stack of résumés by those applicants older than thirty-five and those younger than thirty-five. I thought about Adrian, the friend who was downsized, bought a travel agency franchise, and was now in law school, expecting to graduate at age fifty-seven. And I thought of my smart dad, a man who truly believed in the power of a good education, although his good education did not save him in the end. Finally coming out of my private thoughts, I said to Kim, "Sounds like old economy ideas versus new economy ideas."

"You can tell that she has new economy ideas and he has old economy ideas?" Kim asked.

I nodded. "We can even leave off the word *economy*. Just say that she has new ideas, and he is still operating on ideas he developed in high school. They're only a few years apart, but her ideas are new . . . not original, but for her they are new, refreshing, and exciting, so she seems new and refreshing. His ideas are not new, not original, and he has held on to them for forty years, since we were kids."

"So people don't become obsolete. Their ideas can become obsolete."

"Yeah. Sure seems that way. Their ideas, but more specifically their winning formula becomes obsolete," I replied. "He gets up and goes to work, but instead of being the new wonder kid in town, the new mover and shaker with the new ideas, he is now the old guy with the old ideas, and he is only fifty years old. The trouble is, he was old and obsolete ten years ago, and he didn't know it. He is still operating with the same old winning formulas, and the trouble is that he is not willing to change his formula. Today he is going around town with his résumé in hand, competing for a job with kids his kids' age."

"So the advice of 'Go to school, get good grades, get a good job' was good advice when he was a kid," Kim said, "but it is bad advice for him as an adult."

"And the trouble is, he is trapped by his winning formula and doesn't know it," I added softly. "He does not realize that his good advice in the past is bad advice in the present, so his future is bleak."

"Trapped and doesn't know it?" asked Kim.

"That happened to my dad at age fifty. The advice of 'Go to school and get a job' was good advice for him as a kid. It was a great formula. He got the good grades, he got the great job, and he did rise to the top. But then the formula stopped working and his downhill slide began."

"And he kept using the same formula," said Kim.

"Not only did he continue to use it . . . the less it worked for him, the more insecure he got, the *more* he told other people to follow his advice—his formula—even though it was not working for him."

"The less it worked for him, the more he told others to follow his advice?" Kim said quietly, more to herself.

"I think he is stuck in two places," I said. "He is stuck in what is not working, and he is frustrated and tired . . . yet he continues on. And he is stuck in the past, a time in his life when the formula did work. And because it worked in the past, he wants to reassure himself that he is doing the right thing today."

"So he tells everyone else to do what he did," Kim said. "Even though it stopped working."

"I think he says it because that is all he knows about what worked for him. He has not yet figured out what isn't working."

"The moment he figures that out, he will tell everyone else what he did do," said Kim. "He might become the evangelist for the new way of doing things. When he finds it, he'll go around shouting, 'I found the way! I found the way!' But until then, he will preach about the old way until he finds the new winning formula for his life."

"If he finds it," I replied. "When you graduate from school, no one hands you a roadmap to success. Once the trail disappears, many of us wind up hacking our way through the jungle, hoping to find the trail again. Some find it again, and some don't. And when you don't find the new trail, you often sit and think about the old trail. That is real life."

High School Heroes

Earlier I mentioned Al Bundy, the character in the television sitcom *Married with Children*. Al Bundy is a tragic comic characterization of someone who was a hero in high school but did not change his formula. In the show, Al stands in his shoe store reminiscing about the day he scored four touchdowns and won the game for his high school. Someday we may all become like Al Bundy, sitting in our rocking chair, looking back upon the times when life was magic. But problems arise when you're not ready to look back—and you still want to accomplish something more with your life. Problems arise when you live in the present trying to recapture the joys of the past. People who cannot stop when they should stop are often like old prizefighters who enter the ring and get pounded by a younger opponent. They fight on with an old winning formula, just so the old fighter can relive the memories of days gone by.

Many people may have done well in school or in their last job, but something has stopped working for them. High school reunions are great places to see the football star who never went any further . . . or the academic star who never went any further. You meet them again after ten, twenty, or thirty years, and you know the magic is gone. For them, if they are unhappy, it might be time to change an old winning *professional* formula and to recognize that they may need to change their old winning *learning* formula. And today it is important to let your children know that change is part of their future. In fact, it might be important to let your children know that their ability to change and learn quickly is probably more important than what they are learning in school today.

Ideas for Parents

A couple of years ago I saw a television program where mothers were taking their daughters to work to show their daughters what they did. The TV commentator just gushed at the idea, saying, "This is a bold new idea—mothers teaching their daughters to be the good employees of the future."

All I could say to myself was, What an old idea.

When I talk to young adults today, I often ask them whose winning formula they are operating with. Is it their formula or their parents' formula?

When I was a kid in the 1960s, most parents were saying to their kids, with panicked tones in their voices, "Get a good education so you can get a good job." The reason for the panic was that many parents grew up in the Great Depression, a period when there were no jobs. For many people of my parents' era—generally those born between 1900 and 1935—their emotional fears, the fear of unemployment and the fear of not having enough money, greatly affected their thoughts, words, and actions.

If you take a look around today, there are "Help Wanted" signs every-where. Employers are desperately looking for anyone who can read and write, is pleasant, can smile, and is trainable. While technical skills are im-portant, the fact remains that there are many other attributes that mean more to an employer than technical skills. Although there are plenty of jobs around, I continue to hear young people repeating to their kids the same words, with the same emotional panic, their parents said to them: "Get a good education so you can get a good job."

When I hear someone say, "But you've got to have a job," I say, "Take it easy. Calm down. Take a break. Take a look around. There are plenty of jobs. The Depression is over. Capitalism won. It saved the world. Communism is dead. The Internet is up and running. And stop handing down advice based upon ancient history. Today, if you want a safe, secure job you can find a job. So take a moment to stop and think."

Some people calm down, but many don't. Most people I meet are abso-lutely terrified of not having a job, not having money coming into the house, and most people cannot think rationally because of old fears handed down from parent to child.

One of the most important things a parent can do is stop, think, and look into the future, rather than hand out advice based upon events from the past. As I said, the Depression is over.

Many kids are dropping out of school or are not taking their education seriously because the threat of not being able to get a safe, secure job as a reason for going to school is not working anymore. The kids in school know they can get a job. The kids in school can see that the big dollars aren't paid to academic stars anymore. The kids know that the people who make the most money are people who are stars in sports, music, or movies. The kids today watch Al Bundy on TV and know he got a job. They also see their par-ents go off to work, work hard, not come home, and hire nannies, and the kids then say, "Is that what I am going to go to school to eventually do? Is that what I want for my life? Do I want to do this to my kids?"

I Had to Stop Doing What I Was Good At

When I retired in 1994 at the age of forty-seven, the question "What will I do for the rest of my life" weighed heavily on my mind. Instead of resting for a year, I decided to do what people call "reinvent" myself. That meant I needed to change my winning learning formula and my winning professional formula. If I didn't, I would have been like the aging prizefighter who gets back in the ring after a year off. By reinventing myself, I had to stop doing what I was good at and enjoyed doing. This meant I had to stop teaching business and investing seminars. In order to reinvent myself, I had to start learning something I needed to learn, in order to change the way I did things. To do that, I created a board game to teach what I used to teach, and I had to learn to write, a subject I had failed at twice in high school. Today I am better known as a writer than in any other profession I have had in the past. If not for having a winning learning, professional, and financial formula, I would not have had the luxury of moving on with my life. If I had not moved on, I would have been obsolete at forty-seven . . . spending my life reminiscing about the good old days and the success of my past.

What Has Job Security Done to Family Life?

Parents today need to be smarter because their kids are smarter. Parents need to look beyond school and beyond job security because kids can see that far ahead. They can see what job security has done to their family life. They can see that their parents have a job but may not have a life. That is not the future many kids want. And to be a successful parent with a successful relationship with your child, a parent must look into the crystal ball—but not their crystal ball. A parent today must constantly be looking into their child's crystal ball. A parent today must share the child's vision of the future rather than force the child to see the parent's vision of the future, a vision that is often based on the past.

I stated earlier in this book that many arguments between parent and child are clashes between the winning formula of the parent and the winning formula of the child—for example, a parent saying, "You must go to school," and the child saying, "I am going to drop out." That is an example of a clash of winning formulas. To have a successful relationship, parents must do their best to see what the child sees, for obviously the child sees something, and a good education may not be a part of the vision. At this point, I am not saying parents should cave in and let the child do whatever he or she wants to do. All I am saying is that parents need to look beyond the clash of winning formulas and do their best to find out what vision is in their child's head. I know it may not be easy, but I think it is better than fighting.

Once a parent sees what the child sees and where the child wants to go, there may be a chance of communication and hopefully some guidance. This is crucial, because the moment a parent says to a child, "I don't want you to do that," the child is going to do it or already has done it. Sharing a vision and minimizing the clashes of winning formulas is vital for long-term guidance.

Once good communication is in place, I would recommend that parents begin sharing with their children that they will most likely have many professions in their lifetime, rather than one job for a lifetime. And if a child can grasp that idea, he or she may then have an increased respect for education. If a child can gain an increased respect for education and lifelong learning, it may become a little easier to communicate why the idea of developing a personal winning *learning* formula and why staying in school is so important. I think it is important because I don't think any parent wants their children stuck in a dead-end job, becoming less valuable the older they get.

A COMPARISON OF IDEAS

Industrial Age	Information Age
Job security, tenure	Free agent, virtual companies
Seniority	Paid for results
One job	Many professions
Work until sixty-five	Retire early
Punch a time clock	Work when interested in working
Schools	Seminars
Degrees and credentials	Core talents
Old knowledge	New ideas
Company retirement plan	Self-directed portfolio
Government retirement plan	Don't need it
Government medical plan	Don't need it
Work at company	Work at home

In summary, you and your child will have more options than your parents ever had. The above-listed Industrial Age choices are not better than or worse than the listed Information Age choices. The point is that today there are more choices, and kids know it. The challenge today is for our school system and parents to prepare our children to have the learning skills so they can have as many choices as possible. I don't think any parent wants his or her child stuck in a shoe store because the child followed the parent's advice of "Go to school so you can get a job." Today children need to be better educated than that.

A Final Note

I teach adults. When I say to them that it is the advice of "Go to school and get a job" that is trapping them, many hands go up and ask for further clarification. Many do understand that it was good advice as a kid but bad advice as an adult . . . but now they want to know more.

In one of my classes where this discussion took place, a participant asked, "But how does having a good job trap you?"

"Good question," I said. "It's not the job that traps you. It's the tag line that is added to the statement to 'Go to school to get a job' that traps you."

"Tag line?" asked the participant. "What tag line?"

"The tag line that goes, 'Play it safe and don't make mistakes.'"

Chapter 7

Will Your Child Be Able to Retire Before Thirty?

One day I asked my rich dad why he was so rich. His reply was, "Because I retired early. If you don't have to go to work, you have a lot of time to become rich."

Through the Looking Glass

In the earlier chapter on homework, my rich dad said, "You don't get rich at work, you get rich at home. That is why you must do your homework." Rich dad did his homework by teaching me the formula for great wealth by playing the game of Monopoly. Taking the time to play the game with his son and me, he was doing his best to take our minds into a world that very few people see. Somewhere between the ages of nine and fifteen I crossed over mentally from the world of my poor dad into the world of my rich dad. It was the same world everyone could see; it was just that the perception was different. I could see things I had never seen before.

In Lewis Carroll's *Alice in Wonderland,* Alice goes through the looking glass into a different world. Rich dad took me through his looking glass via the game of Monopoly and let me see the world through his eyes . . . from his perspective. Instead of saying to me, "Go to school, get good grades, and find a safe, secure job," he kept encouraging me to change my mind and think differently. He kept saying, "Buy four green houses, sell them, and then buy one red hotel. That is the formula that will make you a rich man when you grow up." I did not know what he wanted me to see, but I knew he wanted me to know something he could sense that I did not see at that moment.

Being a kid, I did not understand what he was trying to do. I just knew that he thought that buying four green houses, selling them, and then buying one red hotel was a very important idea. Through constantly playing the game with my rich dad, treating it as something important rather than just a silly kid's game, I began to change my thinking. I began to see things differently. Then one day, while we were visiting his banker, my mind made the transition. For a moment I could see into my rich dad's mind and see the world my rich dad saw. I was going through the looking glass.

A Change in Self-Perception

The mental change came when I sat in on a meeting rich dad had with his banker and his real estate agent. They discussed a few details, signed some documents, rich dad handed the banker a check, and then he took possession of some keys from the real estate agent. It dawned on me that he had just bought another green house. Getting in his car, the banker, the real estate agent, rich dad, Mike, and I drove over to the property to inspect his new green house. As we drove, I was beginning to realize that I was actually seeing in real life what I was doing on the game board of Monopoly. Getting out of the car, I watched rich dad walk up the steps, put the key in the door, turn the key, push the door open, step inside, and say, "It's mine."

As I said, I learn best by seeing, touching, feeling, and doing. I don't do well by sitting, listening, reading, and taking tests on paper. When I understood the tangible relationship between the game, the little green house, and the house he had just bought, my mind changed and my world changed because my perception of myself was changing. I was no longer a poor kid who came from a family that was having financial difficulties. I was becoming a rich kid. My perception of myself was changing. I was no longer hoping to be rich. In my soul I was beginning to know with certainty I was rich. I was rich because I was beginning to see the world through my rich dad's eyes.

When I saw him write a check, sign some papers, and take the keys, I got the relationship between the game, the deeds, and the little green house. I said to myself, I can do this. This is not hard. I don't have to be that smart to be rich. I don't even need good grades. It felt as if I were going through the looking glass and entering another world. But entering this world also caused some problems with the world I was leaving behind. I had found my winning formula. It was a formula that would require a winning learning, professional, and financial formula. It was the formula I would follow for the rest of my life. At that moment I knew I was going to be rich. I had no doubts. I understood the game of Monopoly. I liked the game of Monopoly. I saw my rich dad play the game with real money, and if he could do it, I knew I could do it, too.

Back and Forth Between Two Worlds

Mentally I was going back and forth through the looking glass. The problem was, the world I was entering, the world of my rich dad, seemed to make sense. The world I was leaving seemed to be the world that seemed insane. The world I returned to on school days seemed like the world of the Mad Hatter, the marching cards, and the Cheshire cat. On Mondays the teacher would ask us to hand in our homework. She would then hand out more assignments and ask us to study things I really could not see, touch, or feel. I was asked to study subjects that I knew I would never use. I would solve complex math problems and know that I would probably never need to use such complex math formulas in real life. I saw how much math my rich dad used to buy his green house, and he did not use any algebra formulas to buy it. Simple addition and subtraction were all it took. I knew that buying those four green houses was not that hard. Once I had the four green houses to sell, buying the one red hotel seemed easy, even logical—but it made sense only if you really wanted to get rich and have more free time. One large hotel made more money with less effort. I was confused, because each time I went through the looking glass one side definitely looked much saner to me than the other.

I never understood why we studied subjects that we knew we would never use . . . or at least were never told how to use. And then to have to take tests on those same subjects in which I was not interested, and to be labeled smart or stupid depending on how I did on those tests, really seemed like Alice's Wonderland to me.

Why Am I Studying These Subjects?

One day I decided to ask the question that had been puzzling me for years. I finally worked up enough courage and asked my teacher, "Why am I studying and taking tests on subjects I am not interested in and will never use?"

Her reply was, "Because if you don't get good grades, you won't get a good job."

It was the same reply I heard from my real dad. It sounded like an echo. The problem was that the reply did not make much sense. What did studying subjects I was not interested in and would not use have to do with getting a job? Now that I had found my winning formula for life, the idea of going to school and studying subjects I would not use to get a job, a job I now did not plan on getting, made even less sense. After thinking about it for a while, I replied, "But what if I don't want a job?"

With that I was soundly told to "sit down and get back to your schoolwork."

School Is Important

I am not suggesting that you take your child out of school and buy a game of Monopoly. A sound education is very important. School teaches basic scholastic and learning skills, and then it teaches professional skills. Although I do not agree entirely with how the system teaches or what it teaches, going to school and getting through college or trade school is still basic to most success in life today.

The problem is, school does not teach basic financial skills, and because it does not teach those skills, many kids leave school without a winning financial formula. In fact, many leave with a *losing* financial formula. Many young people today leave school with credit card debt and debt from school loans. Many never get out of debt. Many leave school and begin buying cars, homes, boats, and so on. Many will die and pass that debt on to their kids. In other words, they may leave school well educated, but they also leave school without one very important formula—the winning *financial* formula for their life.

Both Dads Were Concerned

My schoolteacher dad realized that something was missing from education, but he never really identified what was missing.

My rich dad knew what was missing. He knew that schools did not teach much, if anything, about money. He knew the lack of a winning financial formula kept many people working hard, clinging to job security, and never getting ahead financially. When I told him my dad's story of the plantations using the school system to insure a steady stream of workers, all he said in a quiet voice was, "Not much has changed." He knew that people held on to a job and worked hard simply because they had to. He knew he would always have a steady stream of workers.

He too was concerned about the financial welfare of those who worked for him. It bothered him to see people work hard for him only to go home and get further in debt. As he said, "You don't get rich at work. You get rich at home. That is why you must do your homework." He also knew that most of his workers did not have the basic financial education to do their financial homework, and that was what concerned and saddened him.

Rich Dad's Way of Teaching

I learned so much from my rich dad because he had a unique way of teaching, a way of teaching that worked best for me.

Once more I refer to the story from *Rich Dad Poor Dad* where rich dad paid me ten cents an hour after he promised to teach me how to become rich. I worked for him for three Saturdays for three hours, making a grand total of thirty cents each day. Finally very upset, I went to his office and told him that he was taking advantage of me. Shaking and crying, I stood in front of his desk, a nine-year-old boy demanding that he keep his end of the bargain.

"You promised to teach me how to be rich. I've now worked for you for three weeks, and I've not seen you at all. You don't come and watch me work, much less teach me anything. I get paid thirty cents, and that is not going to make me rich. When are you going to teach me something?"

Rich dad rocked back in his chair, looking over his desk at a very upset nine-year-old boy. After a very long minute of deathly silence, he smiled and said, "I am teaching you something. I am teaching you the most valuable lesson you can learn if you want to be rich. Most people work all their lives and never learn the lesson you are learning, if you learn it." He went silent, rocked in his chair, and continued to look back at me as I stood shaking, letting his words sink in.

"What do you mean, 'If I learn it?' If I learn what? What am I supposed to be learning that other people never learn?" I said, rubbing my nose on the sleeve of my T-shirt. I was calming down, yet it upset me to hear him saying to me that he was teaching me something. I had not seen him since I had agreed to work for him, and now he was telling me that he was teaching me something.

Over the years I would realize how important that lesson was—that most people do not get rich by working hard for money and job security. Once I understood the distinction between my working for money and having money work for me, I became a little more intelligent. I realized that schools teach us to work for money, and if I wanted to be rich, I needed to learn how to have money work for me. A small distinction, but it changed my choices in education and what I chose to spend my time studying. As stated earlier, intelligence is the ability to make finer distinctions. And the distinction that I needed to learn was how to have money work for me if I wanted to be rich. While my classmates were studying hard to get a job, I was studying hard to not need a job.

I realized what rich dad meant when he said, "Most people never learn the lesson." Rich dad would later explain to me that most people go to work, collect their paycheck, go to work, collect their paycheck, go to work . . . forever . . . and never learn the lesson he was teaching me. He said, "When you asked me to teach you to be rich, I thought the best way to teach you this first lesson was to simply see how long it would take you to learn that working for money will not make you rich. It took you only three weeks. Most people work all their lives and never get the lesson. Most people come back and ask for a raise, and while they may get more money, they rarely get the lesson." That's the way rich dad taught his lessons, and his style of teaching involved action first, mistakes second, and lessons third. And for those of you who read the first book, rich dad then took the ten cents an hour away, and I had to work for free. The next lesson had begun, but only if I wanted it.

The Other Side of the Table

Another lesson that greatly influenced me was the lesson I often call "the other side of the table." After that first lesson at age nine, rich dad realized that I was serious about learning to be rich, and he began inviting me to watch him do different things, as he did with taking me to watch him buy a rental house. At around the age of ten he began inviting me to sit with him while he interviewed people for job positions he was filling. I would sit next to him, on the other side of the table, as he asked job applicants questions about their résumés or about their attitude toward working for his companies. It was always an interesting process. I saw people with no high school education willing to work for less than $1 an hour. Although only a kid, I knew that it would be hard to support a family on less than $8 a day before taxes. When I looked at their résumés or job applications and saw how many kids some of these workers had to support, my heart grew heavy. I realized that my family was not the only one having a tough time financially. I wanted to help them as I wanted to help my family, but I still did not know how.

The Value of a Good Education

Seeing the difference in pay scales was an important lesson I got from sitting at my rich dad's side. Seeing the difference in pay scale between a worker without a high school degree and a worker with a college degree was incentive enough for me to stay in school. After that, any time I thought about quitting school, the memories of the differences in basic pay came back to remind me why a good education was important.

What fascinated me the most, though, was the occasional person who had a master's degree or doctorate degree who still applied for jobs that paid so little. I did not know much, but I knew that rich dad made much more money per month, when you included all his different sources of income, than these very educated individuals. I also knew that rich dad had not graduated from high school. While there were pay differences between workers with a good education and those who had dropped out of high school, I also realized that my rich dad knew something these college graduates did not know.

After going through this process of sitting on the other side of the desk about five times, I finally asked rich dad why he had me sit there. His reply was, "I thought you would never ask. Why do you think I ask you to just sit and watch me interview people?"

"I don't know," I replied. "I thought you just wanted me to keep you company."

Rich dad laughed. "I would never waste your time like that. I promised I would teach you to be rich, and I am giving you what you asked for. So what have you learned so far?"

Sitting at the desk next to my rich dad's side in the room now empty and without people applying for jobs, I sat and pondered his question. "I don't know," I replied. "I never thought of this as a lesson."

Rich dad chuckled and said, "You're learning a very important lesson . . . if you want to be rich. Again, most people never get the opportunity to learn the lesson I want you to learn, because most people only see the world from the other side of the table." Rich dad pointed to the empty seat in front of us. "Very few people see it from this side of the table. You're seeing the real world—the world people see once they leave school. But you have an opportunity to see it from this side of the table before you leave school."

"So if I want to be rich, I need to sit on this side of the table?" I asked.

Rich dad shook his head. Slowly and deliberately he began, "More than just sit on this side of the table, you have to study and learn what it takes to sit on this side of the table . . . and most of the time, those subjects are not taught in school. School teaches you to sit on that side of the table."

"It does?" I replied, a little bewildered. "How does it do that?"

"Well, for what reason does your dad say to go to school?" rich dad asked.

"So I can go look for a job," I replied quietly. "And that is what these people are looking for. Isn't it?"

Rich dad nodded and said, "And that is why they sit on that side of the table. I'm not saying one side is better than the other. All I want to point out to you is that there is a difference. Most people fail to see the difference. That is my lesson for you. All I want to offer you is a choice of which side of the table you eventually sit on. If you want to be rich at a young age, this side of the table gives you a better chance of attaining that goal. If you are serious about being rich and not having to work hard all your life, I will teach you how to do that. If you want to sit on the other side of the table, then follow your dad's advice."

Lessons Learned

That was an important life-directing lesson. Rich dad did not tell me which side to sit on. He offered me a choice. I made my own decisions. I chose what I wanted to study rather than fight against what I was being required to study. And that is how my rich dad taught me over the years. It was actions first, mistakes second, lessons third. After the lesson, he would give me a choice of what I was to do with the lesson I learned.

You Often Cannot See What Is Right in Front of You

"The other side of the table" lesson included other life-changing lessons. Intelligence is the ability to make finer distinctions, or to multiply by dividing. By sitting at the table, I began to make more distinctions, or learn new lessons, of watching and learning from what was happening in front of me. I sat there for long hours, just watching but learning nothing. Once rich dad pointed out to me that there were two sides of the table, I could see the different worlds that each side came from. I could sense a difference in self-perceptions each side required. Over the years I realized that the people sitting across the table from me were doing only what they were told to do, which was go out and look for a job. They were taught in school to "get the skills employers are looking for."

They were not taught to get the skills so they could sit on the other side of the table. Because of those early instructions, most people spend their lives sitting on the other side of the table. How would their lives have been different if they had been told, "Get the financial skills so you can own the table"?

People Find What They Are Programmed to Look For

I also learned that people look for different things. Rich dad said to me, "Most people leave school looking for a job, and that is why they find a job." He explained to me that what you look for in your mind is what you find in the real world. He said, "People who go looking for work often find work. I don't look for work. I don't look for a job. I've trained my mind to look for business opportunities and investments. I learned long ago that you find only what you train your mind to look for. If you want to be rich, you need to educate your brain to look for things that make you rich . . . and a job will not make you rich, so don't go looking for one."

When I say to people that our Western system of education came from Prussia, many people just let that remark go past them. But when I state that the purpose of the Prussian system was to create employees and soldiers, many of them take notice and return my words with stares of cynical, sometimes hostile, skepticism. The people who get the angriest often did the best in that same system. When challenged as to the validity of my comment, I often ask them this question: "What is one of the first things students leave school looking for?" And the answer is, "A job." They look for a job because that is what they have been programmed to do, and they respond like good little soldiers. I say this because Prussia is no longer around, but its centuries-old ideas remain.

We are now in the Information Age, and it's time to teach people to look beyond looking for a safe, secure job. In the Information Age, we need to be educated beyond just *getting the skills employers are looking for.* In the Information Age, the chances are your children will be technically obsolete by age thirty. If that is possible, why not give them the financial skills so they can retire before they turn thirty?

You Cannot Change What You Cannot See

I am not saying that being an employee or being a soldier is good or bad, right or wrong. I have been both. I simply state that when my schoolteacher dad realized that something was wrong with the system, he began to change the system. He wanted to find ways to better prepare students for the real world. The problem was, he was educated by the very system he wanted to change, and he could not see what he could not see. My rich dad could see with different eyes simply because he was not a product of the system. He dropped out of school at the age of thirteen because his father died and he had to take over the family business. At the age of thirteen he learned the skills required to sit on the other side of the table.

I Needed to Learn More to Sit on One Side of the Table

Once I realized that there were two sides to the table, I became more interested in educating myself as to what it would take to sit on my rich dad's side of the table. It was not long before I realized how much I had to study. I realized that not only did I have to study subjects in school, I also needed to study subjects not taught in school. I became much more committed to my education. I would need to learn much more than what was taught in school if I was to earn the right to sit across from the table from those who only went to school. I knew I had to be smarter than the smart kids in school if I wanted to sit on the other side of the table. I needed to learn more than just job skills that employers were looking for.

Finally I had found something that challenged me, gave me a reason to study, something I was interested in studying. Between the ages of nine and fifteen, I began my real education. I became a lifelong student who knew that my education would continue on long after I left school. I had also found what my real dad was looking for, that which was missing from the educational system—a system that was designed to keep a steady flow of workers looking for a safe, secure job, but that never taught them what the rich, the people who sat on the other side of the table, really knew.

The Learning Pyramid

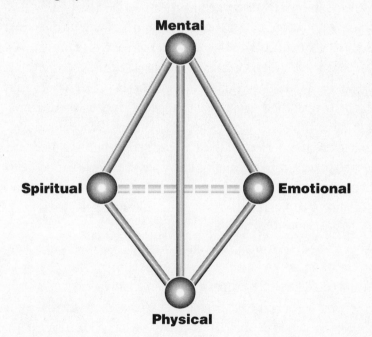

When I speak about education and learning, I often use this diagram I call "the learning pyramid." It is a synthesis of Gardner's seven different geniuses and some of my personal experiences as a teacher of entrepreneurship and investing. Although the pyramid is not based on an accurate science, it does provide some useful references for discussion.

I personally learned so much playing the game of Monopoly because the game involved me mentally, emotionally, and physically. Playing the game caused me to think mentally, my emotional state was excitement, and I had to do something physically. The game held my attention because it involved a lot of me, especially since I am a competitive person.

When I am in a classroom, required to sit still and listen to someone speak on a subject I have no interest in or understanding of in terms of personal relevance, my emotions segue from anger to boredom. Physically I begin to squirm, or I try to go to sleep just to escape my mental and emotional pain. I don't do well just sitting still, trying to take in information mentally, especially if I am not interested or the speaker is boring. Could this be the reason parents and schools are using more and more drugs to keep hyperactive kids still and sitting in their seats? The kids are probably physical learners and not interested in what they are being asked to learn. So when they rebel, is the system drugging them?

Where spiritual learning comes in, is not necessarily in the formal religious sense, although it can come from there also. What I mean by spiritual is the feeling we get when we go to something like the Special Olympics and we see physically challenged kids running or pushing their wheelchairs with all their body, mind, and soul. I went to a special program a year ago, and the spirit of these young people touched the entire audience. I too got to my feet and cheered as I watched these young people pushing their physically challenged bodies, harder than I push my physically able body. Their spirits reached out and touched all of our spirits. Those young spirits reminded all of us of who we really are and what we are really made of. That is the kind of spiritual learning I am talking about.

When I was in Vietnam, I saw young men fight on even when they knew they were dying. It was their spirit that carried them, giving their lives so their team could live. I also witnessed in Vietnam things that I dare not write about for fear of sounding too off-the-wall. Nonetheless, there were times I witnessed young men do things that cannot possibly be explained from the mental, emotional, or physical perspective. That is the kind of spiritual power I am talking about.

When you go to a wedding and see two people getting married, in my mind it is two physical beings joining together before God, spiritually. It is a commitment of two souls joining together and going forward into the world.

Unfortunately, with the divorce rate so high, it seems that many people are getting together mentally, emotionally, physically, and not spiritually. That is why when things get tough they split apart. Anyway, in an ideal sense, that is the kind of spiritual education I am talking about. I mean no personal offense, nor do I wish to impose my personal views on anyone's particular religious or spiritual views. I simply speak of a power that is beyond our mental, emotional, and physical limits.

A Change of Perception

Between the ages of nine and twelve, I remember going through a fundamental change with my personal learning pyramid. I know I changed my perception of myself mentally, emotionally, physically, and spiritually. When I saw my rich dad sign the papers, hand over the check, and take possession of the keys, something inside of me changed. When that happened, the relationship between the game of Monopoly and real life became real. After years of feeling bad about myself because I was not smart, at least not as smart as my smart dad and Andy the Ant, I changed. I felt good about myself. I knew I could make it in life, and I knew I could survive. I knew I would be successful in my own way. I knew that I did not need a high-paying job or even money to do well financially. I had finally seen something that I wanted to be good at, and I knew I could do it well. I had found what I wanted to study. As I said, something changed spiritually, and I felt confident, excited, and good about myself. I had not felt this good in school or at home seeing my mom cry as she looked at the stack of unpaid bills on the kitchen table. A warm feeling filled my heart and then the rest of me. I was certain about who I was and who I was going to become. I knew I was going to be a rich man. I knew I would find a way to help my mom and my dad. I did not know how I was going to make it, but I knew I would make it. I knew I could be successful at something I really wanted to be successful at, rather than try to be successful at what someone else said I should be successful at. I had found my new identity.

The Nine-Year Change

I recently talked to Doug and Heather, a couple who sit on the board of a Waldorf school in Alaska. They were the friends who introduced me to

Rudolph Steiner's work. They were the ones who told me of his theories and writing on "the nine-year change." When I heard what they said, more pieces of the puzzle on learning came together.

When Doug started telling me what the school was teaching their child, and why they were teaching what they taught, things began to make more sense to me. Doug explained that the reason the school had the children using hammers, saws, and nails to build little shelters was that they wanted them to know they could survive in the real world. That is the same reason they teach them to garden and grow vegetables, cook, and bake. It is physical, mental, emotional, and spiritual education. It involves the whole child at this critical period of life that Steiner identified as the nine-year change. It is the time of life when the child no longer wants to be a part of his or her parents' identity and wants to seek his or her own identity. It is a lonely and often frightening time of life. It is a period of uncertainty. The child is stepping into the unknown to find out who he or she really is, not what his or her parents want him or her to be. Learning mentally, physically, emotionally, and spiritually that they can survive on their own is vital for children's self-perception.

Now I know that many educators do not agree with Steiner's work on the nine-year change, and I am not here to change their minds. All I can faithfully relate to you is my own experience. I know that at the age of nine I began to look for something different. I knew that what my mom and dad were doing was not working, and I did not want to follow their lead. I still have memories of the fear in our house every time money was discussed. I still remember my mom and dad arguing about money, and my dad saying, "I'm not interested in money. I'm working as hard as I can. I don't know what else to do." I wanted to find out what else I could do so I did not wind up like my parents, financially at least. I know in my heart, more than anything else, I wanted to help my mom. It broke my heart to see her crying over something as silly as a stack of bills. I knew that every time I heard my dad say, "You need to study hard so you can get a good job," something inside of me rejected his advice. I knew that something was missing . . . and that was why I went looking for new answers and my own reality.

By learning the lessons from my rich dad, and physically playing Monopoly over and over again, probably fifty times a year, I was changing the way my mind worked. I felt I was going through the looking glass and beginning to see a world my mom and dad could not see, although it was right in front of them. In retrospect, I believe they could not see the world my rich dad saw because *mentally* they were taught to look for a job, *emotionally* they were taught to look for security, and *physically* they were taught to work hard. I believe that because they had no winning financial formula, spiritually their financial self-perception got weaker instead of stronger, and the bills just piled up. My dad worked harder and harder, got pay raise after pay raise, but never really got ahead financially. When his career peaked at age fifty, and he was not able to recover from his professional downslide and stagnation, I believe his spirit was finally broken.

Students Leave School Unprepared

Schools do not teach the survival skills needed for today's world. Most students leave school financially needy and looking for security . . . security that cannot be found outside. Security is found on the inside. Many students leave school unprepared, mentally, emotionally, physically, and spiritually. The school system has performed its duty by providing a steady stream of employees and soldiers, looking for a job, a job in big business and in the military. Both my dads were aware of this, but each dad saw it from a different perspective. One dad saw it from one side of the table, and one dad saw it from the other side.

When I say to people, "Don't depend upon job security. Don't depend upon the company to take care of you financially. Don't expect the government to take care of your needs when you retire," people often flinch or squirm. Instead of fire and excitement, I see more fear. People cling to job security rather than trust in their personal abilities. Part of this need for security happens because people never found their new identity and do not trust in their ability to survive on their own. They follow in their parents' footsteps, doing what their parents did and following their parents' advice of "Go to school so you can get the job skills employers are looking for." Most will find a job, but only a few will find the security they truly look for. It is hard to find true security when your survival is dependent upon someone else, someone who happens to be sitting on the other side of the table.

In July of the year 2000, Alan Greenspan, chairman of the Federal Reserve Board, spoke about inflation. He said that the reason inflation was not

as high as it could be, given this period of extremely low unemployment, was
that people wanted a secure job rather than ask for a raise. He went on to explain that most people, fearing the march of technology and the possibility
of a computer taking their job, as it has in many industries, would rather lay
low and work for less. That, he said, was why the rich were getting richer but
most people were not sharing in the new wealth. He said it was because they
were afraid of losing their job. I think it was because many people did not
learn that they could survive financially on their own . . . so they followed
their parents' advice and in their footsteps.

A reporter got very angry at what I had to say about education during a
recent interview. He had done well in school, and he had a good, secure
job. Angrily he said to me, "Are you saying that people should not be employees? What would happen if there were no workers? The world would
come to a halt."

I agreed with him, took a breath, and began my reply. "I agree the
world needs workers. And I believe that every worker performs a valuable
task. The president of the company could not do his or her job if the
janitors did not do theirs. So I hold no grudge against workers. I too am
a worker."

"So what is wrong with the school system teaching people to be employees or soldiers?" asked the reporter. "The world needs workers."

Again I agreed and said, "Yes, the world needs educated workers. The
world does not need educated slaves. I think it is time that all students, not
just the smart ones wanted by big business and the military, be given the education that will set them free."

Don't Ask for a Raise

If I thought asking for a raise would solve the problem, I would tell all my
employees to ask for a raise. But what Greenspan says is true. If a worker
wants too much money, relative to the service he or she provides the company, the guy on the other side of the table must look for a new worker. If expenses are too high, the company's future can be threatened. Many
companies are not around today because they could not contain the cost of
labor. Businesses move offshore because they are searching for lower labor
costs. And technology is replacing many jobs—jobs such as travel agents,

stockbrokers, and more. So Alan Greenspan is correct in saying people are afraid of losing their jobs if their demand for wages gets too high.

But the main reason I say "Don't ask for a raise" is that in most instances, more money does not solve the problem. When people get raises, the government gets a raise also, and then the people usually get further in debt. My books and educational games were written and created to shift a person's self-perception. If a person really wants to find financial security, there needs to be a change mentally, emotionally, physically, and then maybe spiritually. Once people begin mentally to learn the appropriate financial education, they begin to change emotionally, physically, and spiritually. Once their self-perceptions improve, they should begin to find that they need their job less and will then begin to do their homework . . . for as rich dad said, "You don't get rich at work, you get rich at home." I have also found that when your self-perception changes and your self-confidence goes up, employers are often more willing to give you a raise. That is why homework is so important.

Your Homework

I tell parents that what they teach their kids at home is as important as what the schools teach them. One thing I suggest parents do is begin to encourage their child to find a way to retire by thirty. Not that retiring at thirty is so important, but at least it begins to make them think a little differently. If they realize that they have only a few years to work and retire, they may ask questions such as "How can I retire at thirty?" The moment they ask that question, they begin to go through the looking glass. Instead of leaving school and looking for a world of job security, they will look for a world of financial freedom. And who knows? They might even find it, if they do their homework.

The End Results

The value of a person's education is not found in his or her report card. Most of us know that there are many people who were A students in school and F students at the end of their lives.

There are many ways to evaluate how good a person's education was, and one of the best measurements is how they fared financially after leaving school. An interesting piece of data I keep to show people why they need to supplement their formal education comes from the U.S. Department of Health, Education and Welfare, referenced earlier in the book. The report states that out of one hundred people studied, at the age of sixty-five, one is rich, four are comfortable, five are still working, fifty-six are needing government support or family support, and the rest are dead.

In my opinion, this is not a very good report card, considering the billions of dollars and hours we spend educating people. That means, from my graduating class of 700 students, 7 will be wealthy and 392 will need support from the government or their families. Not good. And there is one more distinction on these numbers: Of the 7 who are wealthy, approximately 2 will achieve the top position by inheritance rather than through their own efforts.

On August 16, 2000, *USA Today* ran an article titled "Not-So-Easy Money," in which analyst Danny Sheridan calculated the odds against making $1 million seven different ways:

Owning a small business	1,000 to 1
Working for a dot.com that goes public	10,000 to 1
Saving $800 a month for 30 years	1,500,000 to 1
Winning a game show	4,000,000 to 1
Playing the slots in a casino	6,000,000 to 1
Winning the lottery	12,000,000 to 1
Inheriting $1 million	12,000,000 to 1

These stats would show that even fewer people become millionaires through inheritance. By far, your child's best chance at becoming a millionaire is through owning his or her own business and building it to success.

If you can teach your children that they can survive and thrive financially on their own, knowing how to manage their finances, not being trapped by consumer debt, never needing a job, you will be preparing them for the world that is coming.

A system of education that leaves people dependent at the end of their lives is not preparing them for today's real world. The idea of a company or the government taking care of you at the end of your life is an idea whose time has passed. Your children need your help if they are going to be able to develop the financial skills they need for the future.

In Conclusion of Part I

Part I of this book was about money simply being an idea. The same can be said about education. Children's self-perceptions or ideas of themselves academically and financially will often dictate how they operate for the rest of their lives. That is why a parent's most important job is to monitor, guide, and protect a child's self-perception.

Part II

Money Does Not Make You Rich

My rich dad said, "Money does not make you rich." He would go on to say that money has the power to make you both rich or poor . . . and for most people, the more money they make, the poorer they become. Later in life, after he saw the popularity of lotteries, he said, "If money made you rich, why do so many lottery winners go broke?"

My smart dad said much the same about grades.

If a child leaves school with good grades, does it mean the child will be successful in real life? Does success in the academic world insure your child's success in the real world? Part I of this book was dedicated to preparing your child mentally for school and for changes that occur early in life. Part II is dedicated to preparing your child for success in the real world.

Chapter 8

My Banker Has Never Asked Me for My Report Card

At the age of fifteen, I did not pass the subject of English. I received a failing mark because I could not write, or I should say my English teacher did not like what I wrote about, and my spelling was horrible. That meant I would have to repeat my sophomore year. The emotional pain and embarrassment came from many fronts. First of all, my dad was the head of education. He was the superintendent of education for the island of Hawaii and in charge of over forty schools. There was much snickering and laughter throughout the halls of education as word spread that the boss's son was an academic failure. Second, failing meant I would have to join my younger sister's class. In other words, she was moving forward and I was moving backward. And third, it meant I would not receive my athletic letter for playing varsity football, the sport I had played my heart out for. The day I received my report card and saw the F for English, I went behind the building that housed the chemistry lab to be alone. I sat on the cold concrete slab, pulled my knees up to my chest, pushed my back up against the wooden building, and began to cry deeply. I had been expecting this F for a few months now, but seeing it on paper brought out all the emotions suddenly and uncontrollably. I sat alone behind the lab building for over an hour.

My best friend, Mike, rich dad's son, had also received an F. It was not good that he had also failed, but it was good that at least I had some company in this time of misery. I waved to him as he headed across the campus to catch his ride home, but all he did was shake his head as he kept walking to the waiting car.

After the other children had gone to bed that evening, I told my mom and dad that I had failed English as well as my sophomore year of high school. The educational system had a policy requiring a student failing either English or social studies to repeat the entire year. My dad was very familiar with the policy, for he was the one who enforced it. While they had expected the news, the confirmation of my failing was still a difficult reality. My dad sat quietly and nodded, his face expressionless. My mom, on the other hand, was having a much harder time with the news. I could see the emotions showing on her face, emotions that went from sadness to anger. Turning to my dad, she said, "What is going to happen now? Will he be held back a year?" All my dad said was, "That is the policy. But before I make any decision, I will look into the matter."

For the next few days my dad, the man I refer to as my poor dad, did look into the matter. He discovered that out of my class of thirty-two students, the teacher had failed fifteen students. He had given Ds to eight students. One student had an A, four had Bs, and the rest had Cs. Seeing such a high failure rate, my dad stepped in, and stepped in not as my father, but as the superintendent of education. His first step was to order the principal of the school to open a formal investigation. The investigation began by interviewing many of the students in the class. The investigation ended with the teacher being transferred to another school and a special summer school class being offered to students who wanted an opportunity to improve their grades. I spent three weeks of my summer working my way up to a D so I would be able to move on to the eleventh grade with the rest of my class.

Ultimately, my dad decided that there was right and wrong on both sides, the students' as well as the teacher's. What disturbed my dad was that most of the students who failed were the top students in the sophomore class and were headed to college. So rather than take a side, he came home and said to me, "Take this academic failure as a very important lesson in your life. You can learn a lot or you can learn a little from this incident. You can be angry, blame the teacher, and hold a grudge. Or you can look at your own behavior and learn more about yourself and grow from the experience. I don't think the teacher should have awarded so many failing marks. But I do think you and your friends need to become better students. I hope both the students and the teacher grow from this experience."

I must admit I did hold a grudge. I still do not like the teacher, and I did hate going to school after that. I never did like studying subjects I was not interested in or knew I would never use once school was over. Although the emotional scars were deep, I buckled down a little more, my attitude changed, my study habits improved, and I graduated from high school on schedule.

Most important, I took my dad's advice and made the best out of a bad situation. Upon reflection, I can see how failing the tenth grade was a blessing in disguise. The incident caused me to make corrections in my attitude and study habits. I realize that if I had not made those corrections in the tenth grade, I would surely have flunked out in college.

My Mom Was Very Concerned

During this period, my mom was very upset. She kept saying, "Your grades are so important. If you don't have good grades, you won't get into a good college, and then you won't get a good job. Good grades are so important in your life." She had said the same thing many times. But during this traumatic and trying period, she was repeating herself with much more fear and anxiety in her voice.

This period was also traumatic for me. Not only did I have a failing grade, I had to attend summer school in order to make up the failing grade so I could go on with the rest of my peers. It was the summer school my dad had set up for all the kids who had failed this one teacher's class. I hated summer school. The subject was boring, the room hot and humid. It was hard to keep my attention on the subject of English. My mind often drifted as I gazed out the window, past the coconut trees and out to the ocean where my friends were surfing. To make things worse, many of my surfing friends would snicker, laugh, and call us "the dummies" whenever we ran into them.

When the four-hour class was over, Mike and I would go across town to his dad's office and do whatever he wanted us to do for a few hours. One day while waiting for rich dad, Mike and I were discussing the impact poor grades would have on our futures. Failing and being called "dummies" was very traumatic for us.

"Our friends are laughing because they have better grades than we have and they will get into better colleges than we can," said Mike.

"I've heard that, too," I replied. "Do you think we've failed and messed up our lives?"

Having just turned fifteen and knowing little of the real world, we found that being labeled "dummies" and "failures" was taking its toll on our psyche. Emotionally we were hurt, mentally we doubted our academic abilities, and our future seemed pretty bleak. And my mom tended to agree with us.

Rich Dad's Comments

Rich dad was very aware of our academic failure. His son's F in English disturbed him. He was grateful that my dad intervened and set up a summer school program for us to make up our failing grades. Both dads were looking on the bright side of things, and both had lessons that we could gain from this experience, although their lessons were different. Up to this point, rich dad had not said very much. I believe he was just watching the two of us to see how we would respond to our situation. Now that he had overheard what we were thinking and feeling about our academic setback, it was time for him to comment. Taking a seat in the room, rich dad said, "Good grades are important. How well you do in school is important. How much you learn and how smart you are is also important. But once you leave school, good grades aren't that important."

When I heard him say that, I pushed back in my seat. In my family, a family where almost everyone was employed by the school system, from my dad to his brothers and sisters, to say that grades were not important was nearly sacrilegious. "But what about our grades? Those grades will go with us for the rest of our lives," I added with shock and a slight whine.

Rich dad shook his head and then leaned over, saying sternly, "Look, Mike and Robert. I will tell you both a big secret." Rich dad paused to make sure we were listening attentively to his communication. Then he said, "My banker has never asked me for my report card."

That comment startled me. For months now Mike and I had been worrying about our grades. In school grades are everything. My parents, my relatives, and our friends thought good grades were everything. Now rich dad's words were jolting me out of my chain of thinking . . . the chain of thought that was saying my life was ruined because of bad grades. "What are you saying?" I responded, not fully understanding where he was going with this statement.

"You heard me," rich dad said, also rocking back in his chair. He knew we had heard him, and he was now letting his statement set in.

"Your banker has never asked you for your report card?" I repeated quietly. "Are you saying grades aren't important?"

"Did I say that?" rich dad asked sarcastically. "Did I say grades *aren't* important?"

"No," I replied sheepishly. "You did not say that."

"So what did I say?" he asked.

"You said, 'My banker has never asked me for my report card,'" I replied. It was a difficult thing for me to say because in my family of educators, good grades, test scores, and a good report card meant everything.

"When I go to see my banker," rich dad began again, "he does not say, 'Show me your grades.'" Rich dad asked again: "Does my banker ask, 'Were you a straight A student?' Does he ask me to show him my report card? Does he say, 'Oh, you had good grades. Let me lend you a million dollars.' Does he say things like that?"

"I don't think so," said Mike. "At least he has never asked you for your report card when I was with you in his office. And I know he does not lend you money based on your grade-point average."

"So what does he ask for?" asked rich dad.

"He asks you for your financial statements," Mike replied quietly. "He always asks for your updated financial statements. He wants to see your profit and loss statements and balance sheets."

Your Report Card After You Leave School

Nodding, rich dad continued. "Bankers always ask for a financial statement. Bankers ask everyone for their financial statements. Bankers don't care if you are rich or poor, educated or uneducated. Regardless of what you are, they want to see your financial statement. Why do you think bankers do that?"

Mike and I shook our heads silently and waited for the answer. "I've never really thought about it," Mike said finally. "Will you tell us?"

"Because your financial statement is your report card once you leave school," rich dad said in a strong, low voice. "The problem is, most people leave school and have no idea what a financial statement is."

"My financial statement is my report card when I leave school?" I asked suspiciously. "You mean it's the report card for grown-ups?"

Rich dad nodded. "It is a report card for grown-ups. Again, the problem is, most grown-ups do not really know what a financial statement is."

"Is it the only report card adults have?" I asked. "Are there other report cards?"

"Yes, there are other report cards. Your financial statement is a very important report card, but it's not your only report card. Other report cards are your annual health checkup, which through blood tests and other important procedures tells you how well you're doing and what you might need to improve on. Another report card is the scorecard on your golf game or bowling game. In life there are many different types of report cards, and a person's personal financial statement is an important one."

"So a person could have straight As on their report card in school and have Fs on their financial statement in life?" I asked. "Is that what you are saying?"

Rich dad nodded. "Happens all the time."

Good Grades Count in School, Financial Statements Count in Life

Receiving a failing grade at age fifteen in English turned out to be a very valuable experience for me, because I came to realize that I had developed a bad attitude toward school and my studies. That failing grade was a wake-up call for me to make corrections in my attitude and in my study habits. I also realized early in life that while grades are important in school, financial statements would be my report card once I left school.

Rich dad said to me, "In school, students are given report cards once a quarter. If a child is in trouble, the child at least has time to make the proper corrections, if he or she chooses to. In real life, most adults never receive a quarterly *financial report card*, which is why so many people struggle financially. Many adults do not really look at their financial situation until they lose their job, have an accident, think about retirement, or until it's too late. Because most adults do not have a quarterly financial report card, many adults fail to make the financial corrections necessary to lead a financially secure life. They may have a high-paying job, a big home, a nice car, and be doing well at work, yet have failing financial grades. Many smart students who had good grades in school could spend their life scoring failing financial grades. That is the price of not having a financial report card, at least once a quarter. I want to look at my financial statement so I know where I am doing well, where I am doing poorly, and what I need to improve on."

Report Cards Indicate Where Improvement Is Needed

That failing grade turned out to be a good thing in the long run because both Mike and I buckled down a little more in school, although we were never great students. I received congressional nominations from my state senator to the U.S. Naval Academy at Annapolis, Maryland, and the U.S. Merchant Marine Academy at Kings Point, New York. Mike decided to stay in Hawaii to continue his apprenticeship with his dad, so he attended the University of Hawaii, where he graduated in 1969, the same year I graduated from Kings Point. In the long run, that failing grade proved to be priceless, for it caused both Mike and me to change our attitude toward school.

At the academy I overcame my fear of writing and actually learned to enjoy it, although I am still a technically poor writer. I thank Dr. A. A. Norton, my English teacher for two years at the academy, for helping me overcome my lack of self-confidence, my past fears, and my grudges. If not for Dr. Norton and Sharon Lechter, my coauthor, I doubt I would have become a *New York Times* and *Wall Street Journal* best-selling author today. I sometimes think that if I had not received a failing grade at age fifteen and had the support of my family during this tough period, I would not have made changes in my life and become a best-selling author. That is why report cards are so important, especially if they are bad ones.

In the end I realized that report cards measure not what we know, but what we need to improve upon in our lives. The same is true with your personal financial statement. It is your report card on how well you are doing financially. It is your report card for life.

Your Child Needs a Financial Report Card Now

I received a financial head start at the age of nine. That was the year rich dad introduced me to my financial report card. Those of you who read *Rich Dad Poor Dad* will recall that lesson number two of rich dad's lessons is the importance of financial literacy, or the ability to read financial statements once you leave school.

I did not realize that rich dad was preparing his son and me for the real world, the world we enter once we leave school. He was preparing us by teaching us the basics of financial literacy, a subject generally not taught to preteens in school, or to adults, for that matter. Understanding a basic financial statement gave me tremendous financial confidence and maturity around money. I understood the difference between assets and liabilities, and between income and expenses, and I learned the importance of cash flow. Many adults do not know the subtle differences, and that lack of education causes them to work hard and make lots of money yet not get ahead financially.

But there was something more than confidence I gained by understanding how a financial statement works. Rich dad often referred to "the three Cs," which stand for confidence, control, and correction.

He would say to his son and me, "If you understand how financial statements really work, you will have more confidence over your finances, you will have more control over your finances, and most important, you will be able to make corrections when things are not going your way financially. People who lack financial literacy simply have less financial confidence, so they lose control and rarely make corrections until it is too late in life."

At an early age I began learning mentally, emotionally, physically, and then spiritually the ins and outs of the three Cs. I did not fully understand it then, and I still do not fully understand it today. Yet that basic financial education was the foundation for constant, lifelong financial learning. This basic financial education gave me a financial head start in life . . . and it all began with understanding the financial statement.

My First Drawings

Rich dad began with simple drawings.

Once we had the simple drawings down, he wanted us to understand the words, the definitions, and relationships. I learned how the words and diagrams were related. When I talk to people who are financially trained, they say that although they took accounting in school, they did not truly understand the relationships among the words—and as rich dad said, "It is the relationships that are most important."

Income
Expense

Assets	Liabilities

Where Financial Problems Begin

My poor dad often said, "Our house is an asset." And that is where most of his financial problems began. It is this simple misunderstanding, or lack of a finer distinction in the definition, that caused my dad and most people their financial troubles. When you throw a pebble in a pond, ripples radiate out from the spot where the pebble hit. When a person begins life not understanding the difference between an asset and a liability, the ripples can cause financial problems for the rest of his or her life. And that is why rich dad said, "It is the relationship that is important."

Although I have covered this subject in my other books, it is important to go over it one more time. It is an important first step for giving your child a financial head start in life.

What Defines an Asset or Liability?

What defines an asset and what defines a liability? When I look up the definitions in a dictionary, I become only more confused. That is the problem with learning things only mentally and not including physical learning in the definition. The simple diagram of a financial statement gives some physical learning to the definition, even if it is only some lines on a piece of paper.

To illustrate my point, here is the definition of the word *asset,* from one of my dictionaries:

> **As-set**   a: the property of a deceased person. b: the entire property of all sorts of a person, association, corporation. c: the items on a balance sheet showing the book value of property owned.

For people who are of the verbal-linguist genius and high IQ, a definition like this may be adequate. Maybe they can read into the words and gain insight into what an asset really is. But for a nine-year-old boy, the words alone would not make much sense. For a nine-year-old boy who was learning to be rich, the dictionary definition is inadequate and misleading. If intelligence is a function of making finer distinctions, to be rich I needed much finer distinctions than those provided by the dictionary, and I needed them in more than word form.

My rich dad added the distinctions by adding physical mass and motion to the definition, so that I could make a life-changing finer distinction. He did so by using a piece of paper and showing me the relationship between the income statement and the balance sheet. He said, "What determines if something is really an asset, and not just a piece of junk you list on your balance sheet, is cash flow. Cash flow could be the most important word in the world of money, yet it is often the least understood word. You can see cash, but most people do not see the flow. Hence it is cash flow that determines if something is really an asset, or a liability, or a piece of junk."

The Relationship

"It is the cash flowing between the income statement and the balance sheet that truly defines what is an asset or liability," rich dad said over and over.

If you want to give your child a financial head start in life, memorize this line and repeat it over and over to your child. Your child must understand this

statement and repeat it often if it is to sink in. If your children do not understand that statement, the chances are they will go out, buy golf clubs, stick
them in the garage, and list them as an asset when they fill out a financial statement for the bank and apply for a loan. In my dad's world, a set of golf clubs
sitting in your garage is not an asset. But on many credit applications, you can
count those golf clubs—aka a bag of junk—as assets. They are listed under
the asset column in a section called "Personal Effects." That is where you can
list your shoes, your purses, your ties, your furniture, your dishes, and your
old tennis rackets as assets in the asset column—and this is why most people
do not become rich. They do not know the relationship between the income
statement and the balance sheet.

So this is the cash flow pattern of an asset.

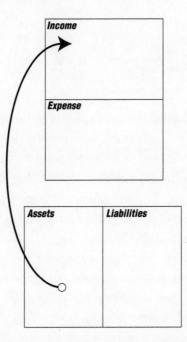

In other words, the asset is cash flowing money *into* the income column.
On the following page we see the cash flow pattern of a liability:

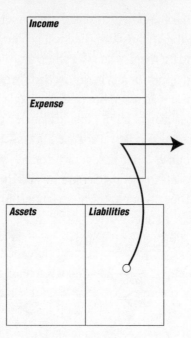

In other words, the liability is cash flowing money *out* of the expense column.

You do not need to be a rocket scientist to know that there is a difference between money going in and money going out. To reinforce this basic idea to Mike and me, rich dad would often say, "Assets put money into your pocket, and liabilities take money from your pocket." As a nine-year-old kid, I understood this. Many adults do not.

As I got older and understood that many adults were clinging to job security, rich dad would upgrade his definition. He would say, "If you lose your job, assets will feed you and liabilities will eat you." He would also say, "Most of my employees cannot stop working because they are buying liabilities they think are assets, and they are being eaten alive every month paying bills to feed those liabilities they think are assets." Again, it was a little more sophisticated definition, but sitting across the table as people applied for jobs, or cried when they were fired, I understood why knowing the difference between assets and liabilities was so important. I understood the importance of knowing the definitions before I was fifteen years old. That was a huge financial head start in life for me.

The Next Steps

So step one started with simple drawings and a little repetitive reinforcement over a number of years. Today people still argue that their house is an asset. And again, at one level of financial sophistication, that can be true. But if intelligence is the ability to make finer distinctions, then for anyone who wants to be rich, knowing the more precise distinctions based upon financial statements and actually seeing how cash flows is vitally important. I think one of the reasons only one out of one hundred people is rich at age sixty-five is that most people do not know the difference between an asset and a liability. People work hard for job security and collect liabilities they think are assets.

If your children buy liabilities they think are assets, chances are they will not be able to retire before they are thirty. If they insist on buying liabilities they think are assets, chances are they will work hard all their lives, not getting ahead financially regardless of what school they graduate from, how good or poor their grades were, how hard they work, or how much money they make. That is why the basics of financial literacy are so important. Just knowing something as simple as the difference between an asset and a liability is like a pebble hitting the water of a pond. The ripple effect will go on for the rest of your child's life.

I am not saying do not buy a house, and I am not saying pay off your mortgage. All I am saying is that for people to be rich, they need greater financial intelligence, which is the ability to make finer distinctions than the average person does. If you want further distinctions for yourself, review my other books, which spend quite a bit of time on the subject of financial literacy:

> *Rich Dad Poor Dad*
> *Rich Dad's CASHFLOW Quadrant*
> *Rich Dad's Guide to Investing*
> *Rich Dad's Guide to Getting Rich* (an electronic book)

Each book goes into different aspects or offers greater distinctions on this subject of financial literacy, which helps increase your financial intelligence. If you are better informed, you have a better chance of influencing your child's financial future. After all, one of the reasons the rich get richer, the poor get poorer, and the middle class is mired in debt and paying more than their fair share of taxes is that money is a subject that is taught at home, not at school. Financial education is handed down from parent to child.

My Banker Wants to Know How Smart I Am

The first step in preparing me for the real world was to acquaint me with the report card of the real world, which is the financial statement, a report that is made up of the income statement and the balance sheet. As my rich dad said, "My banker has never asked me for my report card. All my banker wants to see is my financial statement." He would go on to say, "My banker is not interested in how smart I was academically. My banker wants to know how smart I am financially."

The next few chapters are on more specific ways of increasing your child's chances of becoming financially smarter before entering the real world.

Chapter 9

Kids Learn by Playing

One day my dad and I were watching two kittens playing. They were biting each other's necks and ears, clawing, growling, and occasionally kicking each other. If we did not know they were playing, it could have looked as though they were fighting.

My smart dad said, "The kittens are teaching each other survival skills that have been encoded into their genes. If we should ever throw these cats out in the wild, and did not feed them anymore, the survival skills they are learning now as kittens would keep them alive in the wild. They learn and maintain these skills by playing. Humans learn in the same way."

Financial Survival Skills for the Real World

One of the hardest things I have ever had to do was to shut down my factory and let go thirty-five faithful employees. I wrote about this personal ordeal during the 1970s in another book. I had to shut my factory down because I could no longer afford to compete with Asia and Mexico. My labor costs and government compliance costs were too high. Instead of fighting them, I decided to join my competition, which led to moving my factory overseas. I won, but my employees lost. When people ask me why I write about money when I don't need to, I often think of saying good-bye to my employees that day . . . and that is all the reason I need.

When I shut down the factory, I was paying my workers less than $3.50 an hour. Today, some twenty years later, those same workers would be making only a little more than $5 an hour, or minimum wage. They may even have gotten raises in pay, but I don't think the pay raises would do much good. The only survival skills they would have developed, even if they earned more money, would be to go from job to job, work hard, and try and make more money. As my rich dad taught me, "Money alone does not make you rich, just as a safe, secure job does not necessarily make you feel safe and secure."

In order to survive financially and feel secure financially, people need to develop financial survival skills before they enter the real world. If they do not have these skills before entering the real world, the real world has other lessons about money that it wants to teach your child. And today that includes the school system. Not only are young people leaving school now with credit card debt, many are leaving school with debt from school loans. It is important to teach your child about money management as early as possible. The best way to teach those skills is by playing with your children, for it seems that play is how God or nature intended all young to learn . . . even little kittens.

Have Fun Teaching Your Child to Be Rich

I learned so much about money from my rich dad because he made learning fun. He always played games and did not try to cram information down my throat. If I did not want to learn something, he would let me move on to something I was interested in learning . . . or he made what he was trying to teach me more interesting. He usually had something tangible from the real world, something physical for me to see, touch, and feel as part of the lesson. And most important, he did not try to break my spirit. Instead he encouraged my spirit to get stronger rather than weaker. When I made a mistake, he challenged me to learn the lesson rather than give me the *right* answer. He had the patience to teach with love. He did his best to draw out the smart kid in me rather than perceive me as incompetent, or slow, or label me as having a learning disability because I was taking a little longer to understand something. He taught according to my time schedule of learning and my desire to learn, not with a need for me to pass a test. He definitely was not concerned about my competing against other kids for the best grades, as many parents are. My smart dad taught in much the same way.

Teachers Need a Hand

The current system of education does not allow teachers to teach in this way or allow teachers the time to give each child the attention needed. The system wants the teachers to move the kids along to some kind of mass production schedule. The school system is a factory that moves to the factory's production schedule, not the child's learning schedule. Many teachers have tried to change the system, but as I said, the system of education is like an alligator, a creature designed to survive and not to change. That is why parent and child homework is so important, more important than the schoolwork your child brings home.

I was listening to a professor from a major university say, "We know by age nine if a child will do well in our system or not. We know if the child has the qualities we want and is smart enough to handle the rigors of our system. Unfortunately, we do not have an alternative system for children who are not designed to run through our system."

As a child, my house was filled with people who were from the world of education. Very good people. When I went to my rich dad's house, his house was filled with people from the world of business. They were also very good people. But I could tell they were not necessarily the same people.

Give Yourself a Head Start Also

When I was growing up, many people asked me if I was going to follow in my father's footsteps, to be a teacher. As a kid, I remember saying, "No way. I'm going into business." Years later I found out that I actually love teaching. In 1985 I began teaching business and investing for entrepreneurs and loved it. I enjoyed teaching because I taught in the method in which I learn best. I learn best via games, cooperative competition, group discussions, and lessons. Instead of punishing mistakes, I encouraged mistakes. Instead of asking students to take the test on their own, participants were required to take tests as a team. Instead of silence, the room roared with discussion and rock-and-roll music in the background. In other words, actions first, mistakes second, lessons third, laughter fourth.

In other words, I used an opposite method of teaching from the school system's. I taught in much the same way that my two dads taught me at home. I found out that many other people preferred learning in this manner, and I earned a lot of money as a teacher, often charging thousands of dollars per student to attend. I applied my two dads' teaching styles with my rich dad's lessons on money and investing. I found myself in a profession that I swore I would never enter. I may have been in the educational profession, but I catered to people who learned the way I did. As they say in business, "Find a niche and fill it." I found a very big niche, a niche of people who wanted education to be fun and exciting.

In building this education company in the mid-1980s, my wife, Kim, and I sought out other instructors who loved teaching in the same manner. Our first requirement was to find instructors who were successful in the real world and who also loved to teach. Such individuals are often hard to find. In the real world, there are many people who love to teach, but many of them are not successful in business, money, and investing. There are also people who are good at money and business but are not good teachers. The key was to find people who were both.

Student Geniuses

I had the privilege of studying with a man named Dr. R. Buckminster Fuller. He is often referred to as the most accomplished American in our history, since no one has more patents. He is more often called "our planet's friendly genius." He is recognized as a great architect by the American Institute of Architects, although he was not an architect. Harvard University often refers to him as one of their more noted graduates, yet Fuller never graduated from Harvard. He was thrown out twice and never finished. During one of my weeks studying with him, Dr. Fuller said, "The students will be geniuses if the teacher knows what he is talking about." Our job was not to find a teacher. Our job was to find people who knew what they were talking about and encourage them to teach.

Get Smart by Teaching

Beyond enjoying teaching and making a lot of money at it, I found something even more beneficial than fun and money. I found out that I learned more by teaching. When I taught, I had to dig deep inside of myself to find the lessons the class needed to learn. I learned a lot from the interaction among the participants as we all shared our personal insights and discoveries. Because of this phenomenon, I recommend that parents take the time to teach their children, because the parent often learns even more. And if a parent wants to improve his or her own personal financial situation, one way is to search for new financial ideas and pass them on to the child. Look for new financial ideas before teaching your kids your old ideas about money. Many people have financial problems because they are using old financial ideas, often handed down from their parents. They then teach those same ideas about money to their children. That may explain why the poor remain poor and the middle class works hard and gets deeply in debt soon after graduating from school. They are doing what they learned from their parents.

Therefore, one of the best ways to learn something is to teach what you want to learn to others. As they teach in Sunday school, "Give and you shall receive." The more time you personally invest in teaching your kids about money, the smarter all of you will become.

Three Steps to Learning

My rich dad taught me three steps to learning about money:

Step one: Simple drawings. My education began with simple line drawings with an emphasis on understanding the definitions.

Income
Expense

Assets	Liabilities

Step two: Play. As I said, I learn best by doing, so for a number of years rich dad would have us fill out play financial statements. Sometimes when we played Monopoly, he would have us use our four green houses and one red hotel and put them on our financial statements.

Step three: Real life. Real life started for Mike and me at around age fifteen, when we had to fill out financial statements and submit them to rich dad. Just as any good teacher would do, he would grade them, show us what we were doing well at and what we needed to improve. I have continued my education and my financial reports in real life for nearly forty years now.

How to Begin Teaching Your Child About Money

I recommend that most parents start at step two. Although my rich dad started me at step one, the line drawings, I would be careful talking to most kids about mental abstracts such as income statements and balance sheets. When I use these drawings with some adults, their eyes glaze over. In fact, I might not talk about step one until I was certain the child was interested or ready to learn such concepts. I was taught in the manner listed because I was curious, so that was the sequence rich dad chose for me.

I used to recommend beginning with the game of Monopoly. I have noticed that some kids really like the game, while other kids play the game but are not really that interested in the subject. Many of my friends who are investors or entrepreneurs tell me that they also played Monopoly by the hour, fascinated by it. Without that fascination, I would not force the subject of money, investing, and much less financial statements on young people.

CASHFLOW for Kids

In 1996, after I developed CASHFLOW 101, which is the board game that teaches the principles of the financial statement to adults, the market response indicated that a similar game was needed for children. In late 1999 we introduced CASHFLOW for Kids. Our board games are the only games that teach children the fundamentals of the financial statement, the child's report card after he or she leaves school, and cash flow management.

Used in Schools

A very innovative teacher in Indianapolis, Indiana, Dave Stephens, began using CASHFLOW 101 in his high school classes with tremendous success. He
actually noticed the game changing the life attitudes of many of his students.
One student in particular Dave told us about was about to fail out of school
owing to bad grades and poor attendance. Playing CASHFLOW made a big
difference in his life. In the student's own words:

> I went from being a party person, i.e. smoking marijuana, getting
> drunk, etc., to being a very focused and determined high school stu-
> dent, with ambitions of someday being as successful as the man
> whose game I was playing and learning from! . . . I don't remember
> much of the first few days, but I do remember playing CASHFLOW. It
> was a wonderful game that brought the concepts of making money
> into a reality unbeknownst to me at the time, expressing ideas of sim-
> plicity and genius! The game has opened doors for me like no other
> thing within my life to this point. It gave me reason to go to school
> and a yearning to get involved! Since I played the game I have en-
> tered Student Council—where I tutor Junior High students (and tell
> them ideas expressed in CASHFLOW), I became President of the
> Marion County Youth Congress, have taken a leadership role within
> the Academy of Finance, placed first at State DECA competition, and
> competed nationally. I started a Japanese and BPA club at our school
> and am currently, with the cooperation of other investors, working to
> build an East Side Community Center within my own community. As
> you can see, it has given me new light to my drive for success. As well,
> my grades, attitude, and lifestyle have changed considerably. I now
> look forward to the future with a yearning to learn and teach all who
> want to learn what I know. Sometimes you roll the dice and it
> changes everything!
>
> To Mr. Kiyosaki I give my thanks and praise—someday you will
> see the results of all that you do, and I hope to be one of the first to
> prove that your methods do work, and work well. This has become
> a cliché almost, but it sums up exactly my story: "Two roads diverged
> in a wood; I took the one less traveled by, and that has made all the
> difference."

All I can say in response to this student is, "Wow! What an impressive young man." It gives me great honor to know that our products played a role in helping this young man change the direction of his life in such a positive way.

Dave Stephens's support did not stop there. When he heard about the development of CASHFLOW for Kids, he came up with another innovative idea. Already having a group of sixteen- to eighteen-year-old kids well versed in 101, he set up a program where the high school students went into elementary schools to teach seven- through nine-year-old kids CASHFLOW for Kids. The results were spectacular.

First of all, the elementary school teacher was delighted to have approximately eight high school students come in to assist her for an afternoon. Each high school student would play CASHFLOW for Kids with four elementary school students. Instead of one teacher to thirty students, the ratio was one to four. And the results were spectacular. The elementary kids had a great time, and so did the high school kids. The learning was much more personal and specific. Both the high school students and the elementary school students learned a lot more in a short period of time.

The teachers present were thrilled with the hum and activity of active learning. Instead of the drone of lecturing or the noise of chaos, there was instead the sound of fun and very focused learning. When the game was over, the kids all went, "Ahhhh, let's play again."

An Added Bonus

Something else happened that I had not counted on, an added bonus. As the high school students were leaving, many of the younger kids ran up and either hugged their new teachers or shook their hands. These young elementary school children were gaining new role models. Instead of some of the more questionable students who get much of the publicity and attention today, Dave Stephens's students were well groomed, well mannered, very bright, and focused both on their education and on their future.

As the high school students said good-bye to the elementary school students, I could sense that the younger kids were looking up to their new teachers . . . possibly saying to themselves, I want to be just like them. As I watched the young students wave good-bye, I recalled my preteen years and remembered some of the teenage kids who were very influential in guiding me. For two hours these elementary school children had the opportunity to interact with very positive role models rather than the more questionable role models they may come in contact with outside of school.

High School Students' Comments

When I asked the high school students what they had gained from the exercise, their comments included the following:

- "I really found out I enjoy teaching. I may now consider teaching as a profession."
- "I learned a lot more teaching the younger kids. When I had to teach, I learned a lot more."
- "I was surprised at how fast the young kids can learn."
- "I'm going home and treating my young brothers and sisters differently."

I share these comments because I was amazed that high school students could be so mature.

Curriculum on Our Web Site

Dave Stephens is a director for one of the academies sponsored by the National Academy Foundation. He has also assisted us in writing a curriculum for use by teachers in playing CASHFLOW 101 within the classroom setting.

Summary of Step Two

So the key to step two is to have fun, play, and begin to spark the interest in learning about money, money management, and financial statements. Looking at the learning pyramid in the diagram on the following page, you can see how learning can be more effective.

Because a game is a tangible educational tool, it involves all four main points of the learning pyramid. Games give physical learners an equal chance to learn alongside kids who are good at learning mentally or abstractly. It involves the emotions because it is fun and exciting. Games use play money rather than real money, so the mistakes are less painful emotionally. Many adults leave school terrified of making mistakes, especially financial mistakes. Games allow students of all ages to make financial mistakes and learn from them without the pain of losing real money. If you subscribe to Rudolf Steiner's ideas on the nine-year change, then a child who knows he or she can survive financially will be more confident and less dependent on the idea of job security for financial security. The child may be less susceptible to getting deeply into consumer debt as an adult. Most important, learning how to manage money and how a financial statement works may boost a child's self-confidence as he or she prepares to confront the real world.

The Learning Pyramid

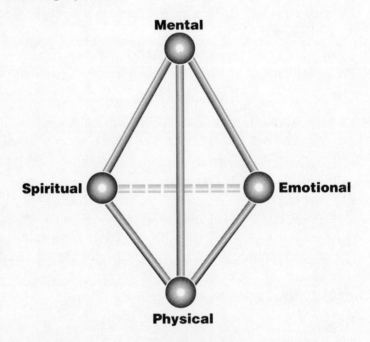

Games Have Been Used for Centuries

Most of the games purchased in stores today are games of entertainment. Yet for centuries games were used for education. Royalty used to teach their children the art of strategic thinking using the game of chess. The game was used to prepare sons for the possibility of leading an army into war. Backgammon was also used to teach strategic thinking. I once read that royalty recognized the need to exercise their bodies as well as their minds, and games were how they exercised their minds. They wanted their offspring to think rather than just memorize answers. Today, while we are not necessarily training our children to go off to war, we do need to teach our children to think strategically when it comes to money. The game of chess and the CASHFLOW games are similar in that they are games without answers. They are games designed to make you think strategically and plan into the future. They are games where each time you play, the outcome is different. With each move or change, the immediate strategy must change, in order to have the long-term plan work.

Games Help Your Child See the Future

One day while playing Monopoly, rich dad made an interesting comment that I never forgot. Pointing to one whole side of the game board, he said, "How long do you think it takes to buy all the properties on this side of the board and put red hotels on them?"

Both Mike and I shrugged. We did not understand what he was getting at. "You mean in the game?"

"No, no, no," said rich dad. "I mean in real life. We've been playing now for about two hours. I finally own all the properties on this side of the board, and I have red hotels on them. My question is, how long do you think this would take in real life?"

Again Mike and I shrugged. At eleven years old, we had little experience with how long things took in real life. We both looked at rich dad's side of the game board and could see six red hotels monopolizing his side. We knew that each time we approached his side of the board, the chances were that we were going to land on one of his properties and were going to pay dearly. "I don't know," Mike finally said.

"I think about twenty years," said rich dad.

"Twenty years!" Mike and I gasped. To a couple of teenagers, twenty years was unfathomable.

"The years go quickly," said rich dad as he launched into his next lesson. "Most people let those years slip by, and they never start. Suddenly they're over forty, often deeply in debt and with kids ready to go to college. So many never get started. They spend most of their lives working hard for money, getting deeply in debt, and paying bills."

"Twenty years," I repeated.

Rich dad nodded, letting the idea sink in. Finally he said, "Your future begins today." Looking at me, he said, "If you do what your dad is doing, which is working hard to pay bills, you will wind up twenty years from now where he is today."

"But twenty years," I complained. "I want to get rich quickly."

"And so do most people," said rich dad. "The problem is, most people simply do as they were taught, which is to go to school and then get a job. That becomes their future. Most will work for twenty years and have nothing to show after all those years of work."

"Or we can play this game for twenty years," said Mike.

Rich dad nodded. "Boys, it is your choice. This may be a two-hour game, but it could also be your future for the next twenty years."

"Our future is today," I said quietly, looking at rich dad's six red hotels.

Rich dad nodded. "Is this only a game or is it your future?"

A Five-Year Delay

In *Rich Dad's Guide to Investing*, I begin with my return from Vietnam and finally being released from the Marine Corps in 1974. I had planned on beginning my twenty-year plan in 1969, the year I graduated from the academy, but the Vietnam War had put a five-year delay in my plans to begin playing the game in real life. In 1994, exactly twenty years after beginning the game, my wife and I purchased one of our largest "red hotels" and retired. I was forty-seven and she was thirty-seven. The game of Monopoly allowed me to see into my future. The game had compressed twenty years of education into two hours.

The Advantage I Had

I believe the advantage I had over other kids who also play Monopoly was that I understood the income statement and the balance sheet—aka the financial statement. I knew the difference between assets and liabilities, businesses, stocks and bonds. In 1996 I developed my CASHFLOW board games to be a bridge between Monopoly and the real world. If you or your child likes the game of Monopoly, and are interested in building businesses or investing, then my games are the next step in the educational process. My educational games are a little bit more difficult to learn and may take a little longer to learn and master. But once you've learned them, you too may see your future in only a few hours.

Your Financial Statement Is Your Real-Life Report Card

As my rich dad often said, "My banker has never asked me for my report card." He also said, "One of the reasons people struggle financially is that they leave school not knowing what a financial statement is."

Financial Statements Are Fundamental to Wealth

A fundamental to creating and keeping great wealth is the financial statement. You have a financial statement whether you know it or not. A business has a financial statement. A piece of real estate has a financial statement. Before you buy a share of stock in a company, it is recommended that you look at the company's financial statement. Financial statements are fundamental to all matters dealing with money. Unfortunately, most people leave school not knowing what a financial statement is. That is why, for most people, Monopoly is only a game. I created my CASHFLOW games to teach interested people what a financial statement is, how it is used, and how they can take control of their future while having fun. My games are the bridge between Monopoly and the real world.

In the next pages you will see examples of the financial statement used in CASHFLOW for Kids and the financial statement used in CASHFLOW 101 and 202, which are the games used to teach adults. You may notice that while both are financial statements, one is a little more appropriate for younger children's minds.

In Conclusion

Step two is a most important part of learning. It is important to learn while having fun. It is much better to learn while having fun than to learn about money via the fear of losing it. Instead of money being related to fun and excitement, I often hear parents reinforcing fear and negativity when it comes to money. The number one argument in houses today is about money. A child learns to associate fear and anger with money. In many households a child learns that money is scarce and hard to get and that you must work hard for it. That is what I often learned when I was at home with my parents. When I was with my rich dad, I learned that making money was just a game, and he had fun playing the game. I chose to have making money a game in my life and to have fun playing the game.

In the next chapters I will go over step three, which includes the more real-life—or should I say more real-money?—exercises you can use with your children to prepare them for the real world.

Chapter 10

Why Savers Are Losers

I have a friend who recently asked me for financial advice. When I asked her what her problem was, she replied, "I have a lot of money, but I am afraid of investing it." She had worked hard all her life and had saved about $250,000.

When I asked her why she was afraid of investing it, she replied, "Because I am afraid of losing it." She went on to say, "This is my hard-earned money. I have worked for years to save it, but now that I am ready to retire, I know that it will not be enough to support me for the rest of my life. I know I need to invest it to get a better return, but if I lose it all at my age, I won't be able to work to get it back. I'm out of time."

An Old Winning Formula

I was watching TV the other day, and a child psychologist turned money adviser came on the program, saying, "It is important to teach your child to save money." The interview continued with the usual banter about starting good financial habits early as well as the usual string of clichés such as "A penny saved is a penny earned" and "Save for a rainy day."

My mom used to say to her four kids, "Neither a borrower nor a lender be." And my dad used to say, "I wish your mother would stop borrowing from the lenders so we could put some money into our savings."

I hear many parents saying to their children, "Go to school, get good grades, get a good job, buy a house, and save money." It was a good win-

ning formula for the Industrial Age, but that advice could be a losing formula for the Information Age. Why? Simply because in the Information
Age, your child will need more sophisticated financial information, sophistication far beyond simply putting money in the bank or their retirement
savings plans.

Rich Dad's Lesson on Savings

My rich dad would say, "Savers are losers." It was not that he was against savings. His reason for saying "Savers are losers" was that he wanted Mike and
me to look beyond just being savers. In *Rich Dad Poor Dad,* rich dad's lesson number one was, "The rich don't work for money." Instead of us working for money, he wanted Mike and me to learn how to have money work
hard for us. And while savings is a form of having money work for us, in his
mind simply saving money and trying to live only off the interest was a game
for losers—and he could prove it.

   Although this was covered in previous books, it is important enough to
be repeated. It points out why rich dad said, "Savers are losers." It may also
reinforce why teaching your child to understand financial statements early in
life is so important.

I Love My Banker

First of all, I love my banker. I say this because after my previous lessons on
the subject, many people thought I was against banks and bankers. Nothing
could be further from the truth. The reality is that I love my banker because
my banker is my money partner and helps me get rich . . . and I tend to like
people who help me get richer. What I am against is financial ignorance, because it is financial ignorance that causes many people to use their banker as
a partner in getting poorer.

   When a banker says to you that your house is an asset, the question is, Is
your banker lying or telling you the truth? The answer is, Your banker is telling
you the truth. He is just not saying whose asset your house really is. Your
house is the bank's asset. If you can read a financial statement, it is easy to understand why this is true.

   On the following page is a true picture of why, for most people, their
house is the bank's asset.

You

Income
Expense

Asset	Liability
	Your Mortgage

When you go across town to the bank and look at the bank's financial statement, you will begin to see and understand how financial statements really work.

Your bank's financial statement:

The Bank

Income
Expense

Asset	Liability
Your Mortgage	

By inspecting your bank's financial statement, you soon notice that your mortgage, which is listed under your liability column, is also listed under the bank's asset column. At this point you are beginning to understand how financial statements really work.

The Complete Picture

When people tell me that this proves nothing and insist that their house is an asset, I go to the litmus test of cash flow, possibly the most important word in business and investing. As by definition, if money flows into your pocket, then what you have is an asset; and if money flows out of your pocket, then what you have is a liability.

Look at the complete cycle of cash flow: That picture is worth a thousand words.

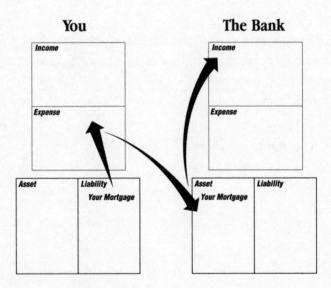

So What About Savings?

The next question is, What does this have to do with savings being for losers? Again the answer is found by reading the financial statement.

Your financial statement:

You

Income

Expense

Asset	Liability
Your Savings	

Yes, your savings are an asset. But to get a true picture, we need to follow the trail left by cash flow to improve our financial intelligence.

Your bank's financial statement:

The Bank

Income

Expense

Asset	Liability
	Your Savings

Again applying the litmus test of which way the cash is flowing, you can see that the test for what defines an asset and what defines a liability holds true.

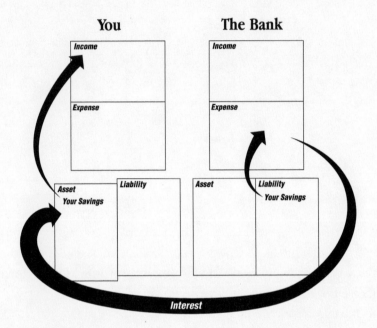

Tax Incentives for You to Be in Debt and Tax Punishment for You Saving

As the year 2000 began, many economists were alarmed at the negative savings rate in America. A negative savings rate means that as a nation we had more debt than cash in the banks. The economists began to say that we needed to encourage people to save more money. They began to sound the alarm bells that as a nation we had borrowed too much money from Asian and European banks and that our nation was on the brink of economic disaster. In one article I read, a noted economist said, "Americans have lost the work and savings ethic of our forefathers." The economist went on to blame the *people* for this problem rather than the *system* we created long after our forefathers were gone.

All one has to do is look at our tax laws, and the reason for this low savings and high debt problem becomes obvious. My rich dad said, "Savers are losers," *not* because he was against saving money. All rich dad was doing was pointing out the obvious. In many Western nations people receive tax breaks for being in debt. In other words, people are offered incentives to get further in debt. That is why so many people take their credit card debt and roll it into their home equity loans.

On top of that, you are not offered a tax break for savings. The exact opposite is true. People who save are taxed, and people who are in debt are offered tax breaks. Not only that. It is the people who work the hardest and are paid the least that pay the highest percentages in taxes, not the rich. It seems obvious to me that the system is designed to punish those who work and save and reward those who borrow and spend. And the more the educational system fails to teach kids about financial statements, the more we have a nation that cannot read the numbers to figure out what is really going on.

The Reward for Saving

My rich dad once said, "You are paid 4 percent for your savings, but inflation is growing by 4 percent, so you're not getting ahead. Then the government taxes you on your interest, so the net result is that you are losing money on your savings. That is why savers are losers."

Rich dad rarely spoke about saving money after that statement. Instead he began teaching us to have money work hard for us . . . and that was by acquiring assets or what he called "converting money into wealth." My mom and dad converted their money into debt, thinking it an asset, and they had nothing left to save. And although they worked hard and had no money to save, they kept saying to their kids, "Get a job, work hard, and save money." That may have been good advice for the Industrial Age, but it is bad advice for the Information Age.

How Fast Is Your Money Moving?

Rich dad was not against saving money. But instead of mindlessly advising us to *save* money, rich dad often talked about the *velocity* of money. Instead of advising us to put money away and "save for retirement," he often spoke about "return on investment" and "internal rates of return," which was another way of saying, "How fast does my money come back?"

Here's an oversimplified example:

Let's say I buy a $100,000 rental house and use $10,000 from my savings as a down payment. After a year, the rental income minus the mortgage payment, taxes, and other expenses is a net $10,000. In other words, I have got my $10,000 in savings back and I still have the house, an asset, paying me an additional $10,000 a year. I can now take that $10,000 and go buy another property, or stock, or business.

This is what some people refer to as "the velocity of money," or as my rich dad said, "How fast does my money come back?" Or "What is my return on investment?" The financially sophisticated want their money back so they can go forward and invest in another asset. Which is another reason why the rich get richer and everyone else is trying to save for a rainy day or saving pennies or saving for retirement.

Playing with Real Money

At the beginning of this chapter, I related the story of an old friend of mine who was nearing retirement age, had about $250,000 in savings, and was wondering what to do next. She knew that she needed about $35,000 a year to live on, and the interest on her $250,000 would not provide that level of income. I used the same simple example of taking $10,000 from savings and buying a $100,000 house to explain how investing could help solve her financial problems. Of course, she would need to learn how to invest in property and find such an investment first. When I explained to her what "the velocity of money" and "return on investment" meant, she froze mentally and emotionally. Although it made sense to her, the fear of losing her hard-earned money closed her mind to the possibility of a new winning formula. All she had known was how to work hard and save money. Today her money still sits in the bank, and when I recently saw her again she said, "I love my work, so I think I will work for a few more years. It will keep me active." As she walked away, I could hear my rich dad say, "One of the main reasons people work so hard is that they never learned how to have their money work hard. So they work hard all their lives, and their money takes it easy."

Teaching Your Children to Have Their Money Work Hard

The following are some ideas that you may want to use to teach your children to have their money work hard for them. Again, I caution parents not to force children to learn this if they do not want to learn. The trick of parenting is to find ways to make a child want to learn rather than forcing the child to learn.

THE THREE PIGGY BANK SYSTEM

When I was a little boy, my rich dad asked me to buy three different piggy banks. They were labeled as follows:

Tithing: Rich dad believed in giving to churches and charities. He took 10 percent of his gross income and tithed it. He often said, "God does not need to receive, but humans need to give." Over the years I have found that many of the richest people in the world began their lives with the habit of tithing.

 Rich dad was certain that he owed much of his good financial fortune to tithing. He would also say, "God is my partner. If you don't pay your partner, your partner stops working and you have to work ten times harder."

Savings: Bank number two was for savings. As a rule of thumb, rich dad believed in having enough savings to cover one year's worth of expenses. For example, if his total expenses per year were $35,000, he thought it important to have $35,000 in savings. After he had that amount in savings, he would tithe the rest. If his expenses went up, then the amount he had in savings had to go up accordingly.

Investing: In my opinion, it is this bank that gave me a very big head start in life. This is the bank that provided the money via which I would learn to take risks.

 My friend who had the $250,000 in savings should have had this bank at the age of nine. As stated earlier, when a child is nine years old, the child begins to seek his or her own identity. I think for me, learning to not need money, not need a job, and to invest at that age helped forge my identity. I learned financial confidence instead of the need for financial security.

 In other words, it was from this third bank that I got the real money to begin taking risks, making mistakes, learning lessons, and gaining the experience that would stand me in good stead the rest of my life.

 One of the first things I began to invest in were rare coins, a collection I still have today. After coins I invested in stocks and then real estate. But more than what assets I was investing in, I was investing in my education. Today when I speak about velocity of money and returns on investment, I speak from over forty years of experience. My friend with $250,000 in savings and approaching retirement age has yet to begin gaining her experience. And it is this lack of experience that causes her to be so afraid of losing her hard-earned money. It is my years of experience that give me a head start in this subject.

By getting your children three piggy banks, you can give them the seed capital to begin gaining this priceless experience while they are young. Once they have the three banks and are developing good habits, you may want to take your children down to a brokerage house and have them open an account, buying mutual funds or stocks with the money emptied from their piggy bank labeled "savings." I recommend letting the children do it so they gain the mental, emotional, and physical experience of the process. I know too many parents who perform this service for their child. Although you're helping your children gain a small portfolio, it robs them of the experience—and in the real world experience is as important as education.

PAY YOURSELF FIRST

Recently I was on the Oprah Winfrey show, and one of the main questions the audience had was "How do you pay yourself first?" I was shocked to realize that for many adults, the idea of paying yourself first was new and difficult. The reason it was difficult was that so many adults were so deeply in debt, they could not afford to pay themselves first. After leaving the show, I realized that by starting my life with the three piggy bank system, my rich dad was teaching me how to pay myself first. Today, as an adult, my wife and I still have three piggy banks sitting on our dresser, and we still tithe, save, and invest.

When I study the lives of very rich people, I see that this idea of pay yourself first is paramount in their minds. It is fundamental to their lives. Recently I was listening to investment guru and fund manager Sir John Templeton, who was saying that he does his best to live on 20 percent of his gross and save, tithe, and invest 80 percent of his gross. Many people are living on 105 percent of their gross and have nothing left over with which to pay themselves. Instead of paying themselves first, they pay everyone else first.

THE PAPERWORK

Rich dad took the idea of the three piggy banks one step further. He wanted to make sure that Mike and I could then relate our piggy banks to our financial statements. As we continued to fill our piggy banks, he would also have us account for our banks on crude financial statements. This is how he would have us account for our piggy banks:

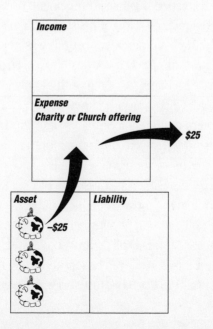

If we moved some money out of our account or bank, we had to account for it. For example, if I moved $25 out of my tithing account and gave it to charity or for a church offering, I had to account for it on my monthly financial statement.

My financials would look like this for the month:

By having three piggy banks and being held accountable for my money on my financial statement, I gained years of financial education and experience that most adults, much less kids, never receive. My rich dad would say, "The word *accounting* comes from the word *accountability*. If you are going to be rich, you need to be accountable for your money."

I cannot tell you how important the idea of accountability and accounting is for me in my life today. And it's important for everyone. When a bank politely turns you down for a loan, in many ways the bank is saying they are concerned with your lack of accountability for your money. When the International Monetary Fund (IMF) says that a country is not "transparent" enough, in many ways it is asking that the country show them clearer financial statements. Transparency means clarity, such that any interested party can easily see where the cash is flowing and to whom it is flowing. In other words, the IMF will hold an entire nation accountable just as my rich dad held Mike and me accountable.

So whether you're a small child, a family, a business, a church, or a large nation, the ability to manage your money and be accountable for it is an important life skill worth learning.

This Is the Beginning

This simple idea of using board games, three piggy banks, and simple financial statements is how my rich dad got his son and me started into the real world of money. Although simple in concept, it was not necessarily easy to keep up. One of the most important lessons I learned from this process was the value of financial discipline. Once a month I knew I had to report my finances to my rich dad. Once a month I knew I had to be accountable for all my money. There were definitely months I wanted to run and hide, yet in retrospect, the worst months were often the months I learned the most . . . because I learned the most about myself. I also know that this discipline helped me in school, because it was my lack of discipline, not my lack of intelligence, that got me in the most academic trouble.

This is how my rich dad taught his son and me to handle money in the real world. In the next chapters I will go into some more advanced exercises you can try and other lessons that can be learned along the way. The following lessons are important to learn because today, just saving your money for a rainy day is a sure way of falling behind financially. In the Industrial Age, saving money may have been an okay idea. But in the Information Age, saving money is an idea that will not keep up with the speed of change caused by the changes in information. In the Information Age, you want to know how fast your money is moving and how hard it is working for you.

Chapter 11

The Difference Between Good and Bad Debt

My mom and dad spent most of their lives doing their best to get out of debt.

My rich dad, on the other hand, spent most of his life trying to get into more and more debt. Instead of advising Mike and me to avoid debt and pay off bills, he would often say, "If you want to be rich, you must know the difference between good debt and bad debt." It was not so much the subject of debt that rich dad was so interested in. He wanted us to know the difference between financial good and bad. Rich dad was more interested in bringing out our financial genius.

Do You Know the Difference Between Good and Bad?

In school, teachers focus most of their time looking for right answers and wrong answers. In church, much of the discussion is about the battle between good and evil. When it comes to money, rich dad also taught his son and me to know the difference between good and bad.

The Poor and Banks

When I was a kid I knew of many poor families that did not trust banks and bankers. Many poor people feel uncomfortable talking to a banker in a suit.

So rather than go into a bank, many of them simply hide their money under a mattress or some other place of safekeeping . . . as long as it's not in a bank. If someone needs money, the people group together, pool their money, and lend their combined money to the group member in need. If they cannot find some friend or family member to lend them money, the poor often use pawnshops as their bank. Instead of putting up their house as collateral, they will put up their chain saw or TV and be charged very high interest rates. Today the poor can be charged interest rates over 400 percent on short-term money in some states in the United States. They are often called "payday loans." Many states do regulate the maximum amount of interest that can be charged, but it is still a very high price for borrowing money. When I realized how badly these types of financial institutions treat the poor, I knew why so many poor people distrusted the men in suits . . . and I also know that trust is a two-way street. To them, all banks and bankers were bad and out to exploit them, and banks and bankers often had a similar view of them.

The Middle Class and Banks

My parents, on the other hand, like much of the middle class, viewed the bank as a safe place to keep money. They often said to the kids, "It's as safe as money in the bank." So they viewed the banks as a good place to keep their money, but they also viewed borrowing too much money as bad. That is why my mom and dad were always trying to pay off their bills early. One of their goals was to pay off their house and own it free and clear. To summarize their view, they thought banks were good, savings were good, and borrowing was bad. That was why my mom said repeatedly, "Neither a borrower nor a lender be."

The Rich and Banks

My rich dad, on the other hand, taught Mike and me to be more financially intelligent. As stated earlier in this book, one of the definitions of intelligence is the ability to make finer distinctions, or multiply by dividing. More specifically, rich dad did not just blindly think that saving money was good or that debt was bad. Instead he spent a lot of time teaching us the difference between good savings and bad savings, good expenses and bad expenses, good debt and bad debt, good losses and bad losses, good income and bad income, good taxes and bad taxes, good investments and bad investments.

Rich dad taught us to think and raise our financial intelligence by making finer distinctions. In other words, the more you can tell the difference between good debt and bad debt, good savings and bad savings, the higher your financial IQ. If you see something such as debt as only good or only bad, then that means your financial IQ could be higher.

This book will not go into the specific differences between the goods and the bads. But if you are interested in finding out more, book number three, *Rich Dad's Guide to Investing*, will explain further some of the differences between good and bad debt, expenses, losses, taxes, and so on.

The point of this book is to caution parents about saying such things as

- "Get out of debt."
- "Save money."
- "Pay off your bills."
- "Cut up your credit cards."
- "Don't borrow money."

Repeating what was said earlier, the poor tend to think banks are bad and avoid them; the middle class think of certain services of banks as good and certain services of banks as bad; and my rich dad taught us to see the good and bad in everything. By encouraging us to see both the good and the bad in most financial matters, he increased our ability to make finer distinctions, and hence we raised our financial intelligence.

Developing Your Child's Financial Genius

One of the most important lessons rich dad taught us was the lesson he called "think like a banker." He also called it "the alchemy of money . . . how to turn lead into gold." Or "how to make money with nothing."

Those of you who read *Rich Dad Poor Dad* will recall the comic book story. That was a story about me learning to think like a banker or like an alchemist, which is a person who can turn lead into gold.

Instead of viewing the bank as bad, as many of the poor do, or that parts of the bank are good and some parts of the bank are bad, as many of the middle class do, rich dad wanted Mike and me to understand how banks work. During this period of our development, he would occasionally take us to his bank and have us sit in the lobby, watching people come and go. Finally, after we had done this exercise a number of times, he asked us, "Well, what do you boys see?"

Being about fourteen years old, we did not see too much. Mike and I shrugged and looked bored, as most teenagers do when they are asked a question. "People coming in and going out," said Mike.

"Yeah," I replied. "That's all I see."

"Okay," said rich dad as he guided us to the teller's counter. There he had us watch a woman make a deposit. "See that?" he said.

We nodded.

"Good," he said as he then led us to a desk where one of the officers of the bank sat. "What do you see here?"

Mike and I watched as a man in a suit was sitting there filling out a financial statement and talking to the banker. "I don't really know," I replied. "But if I were to guess, I would say that he is borrowing some money."

"Good," said rich dad, indicating that it was time for us to leave. "You finally saw what I wanted you to see."

Climbing into his car, which was very hot from the Hawaiian sun, Mike asked, "What did we see?"

"Good question," rich dad replied. "What did you see?"

"I saw people going in and putting money in the bank," I said. "And then I saw other people going into the bank and borrowing the money out. That is all I saw."

"Very good," said rich dad. "And whose money was it? Was it the bank's money?"

"No," said Mike. "It was the people's money. The bank is making money with other people's money. They take money in and lend money out, but it is not their money."

"Good," rich dad said again. Then, turning to me, he said, "And what are your parents trying to do every time they go to the bank?"

After thinking for a moment, I replied, "They try their best to save money. And if they borrow money, they then try their best to pay off the debt from the money they borrowed. They think that savings are good and debt is bad."

"Very good," said rich dad. "You are very observant."

Pushing my baseball hat back, I just shrugged, saying to myself, big deal, as we rode back to rich dad's office.

Sitting at his desk, rich dad took out his yellow legal tablet and drew the following diagram, the diagram of a financial statement:

The Bank

Income

Expense

Asset	Liability
Loans 6%	Savings 3%

"Do you understand this financial picture?" rich dad asked as he pushed the legal tablet in front of us.

Mike and I studied it for a moment. "Yes, I understand it," said Mike as I nodded. By now we had run so many of these different financial scenarios that it was getting easy to understand how rich dad thought. "The bank borrows or holds the money and pays 3 percent to the saver and then lends it out at 6 percent to the borrower."

Nodding, rich dad said, "And whose money is it?"

"It's the saver's money," I replied quickly. "As soon as it comes in, the banker wants to lend it out."

Rich dad nodded. After a long period of silence, letting us digest what he wanted us to understand, he said, "When I play Monopoly with you boys, I often say to you that you are looking at the formula for great wealth. Is that correct?"

We nodded. "Four green houses, one red hotel," I replied quietly.

"Good," rich dad said. "The one good thing about real estate is that you can see it. But now that you are older, I want you to see what the eyes cannot see."

"What the eyes cannot see?" I repeated, now confused.

Rich dad nodded. "You're older now. Your brain is more developed. I want to begin teaching you to see with your brain what the poor and middle class rarely see . . . and they often do not see it because they are not familiar with financial statements and how they work."

Mike and I sat quietly, waiting. We knew that he was about to show us something simple yet profound—but it would be profound only if we could see beyond the simplicity.

Rich dad then took back his legal tablet and drew the next diagram.

Rich dad's financial statement:

Rich Dad

Income	
Expense	

Asset	**Liability**
Consumer Loan 12%	**Bank Loan 6%**

Mike and I just sat and stared at the diagram for a long time. As I said, it was a simple diagram, but it would be profound if we let the lesson come through in spite of its simplicity. Finally I said, "So you borrow the money and lend it back out, just like the bank does."

"That is correct," said rich dad. "Do you know how your parents often say, 'Neither a borrower nor a lender be'?"

I nodded.

"That is why they struggle with money," said rich dad. "First they focus on saving money. If they do borrow money, they borrow money for liabilities they think are assets—things such as houses and cars—things where the cash flows out rather than in. Then they work hard to pay off that debt so they can say, 'I own this free and clear.'"

"Is it bad that they do that?" I asked.

"No," said rich dad. "It is not a matter of good or bad. It is a matter of education."

"Education?" I replied. "What does education have to do with this?"

"Well," said rich dad, "since your parents are not well educated when it comes to money, it is best that they save money and do their best to pay off debt quickly. Given their level of financial education, or what I call 'financial sophistication,' that type of money management is best for them."

"But if they want to do what you do," said Mike, "they must increase their financial education."

Rich dad nodded. "And that is what I want to do with you two before you get out of school. If you do not learn what I am about to teach you before you leave school, the chances are you will never learn it. If you leave school without this education, the chances are the world will take unfair advantage of you simply because you do not know much about money."

"You mean the real world will educate us?" I asked.

Rich dad just nodded.

"So you borrow money to make money," I said.

"That is correct," said rich dad.

"And my parents work for money and then try to save money and not borrow money."

Rich dad nodded. "And that is why it is hard for them to get rich."

"Because they work hard for money," I added, seeking more clarification.

Nodding, rich dad said, "And you can work only so hard and you can get paid only so much for your hard work. For most people, there is a limit as to how much money hard work can produce."

"So then there is a limit as to how much you can save," Mike added. "As you said, taxes take a large chunk from employees' wages before the employee even gets paid."

Quietly rich dad leaned back in his chair. He could tell the lesson was coming through.

Turning to the diagram on rich dad's legal tablet, I pointed to the asset and liability column.

Rich Dad

Income	
Expense	

Asset	Liability
Consumer Loan 12%	**Bank Loan 6%**

"So you do exactly as the bank does: borrow the money from the bank, then find a way to have that borrowed money make more money."

Rich dad stared back at me and said, "Now let's look at your parents' financial statement."

With that statement, I rocked back in my chair. I knew what he was getting at. It was clear as a bell. Using the legal tablet, he drew my parents' financial statement.

Poor Dad

Income	
Expense	

Asset	Liability
Savings 3%	**Mortgage 6%**

Rich dad, Mike, and I sat there looking at the differences in the two financial statements. I really did not know how profound this simple lesson would be for me in my life, yet it did affect the way I looked at the world after that day. There were so many lessons to be learned from this simple example, and I continue to learn the lessons today.

Many of the lessons are hidden. I would suggest sitting down with friends and discussing the impact the subtle differences can have over a lifetime. I would suggest investing the time to discuss the following:

- What happens to people if their financial mind allows assets to earn less than the cost of their liabilities over their lifetimes?
- How much time does it take to save money instead of borrow money? For example, how long would it take you to save $100,000 versus borrow $100,000 if you made only $50,000 a year and had a family to feed, clothe, and educate?
- How much faster could you get ahead if you could borrow money and make money, versus work hard and save money and then try to make money with what you saved?
- How did one dad take an asset, his savings, and turn it into a liability (savers are losers), while the other dad took debt and turned it into an asset?
- What financial skills would you need in order to be a person who could borrow money to make more money?
- How would you learn to get those skills?
- What are the long- and short-term risks of both types of financial statements?
- What do we teach our children?

If you will invest the time to discuss these questions, I think you will see why a few people get rich and why most people struggle financially all their lives. Many of life's financial struggles and financial wins revolve around the subject of money, savings, and debt.

A WORD OF CAUTION—
START SMALL

Rich dad always said, "Treat all debt the way you would treat a loaded gun." The reason rich dad often said that it was important to know the difference between good debt and bad debt was that debt had the power to make you both rich and poor. Just as a loaded gun can protect you or kill you, so it is with debt. In America today, credit card debt is choking the life out of many families, even well-educated ones.

The main point of this chapter is to give you some time to think about what you are teaching your children about debt. If you want your child to grow up and have the opportunity to become very rich in a short period of time, then you as a parent need to teach your child the basic skills of debt and debt management. That education begins with the financial statement.

If you teach your children little to nothing about debt, the chances are that your children will struggle financially for most of their lives, doing their best to work hard, save money, and get out of debt.

The next chapters are on how parents can begin to increase their child's financial IQ. A child with a high financial IQ will be better able to harness the awesome power found in debt. As rich dad said, "Always treat debt like a loaded gun." And, "You must know the difference between good debt and bad debt."

When you begin to teach your child about good debt and bad debt, good expenses and bad expenses, you begin to bring out your child's financial genius.

Chapter 12

Learning with Real Money

When my mom and dad announced that they did not have the money to send me to college, all I said was, "That's okay. I don't need your money to go to school. I will find my own way to pay for my education." I could say that with confidence because I had already been earning my own money. But it was not the money I earned that was going to put me through school. It was the lessons I learned earning the money that put me through school. It began with the lesson of my rich dad taking the ten cents an hour away. At the age of nine I was learning that I could survive on my own.

I Stopped Helping My Son and Began Teaching Him

A father came up to me recently and said, "I think my son could be the next Bill Gates. Brian is only fourteen years old, but he already has a strong interest in business and investing. I also realized after reading your books that I was spoiling him. By my wanting to help him, I was actually getting in his way. So when he came to me and said he wanted new golf clubs, I offered him a new challenge."

"How were you getting in his way?" I asked.

"I was teaching him to work for money," said the dad. "Normally, if he had come to me and asked for golf clubs, I would have told him to go earn the money and buy the clubs. After reading your books, I realized that I was programming him to be a hardworking consumer. He was being programmed to be a hardworking man instead of a rich man who knows how to have his money work hard for him."

"So what did you do differently?" I asked.

"Well, I told him to go around the neighborhood and look for jobs that needed to be done. Normally I would have given him the money via an allowance and told him to save enough to buy the golf clubs."

"That's interesting," I replied. "Instead of teaching him that he automatically deserved money, you told him to go look for opportunities and earn the money."

Nodding, the proud father said, "I thought he would be angry, but he was really excited about starting his own business, something on his own rather than asking me for the money. So he went out and mowed lawns for the summer and soon had $500, which would have more than paid for his clubs. But then I did something else that was different."

"What did you do?" I asked.

"I took him down to a stockbrokerage company, and he bought $100 worth of high-growth mutual funds. I told him this was money for his college education."

"That's good," I said. "Then did you let him buy his golf clubs?"

"Oh no," said the proud father, beaming with pride. "I then did something your rich dad would have done."

"And what was that?" I asked cautiously.

"I took his $400 and told him I would hold it until he found an asset that would buy the golf clubs for him."

"What?" I asked. "You told him to go buy an asset? So you delayed his need for gratification even longer?"

"Yeah," said the dad. "You said that delayed gratification was an important emotional intelligence to develop. So I took his money and delayed his gratification."

"What happened then?" I asked.

"Well, he got angry for about half an hour, but then he realized what I was doing. Once he realized that I was trying to teach him something, he began to think. And once he understood what I was doing, he got the lesson," said the dad.

"And what was the lesson?" I asked.

"He came back to me and said, 'You are trying to preserve my money, aren't you? You don't want me to blow it on a set of golf clubs. You want me to get the golf clubs and still hang on to my money. That is what you want me to learn, isn't it?'" said the dad, beaming. "He got the lesson. He understood that he could now keep his hard-earned money and get his golf clubs. I was so proud of him."

"Wow," was all I could say. "At the age of fourteen he understood that he could keep his money and get his golf clubs?"

"That's right," said the dad. "He understood he could have both."

Again, all I could say was, "Wow." Then I said, "Most adults never learn that lesson. So how did he do it?"

"He began reading the want ads in the newspapers. Then he went to the golf shop and talked to the pros to find out what they needed and wanted. Then one day he came home and told me he needed his money. He had found a way to keep his money and get his golf clubs."

"So tell me," I pushed, waiting for the answer.

"He found a person with candy vending machines for sale. He then went to the golf pro and asked if he could place two machines in the golf shop. The pro said yes, and he came home to me and asked for the money. We went back to the candy vendor, bought two machines and a supply of nuts and candy for about $350, and set the machines up in the golf shop. Once a week he ran over to the golf shop and collected the money from the machine and restocked the machine. After two months he had made more than enough money to buy his golf clubs. So now he has his golf clubs, and he has steady income from his six machines, his assets."

"Six machines," I said. "I thought he only bought two candy machines?"

"He did," said the dad. "But as soon as he realized that his machines were assets, he went out and bought more assets. So now his college fund is increasing steadily, his candy machines are increasing, and he has the time and money to play all the golf he wants because he doesn't have to work for the money to pay for his golf games. He plans on being the next Tiger Woods, and I don't have to pay for it. Most important, he is learning much more than if I had just given him the money."

"Sounds like you have a cross between Tiger Woods and Bill Gates coming up."

The proud father laughed. "You know, it doesn't really matter. What does matter is that he now knows that he can grow up to become anyone he wants to be."

He Can Become Whoever He Wants to Become

We discussed at length the importance of his son knowing that he can grow up to become whoever he wants to become. "My dad said, 'Success is becoming whoever you want to become' . . . and it sounds like your son is already successful."

"Well, he is happy," said the dad. "He is not in with the 'in' crowd at school. He sort of follows the beat of a different drum, as they say. So now that he has his own business and his own money, he has his own identity . . . a sense of personal security. He is not trying to see how popular he can be with the rest of the 'in' crowd. I think having the security of his own identity gives him time to think more about what he wants to become rather than try to be what his friends think is cool. He has gained a lot of self-confidence in the process."

I nodded, reflecting back to my high school days. I painfully remember being an *outsider,* not an *insider.* I remember not being in with the "in" crowd and how lonely it felt not to be recognized or accepted by the cool kids. Looking back, I realize that learning from rich dad did give me a sense of personal security and confidence in spite of a "not so cool" identity. I knew that even though I was not the smartest or coolest kid in school, I at least knew that someday I would be rich . . . and that was the identity I wanted the most.

"Tell me," asked the dad, popping me out of my high school memories, "what else would you add to my son's education? He's come this far, he's doing well, but I know he can still learn more. What would you suggest?"

"Oh, great question," I replied. "How is his paperwork?"

"Paperwork?" the dad asked.

"Yes, his records . . . his financial statements. Are they up-to-date?"

"No. He just verbally reports in to me on a weekly basis, and he shows me what he collected from the machines and his receipts from his purchases of candy to fill the machines. But there are no formal financial statements. Isn't that too difficult?"

"It doesn't have to be. It can be very simple. In fact, it is better if at first it is really simple."

"You mean keep an actual financial statement the way he does while playing CASHFLOW?" asked the dad.

"Yes," I said. "Not even that difficult. What is most important is that he sees the big picture of what financial statements do, and then he can slowly but surely add in more detail, finer distinctions. When he does that, his financial IQ will go up and up and his financial success will increase."

"We can do that," said the dad. "I'll send you a copy of the first financial statement we do."

We shook hands and went our own way. About a week later I received in the mail a copy of his son's financial statement. It looked like this:

Brian's Business Financial Statement for the Month of June

Income	
Income from 6 Candy Machines	$465

Expense	
Candy & Nuts	$ 85
Brian's Salary	$100
College Fund	$150
Savings	$130

Asset		Liability
Savings	$ 680	$0
College Fund	$3700	
6 Candy Machines	$1000	

I sent back my congratulations and comments. My comments were, "Where are his personal expenses?" His dad e-mailed back, "He now keeps his personal expenses on a separate financial statement. He does not want to confuse business expenses with personal expenses."

I e-mailed back, "Great training. It is important to know the difference between personal finances and business finances. But what about taxes?"

His dad replied, "I don't want to shock him just yet. We'll address that

next year. I'm just letting him win for now. He will be learning about taxes
soon enough."

Eight Months Later

About eight months later his dad sent me an e-mail and a copy of Brian's latest financial statement. "Just want to let you know about Brian's progress.
The mutual fund he has his college fund in did very well, even in a bad market, and he now has almost $6,000 in it. He has nine candy machines and is
now thinking about buying a business, a coin-operated automatic business
. . . just like on game cards from CASHFLOW. He has hired a part-time book-
keeper because his paperwork got too complicated. It is now time to talk to
him about taxes and introduce him to an accountant. He just turned fifteen,
and I think he is ready for the real world. His financial report card is in great
shape, and so is his academic report card. As his self-confidence increased,
so did his grades."

At the bottom of the note was written, "P.S. Brian even has a girlfriend
now, and he is teaching her what he has been learning. She says she likes
him because he is not like all the other boys, and she thinks he has a future.
Besides, I think she is more interested in business than he is. His self-esteem
and his self-confidence are now sky-high. The most important thing is that
he is learning to become who he wants to become . . . rather than trying to
become what the other kids think he should become. Thanks. Brian's dad."

The Most Satisfying Part of My Work

Most of the mail we receive, electronic or on paper, is very positive and uplift-
ing. I thank all of you who send your words of kindness to us. It inspires us as
a company to keep on going. While 99 percent of our letters are positive, there
are those that are negative. We receive comments such as "You're wrong. I
don't agree with you" or "You offended my beliefs." As I said, a vast majority of
our incoming correspondence is positive, and we thank you, because it is the
positive support that gives us the energy to keep going. Not that we don't appreciate people pointing out our mistakes for correction. So keep those comments coming in, positive and negative. We do appreciate them.

Another repeated response I receive is, "I wish I had read your books
and played your games twenty years ago." And to these people I say, "It is

never too late, and I commend you for admitting that you could have done a few things differently." Some people will defend what they did in the past, accuse me of insulting their beliefs, and then continue on with what they did in the past, even though what they did in the past is no longer working. These people often had a winning formula that worked for them in the past but is not working today . . . and to continue on with an old winning formula that is not working anymore is a loser's way of living life.

The most satisfying part of my work is to hear from parents whose children are learning to be financially secure, financially independent, and financially confident. The children who are not waiting twenty years to begin their financial education make this work especially worthwhile. Children given the opportunity to gain some degree of financial security and financial confidence early in life have a great opportunity to create a life exactly the way they want it to be.

A strong financial foundation does not give your child the answers to life. A foundation is just that, a foundation. Yet if the foundation is strong, the children can grow and find the answers they need to find so they will have the freedom to live life exactly the way they want to live it.

Young Future Millionaires

Ever since *Rich Dad Poor Dad* was released, more and more proud parents come up to me and tell stories such as the three that follow. Each story, illustrating the initiative and creativity of a particular child, amazes me.

One sixteen-year-old boy from Adelaide, Australia, came up to me and said, "After reading your book and playing your CASHFLOW game, I bought my first piece of real estate, sold part of it, and put $100,000 in my pocket." He went on to say that with the help of his father, an attorney, he made the deal on his cell phone while in study hall at school. "My mom is worried that I might let this money go to my head, but it won't. I know the difference between assets and liabilities, and I plan on using the $100,000 to buy more assets . . . not liabilities."

A young woman just nineteen years of age, from Perth, Australia, after reading my book, went out and began purchasing rental properties with her mom as her partner. She said to me, "I already make more from my rental income than I could make as a shop clerk in a retail store. I don't plan on stopping. While most of my friends are drinking in pubs, I am out looking for more investments."

A twenty-six-year-old single mom came to one of my book signings in Auckland, New Zealand, and said, "I was on welfare until a friend who is a medical doctor gave me your book and said, 'Read this.' After reading it, I went back to my friend and said, 'Let's do something together.' And we did. She and I purchased the medical clinic she was an employee of for only $1,000 down, and we financed the rest out of the cash flow from the medical clinic. In one transaction I went from a single welfare mom to a mom who was financially free. Today I watch the doctors who work for my medical clinic go to work, while I stay at home with my child. My friend and I are now looking for other investments, because we now have the time to look."

Encourage and Protect Your Child's Creativity

You may also notice that most of these young people were not afraid of using debt to make them rich. They did not say, "Play it safe and don't take risks." They did not learn to fear making mistakes or fear failing. Instead they were encouraged to take risks and to learn. When a child is taught to fear making mistakes, the child's creativity is crippled, even crushed. The same thing happens when parents say, "Do it my way." And when encouraged to think for themselves, take risks, and seek their own answers, the children's geniuses kick in, and their creativity is encouraged and protected.

I am always amazed at how creative young people are. The previous stories are examples of that creativity. Encourage a child's financial creativity when they're young. Rather than tell kids what to do, allow them to use their natural creativity, and let them find their own ways of solving financial problems and creating exactly the life they want.

The Greatest Risk of All

One of the most frequent comments I receive from parents who play my board game CASHFLOW with their kids is, "The kids always beat me. They learn so much quicker than the adults." There are many reasons why this may happen. One reason is that the children have not yet been conditioned by fear. They are young, and they know that if they fall, they will bounce back up. It seems that for many of us, the older we get, the more we seem to fear falling down.

Since the way we learn is by making mistakes, the greatest risk of all is to wait too long to begin making those mistakes. I have friends who have been doing the same old thing for over twenty years, and many of those friends are in financial trouble. The reason they are in trouble is that they failed to make enough mistakes when they were younger. Now many are out of time and out of money, and of the two, time is much more important. So please encourage your children to begin playing with real money and learning financial habits that will increase their financial well-being as they grow older. Because the greatest risk of all is to not take risks and learn from your mistakes when you're young. The older you get, the bigger the mistakes.

Chapter 13

Other Ways to Increase Your Child's Financial IQ

In June of 2000, a local Phoenix, Arizona, reporter was interviewing me. He was a nice but rather skeptical, bordering on cynical, individual. We were of the same age and of similar backgrounds. His dad was a respected judge in Boston, where he had grown up. Although we were of the same age and socioeconomic and academic backgrounds, there was a tremendous difference in our financial stations in life. At fifty-three years old he had very little to retire on. He said to me, "I had planned to write my great novel once I retired, but it seems now that I will always need to work as a freelance journalist just to pay the mortgage and keep food on the table."

I then asked him, "Why don't you begin to invest? Why not buy a few pieces of rental property here in Phoenix and then take your time to write that great novel that lies inside of you?"

His reply was, "You can't find good deals here in Phoenix anymore. You could do it ten years ago, but good deals just don't exist anymore. The market is way too hot. So when the stock market crashes, the real estate market will probably crash, too. I think that it is too risky to invest."

With that comment I knew that he would wind up working all his life. I could sense that he would probably continue on with his winning formula for the rest of his life. I could tell just by the words he was using. If he did not change his words, he would not change his life.

A Rich Vocabulary

By having two dads, I could compare the similarities and differences between them. I was about fourteen years old when I began to realize that although both my dads spoke English, they did not speak the same language. One spoke the language of a schoolteacher, and the other spoke the language of a businessman and investor. Both spoke English, but what they said was very different.

I am acutely aware of a person's vocabulary. Just by listening to their words, I can learn a great deal about people. For example, I have a friend who really likes sports. He and I can have a great conversation as long as we speak about sports. However, if I should ask him, "What is the debt to equity ratio of your house?" his eyes would glaze over, even though the question is a simple one. If I asked the same question differently, he would understand me better. Instead of asking about the debt to equity ratio, I could ask, "How much do you owe on your house, and how much do you think your house is worth?" By asking him with those words, I am asking almost the same question and seeking much the same answer. The difference is, he can understand me when I use one set of words but not when I use different words. And that is what this chapter is about: the power of words.

Nothing Is Complicated If You Use Simple Words

Both dads taught me not to ever let a word go past that I did not understand. Both dads encouraged me to stop someone in midsentence and ask him or her to explain a word or words I did not understand. For example, I was in my rich dad's attorney's office when the attorney used some words rich dad did not understand. Rich dad said calmly, "Hold it, I did not understand what you just said. Please explain that word to me in my language." Rich dad carried this practice to an extreme, especially with his attorney, who liked to use flashy words. When his attorney said, "the party of the first . . ." rich dad stopped him and asked, "What kind of *party* are you talking about? A formal black-tie party or a casual party at my house?"

My smart dad said, "Many people believe that if they use big words that no one understands, they sound more intelligent. The problem is, they may sound intelligent, but they fail to communicate."

Whenever I was having trouble with some financial terms, rich dad said, "Nothing is complicated if you use simple words."

Many people are in financial trouble simply because they are using words they do not understand. Two classic examples are the definitions of the words *assets* and *liabilities*. Instead of giving me only the definition from the dictionary, which is very confusing, rich dad gave me a definition I could use and understand. He simply said, "Assets put money in your pocket, and liabilities take money from your pocket." For added emphasis, he also said, "If you stop working, assets will feed you and liabilities will eat you."

Examining rich dad's definitions a little closer, you may notice that he uses a physical activity to define his definition instead of stating only a mental or verbal definition, such as the definition of "asset" from *Webster's* dictionary: "items on a balance sheet showing the book value of property owned."

When you look at the dictionary definition, it is small wonder that so many people think their house is an asset. First of all, most people have never bothered to look up the word. Second, most people tend to just blindly accept a definition when they hear someone they perceive to be an authority, someone such as their banker or accountant, tell them, "Your house is an asset." As I said, when your banker says your house is an asset, he or she is not lying. Your banker just is not saying whose asset it is. I also said that intelligence is the ability to make finer distinctions. So having multiple definitions is another way of making finer distinctions. Third, if you have a personal or physical experience of a word, you tend to have a better understanding of it.

When you look at the learning pyramid on the following page, you can begin to understand why so many people blindly accept only mental definitions of words.

Much of the current educational system, after the third grade or approximately by the time a child is nine, tends to be pure mental learning. The blocks and toys are taken away and students begin to study mentally. To expedite the learning process, children are asked to almost blindly accept as fact what they read or hear from an authority figure such as a teacher. The system, at this point, is focused on almost pure mental learning. Emotionally the child learns to fear making mistakes and fear questioning or challenging what is being said. Physical learning, except for art and physical education in the gym or on the athletic field, is almost nonexistent. Children who are verbal-linguistic students do well, and students who learn physically or are more artistically inclined begin to drop back. Children at this stage are often asked to accept mental concepts as facts without any physical proof. This may be why when a banker says, "Your house is an asset," most people just nod and accept that as a statement of fact without any physical proof. After all, it is how we are taught to learn after the age of nine.

The Learning Pyramid

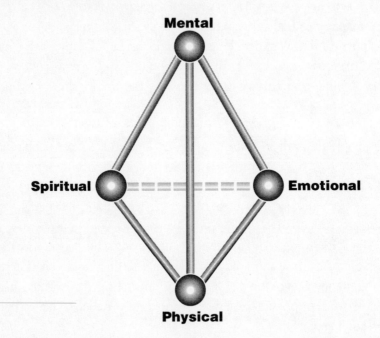

The Power of Nouns and Verbs

My rich dad did his best to have us associate physically with each new word or concept. That is why his definition of assets and liabilities always had some physical references such as "money" and "pocket" and some type of activity, such as "puts money in your pocket." He used *nouns* such as "money" and "pocket" and *verbs* such as "put" in his description—nouns and verbs that Mike and I understood. When investing the time to teach your children about money, please be very careful to use words they understand. And if they are physical learners, please be especially careful about using definitions that your children can see, touch, and feel regardless of how old they are. Games are great teachers because they provide a physical aspect to the new financial vocabulary your child is learning.

The Power of Words

At the start of this chapter I mentioned my conversation with the reporter. He was a very bright man, we were about the same age, and I enjoyed my time with him. We shared many of the same interests in life, but when it came to money, we approached the subject from very different points of view. Two issues immediately tipped me off that I should be careful about what I said around him, for he could misunderstand what I was saying about money. The first issue was that money is a very emotional subject, and the second was that I have tremendous respect for the power of the press. The press has the power to make you and the power to break you . . . so I was especially careful of what I said to him when it came to my views on money.

An example from the interview went like this:

Reporter: "Why do you invest in real estate instead of mutual funds?"

RTK: "Well, I do invest in both, but it is true that I have more money in real estate. First of all, each type of investment has different strengths and different weaknesses. One of the strengths I like about real estate is that real estate gives me the greatest control over when I pay my taxes and how much I pay in taxes."

Reporter: "Are you saying that people should *avoid* paying taxes? Isn't that a little risky?"

RTK: "I did not say *avoid,* I said real estate gave me greater *control* over my taxes."

Just the difference between the definitions and understanding of the words *avoid taxes* and *control over taxes* is vast. It took me a good twenty minutes to explain the differences between the words *avoid* and *control.* In order for me to explain the differences, I needed to explain differences between the tax laws for an employee and the tax laws for an investor. I also had to explain the differences between tax laws of mutual funds and the tax laws of real estate. At the core of the problem in communication was the fact that as an employee, he had very little control over his taxes. Since he had little control, the word *avoid* sounded like *evade* to him, and most of us know that tax evasion is illegal. So when I said "control over taxes," he heard "tax evasion," and all of his red flags went up and he went on the defensive. As stated earlier, "An ounce of perception often takes a ton of education to change." In this case, it did not take a ton of education, but it did take about twenty minutes of hard explaining to calm the situation down. I definitely did not want the awesome power of the press wielded against me simply over a misunderstanding between the definitions of two words.

After that, the interview got back on track:

Reporter: "The problem with your message is that you can't buy real estate anymore. The prices here in Phoenix are simply too high. Besides, how can I find a property, buy it cheap, fix it up, and sell it? I don't have that kind of time."

RTK: "Well, I don't trade real estate. I invest in real estate."

Reporter: "Are you saying that fixing up a property and selling it for a profit isn't investing?"

RTK: "Well, in the broad term definition of investing, I guess you could call buying and selling real estate investing. But in the world of investing, people who buy something they don't plan on using or owning are more often called 'traders.' They buy to sell. An investor usually buys to hold and uses the asset for cash flow and capital gains. It is just a finer distinction."

Reporter: "But don't you have to sell your property to get your capital gains?"

RTK: "No. A true investor will do their best to get their capital gains out without selling or trading their property. You see, the first objective of an investor is to buy and hold, buy and hold, buy and hold. A true investor's primary objective is to increase their assets, not sell them. They may sell, but it is not their primary objective. In a true investor's mind, it takes too much time to find a good investment, so they would rather buy and hold. A trader buys and sells, buys and sells, hopefully increasing their cash basis each time. An investor buys to hold, and a trader buys to sell."

The reporter sat for a while, shaking his head. Finally he said, " It sounds like a lot of mumbo-jumbo to me." Then he got back on track and asked me his next question.

I was feeling bad because I was getting into areas of discussion I should have avoided. I was doing my best to use simple language, but I could tell it was not going well. In my attempt to make finer distinctions, I could tell I was only making things more confusing:

Reporter: "Are you saying that you do not look for run-down pieces of property you can fix up and sell for a profit?"

RTK: "I might look for such properties, especially if I can buy and hold them. But the answer is 'No.' I am not necessarily looking for properties that are run-down and need repair."

Reporter: "So what are you looking for?"

RTK: "First of all, I am usually looking for a motivated seller. People often need to sell quickly, so they are willing to negotiate a good price. Or I look to banks for properties that are in foreclosure."

Reporter: "It sounds like you are picking on people who are in trouble. That doesn't sound fair."

RTK: "Well, first of all, the person needs to sell. He or she is delighted to have an interested buyer. And second, haven't you ever just wanted to get rid of something you no longer needed and were happy to get some money for it?"

Reporter: "Well, it still sounds to me like you look for people to take advantage of. If you didn't, why would you buy a foreclosure? Isn't the reason someone is in foreclosure because they ran upon tough economic times?"

RTK: "Well, I can see how you can see it that way, and from that point of view, you have a point. But the other side of the coin is that the bank foreclosed on the person because the person did not keep their agreements with the bank. I did not foreclose on them, the bank did."

Reporter: "Okay, I understand what you are saying, but I still think it is just another case of the rich picking on the poor and the weak. So after finding a motivated seller or a bank foreclosure, what else do you look for?"

RTK: "Well, the next thing I do is run my numbers and see if the IRR, or internal rate of return, makes sense."

Reporter: "IRR? Why is that important?"

Immediately after saying "IRR," I knew I was in trouble again. Maybe I should have said "ROI" or "cash on cash return." Nonetheless, I could feel I was not winning many points with this reporter. I needed to scramble out quickly. I needed to use the simple definitions that my rich dad used so I could get back into communication:

RTK: "As I said earlier, my objective as an investor is to buy and hold. IRR, or internal rate of return, is important because it measures how fast I can get my initial capital back, often called my 'down payment.' I want my initial capital back quickly because I want to go back out and buy another asset with it."

Reporter: "What about the debt? Aren't you interested in paying off the debt?"

At this point I sort of knew the interview was lost. I gave up trying to be a teacher and simply stated the investment formula I had in my head and let him decide what he was going to do with the newspaper article:

RTK: "No. My objective is not to pay off my debt. My objective is to increase my debt."

Reporter: "Increase your debt? Why would you want to increase your debt?"

As I said, by this point I knew the interview was lost. It went downhill even further when I explained the tax risk involved with mutual fund losses. He did not like what I said about mutual funds simply because all of his retirement account was in mutual funds. The gap in our communication was expanding instead of getting closer. I could tell that when it came to the subject of investing, we not only used different words, we were on opposite sides of the fence.

In the end, nevertheless, he wrote a surprisingly accurate account of my investment ideas, even if he did not necessarily agree with them. He even sent me a copy of the article for my approval before it was to go to press. I sent him a letter of thanks for his objectivity along with my approval of the article. The article was so well written, I had no changes to make. However, he called later to tell me that his editor would not print the article for reasons the editor would not explain.

Why It Does Not Take Money to Make Money

I am often asked, "Doesn't it take money to make money?" And my standard reply is, "No. Money is just an idea . . . and ideas are defined by words. So the more carefully you choose the vocabulary you use, the better chance you have of improving your financial situation."

I recall listening to Dr. R. Buckminster Fuller back in the 1980s. During one of the lectures I attended, Bucky began talking about the power of words. He said, "Words are the most powerful tools ever invented by human beings." Being a student who failed English in high school, I had a dismal point of view on the subject of words until I listened to this great man speak on their power. It was his talk that helped me realize that the difference between my rich dad and my poor dad began with the difference in their words. As stated earlier, my real dad had the vocabulary of a schoolteacher, and my rich dad had the vocabulary of a person in business and investing.

The First Step to Getting Rich

When people ask me what they can do to begin improving their financial position in life, I say, "The first step to getting rich is to add financial words to your vocabulary. In other words, if you want to be rich, start with enriching your vocabulary." I also inform them that the English language is made up of two million words, and the average person has command of only five thousand words. I then say, "If you are truly serious about becoming rich, set a goal to learn one thousand financial words and you will be far richer than people who don't use the same words." I then caution them by adding, "But go beyond simply knowing the mental definition of the words. Push your understanding to include knowing each word mentally, emotionally, physically, and then spiritually. If you have command over your financial words, your self-confidence is bound to improve." I end by saying, "And the best thing about this investment of your time is that words are free."

Words Allow the Mind to See What Your Eyes Cannot

Intelligence is the ability to make finer distinctions. Words allow your mind to make those finer distinctions. Words allow your mind to see what your eyes cannot. For example, there is a world of difference between an *asset* and a *liability* . . . but most people are not aware of the differences. And simply knowing that difference can greatly influence the financial outcome of a person's life.

In previous books I wrote about the differences in the three different types of income: *earned, passive,* and *portfolio.* Again, they all fall under the umbrella of the word *income,* but there is a tremendous difference between each of the three incomes. When you say to your child, "Go to school, get good grades, and get a job," you are advising your child to work for earned income. One big problem with earned income is that it is the highest taxed of the three incomes, and it also gives you the least control over taxes. My

rich dad advised me to work hard for passive income, which is primarily income from real estate. It is the least taxed of the three incomes and offers
you the most control over taxes. Portfolio income is typically income from
paper assets and is in most cases the second-best type of income to receive.
As you may be able to tell, the difference in words is not great, yet the difference in outcome to a person's financial report card is staggering.

The Income of the Rich

When you look at a person's financial statement, it is easy to see what type
of income that person thinks is important. The following is the financial
statement from CASHFLOW 101:

Game Sheet from CASHFLOW®101

© 2000 CASHFLOW® Technologies, Inc. All rights reserved.

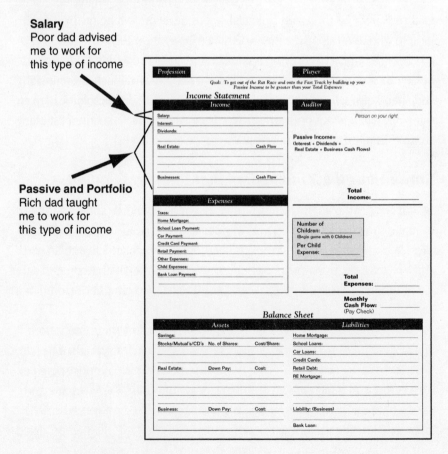

Salary
Poor dad advised
me to work for
this type of income

Passive and Portfolio
Rich dad taught
me to work for
this type of income

It is difficult to get rich working from earned income, regardless of how much money you make. If you want to be rich, you must learn how to convert earned income into passive income or portfolio income. That is what the rich teach their kids to do.

Numbers Further Define the Distinction

When accurate numbers are added to words, the mind becomes supercharged. As most stock investors know, there is a significant difference between a stock with a P/E (price-earnings ratio) of 10 and stock with a P/E of 15. Also, most sophisticated investors would not buy a stock on P/E alone, regardless if it is high or low. A sophisticated investor would need further words and further numbers.

There is also a tremendous difference in useful knowledge between someone who says, "Our business made a lot of money last month," and someone who says, "Our business grossed $500,000 last month, with a 26 percent net profit margin, which was achieved by increasing sales by 12 percent over the previous month and at the same time reducing operating expenses by 6 percent." This information would give me much more insight into whether or not I would invest in this company. This added information, combined with the company's P/E, would reduce my investment risk and increase my chances of making money as an investor.

The Power of Communication

The power of a strong financial vocabulary coupled with an appreciation for numbers can give your child a tremendous financial head start in life. One of the reasons I personally found school so boring was that I learned words without numbers. I learned how to use words in English class and how to use numbers in math class. Separated as subjects, both became boring and unrelated to my real life.

When rich dad began teaching me how to invest playing Monopoly, I gained a whole new vocabulary, and I found a love of doing math. All I had to do was put a dollar sign in front of the numbers and my interest soared in both words and numbers. When children play the CASHFLOW games, they learn a whole new financial vocabulary, and they learn to enjoy mathematics at the same time without realizing it.

My smart dad called the combining of words and numbers "the power of communication." Being an academic scholar, he was always interested in how and what caused people to communicate. He found that when people shared the same words and were excited about measuring the distinctions found in each word, communication between them flourished. He said to me, "The word *communication* finds its base in the word *community.* When people enjoy the same words, a community is formed. People who do not share the same words, or are not interested in their measurement, are people who are excluded from that closed community."

Today we find people who speak computer talk with words such as "megabyte" and "gigabyte." People who love and appreciate the bytes and the differences between mega and giga are all part of the same community. If you do not like those words or do not appreciate the differences, you are not part of that community. And that is the power of words and numbers. They can include you or exclude you.

One way to give your children a financial head start is to begin teaching them the words of money and an appreciation for measuring the differences. If you do, they have a better chance of being included in the community of the financially sophisticated. If they do not possess the words and appreciation for measuring the words, they may be excluded from that same community.

Remember my rich dad's words: "There is a very big difference between an asset and a liability, even though they are simply two words. If you see no difference between these two words, the difference will show up on your financial statement and in how hard you will work all your life." I say, "Make sure your child knows the difference between an asset and a liability, and your child will be given a very big head start in life."

Chapter 14

What Is an Allowance For?

The other day, I watched one of my friends give his child $100. The child took it, put it in his pocket, turned, and walked away without saying anything.

My friend then said, "Aren't you going to say anything? Aren't you even going to say, 'Thank you'?"

The sixteen-year-old boy turned and said, "Thank you for what?"

"The $100 I just gave you," said the father.

"This is my allowance," said the boy. "I deserve it. Besides, other kids in school get much more than this. But if you think I have to say, 'Thank you,' then I'll say it. 'Thank you.'" The boy stuffed the money in his pocket and walked out the door.

This is a prime example of the "entitlement" mentality that many of today's youth have developed. Unfortunately I see this happen all too often. Sharon Lechter refers to it as "Parents have become ATM machines for their children."

Money Is a Teaching Tool

"Money is a teaching tool," said rich dad. "I can train people to do many things. All I have to do is wave a few dollars in the air and people respond.

Just as an animal trainer uses treats to teach his animals, money is used in much the same way for humans."

"Isn't that a cruel way of looking at money and education?" I asked. "You make it sound so crude and dehumanizing."

"I'm glad to hear you say that," said rich dad. "I wanted to sound crude and dehumanizing."

"Why?" I asked.

"Because I wanted to make you aware of the other side of money. I wanted to show you the power that money can have. I want you to know the power, and I want you to have respect for that power. If you have respect for the power, hopefully you will not abuse the power of money when you have it."

"What do you mean, the other side of money?" I asked. I was now seventeen years of age and entering my senior year of high school. Up to this point, rich dad had been teaching me how to acquire, keep, and invest money. Now he was beginning to teach me something new about money.

Rich dad pulled a coin from out of his pocket. Holding it up, he said, "Each coin has two sides. Remember that." Putting the coin back in his pocket, he said, "Let's take a drive downtown."

Ten minutes later rich dad found a parking spot and put some money in the parking meter. "It's nearly five o'clock," he said. "We have to hurry."

"Hurry for what?" I said.

"Come on. You'll see," rich dad said as he looked both ways and then dashed across the street.

Once across the street, he and I just stood and looked down the sidewalk at all the retail shops in a row. Suddenly, just at five o'clock, the stores began to close. Customers hurried to make their last purchases, and employees began to walk out the door, saying, "Good night," and, "See you in the morning," to the store's owner.

"See what I mean by well trained?" said rich dad.

I did not respond. I was seeing the lesson rich dad wanted me to get. And I did not like the lesson.

"Now do you understand what I mean when I say, 'Money is a teaching tool'?" asked rich dad as he and I began walking past the shops that were closed. The quiet, deserted streets gave off a cold, empty feeling as rich dad stopped occasionally and peered into shop windows he found interesting.

I remained silent.

Riding back in the car, rich dad repeated his question. "Do you understand?"

"I understand," I replied. "Are you saying that getting up every day to go to work is bad?"

"No. I am not saying anything is good or bad. I just want you to understand the tremendous power that money has and why money is a teaching tool."

"Explain teaching tool," I said.

Rich dad thought for a while. Finally he began with, "Before there was money, humans roamed as hunter-gatherers, living off the land and the sea. Basically God or nature provided everything we needed to survive. But as we got more civilized and it became too troublesome to barter goods and services, money became more and more important. Today, those who control the money have more power than people who still trade in goods and services. In other words, money has taken over the game."

"What do you mean by 'money has taken over the game'?" I asked.

"Well, up until just a few hundred years ago, humans really did not need money to survive. Nature provided for you. You could grow vegetables if you wanted to eat or roam the woods and hunt if you needed meat. Today money gives you life. Today it is difficult to survive by growing only vegetables in a one-bedroom apartment in the city or in your backyard in suburbia. You can't pay your electric bill with tomatoes, and the government won't accept venison from the deer you shot as payment for taxes."

"So because people need money to exchange for goods and services essential for life, you say that money has taken over the game. Money and life now go hand in hand."

Rich dad nodded. "It is hard to survive without money in today's world. Money and personal survival now go hand in hand."

"And that is why you say that money is a teaching tool," I said quietly. "Because money is linked with personal survival; if you have money, you can teach people to do things they may not necessarily want to do. Things such as get up and go to work every day."

"Or study hard so you can get a good job," added rich dad with a smirk.

"But aren't well-trained and educated workers important to our society?" I asked.

"Very important," said rich dad. "Schools provide the doctors, engineers, policemen, firemen, secretaries, beauticians, pilots, soldiers, and many of the professions required to keep our civilized society civilized. I am not saying that school is not important . . . and that is why I want you to go on to college, even if you do not want to. I simply want you to understand how money can be a powerful teaching tool."

"I understand that now," I said.

"Someday you will be a very rich man," said rich dad. "And I want you to be aware of the power and responsibility you will have when you acquire your money. Instead of using your wealth to keep people enslaved to money, I ask that you use your wealth to teach people to be the masters of money."

"Just as you are teaching me," I said.

Rich dad nodded. "The more our civilized society becomes dependent upon money for life itself, the more power money has over our souls. Just as you can teach a dog to obey with dog biscuits, you can teach a human being to obey and work hard all their life with money. Too many people work for money just to survive rather than focusing on providing goods or services that make our civilized society better. That is the power money has as a teaching tool. There is both a good and a bad side to that power."

What Do You Teach Your Child with Money?

I am surprised at how many young people have the idea that they deserve money or that they are "entitled" to it. I know it is not all kids, but I have noticed more young people with that type of attitude. I have noticed that many parents use money as a way of relieving guilt. Since so many parents are so busy working, some of them tend to use money as a substitute for love and personal attention. I have noticed that parents who can afford a full-time nanny will usually have one. A growing number of single moms who own their own businesses take their children to work, especially during the summer months. But there are still too many kids left alone at home, the so-called latchkey kids. They come home from school and are unsupervised for hours because both Mom and Dad are at work . . . working hard to put food on the table. As my rich dad said, "Money is a teaching tool."

The Importance of Exchange

Parents can teach their child an important lesson about money if they teach them about the concept of *exchange*. The word *exchange* was a very important word to rich dad. He would say, "You can have anything you want as long as you are willing to exchange something of value for what you want." In other words, the more you give, the more you get.

I receive many requests to be a mentor to people. A little over a year ago a young man called and asked if he could take me to lunch. I declined, but the young man was persistent, so I finally agreed. Over lunch the young man asked, "I would like you to be my mentor." I turned him down, but he persisted even harder than he'd persisted in asking me out to lunch.

Finally I asked him, "If I was to agree, what do you want me to do as your mentor?"

He replied, "Well, I want you to take me along to sit in on your meetings, spend at least four hours a week with me, and show me how you invest in real estate. I simply want you to teach me what you know."

I thought about his request for a while and then said, "And what will you give me in exchange?"

The young man flinched with that question, sat up a little straighter, smiled his charming smile, and said, "Well, nothing. I don't have anything. That is why I want you to teach me, just as your rich dad taught you. You didn't pay him, did you?"

I rocked back in my chair, gazing back at the young man. "So you want me to spend time teaching you what I know for free. Is that what you want?"

"Well, of course," said the young man. "What do you expect me to do? Pay you money I don't have? If I had money, I wouldn't be asking. All I am asking is that you teach me something. Teach me to be rich."

A smile came over my face, and old memories of sitting across the table from rich dad came flooding back. This time I was in rich dad's seat, and I had the opportunity to teach in the same way rich dad taught me. Standing, I said, "Thank you for the lunch. My answer is 'No.' I am not interested in being your mentor. But I am teaching you a very important lesson. And if you get the lesson you need to get, you will become the rich man you wish to become. Get the lesson and you will find the answer you look for." The waiter came with the check, and I pointed to the young man. "It's his check."

"But what is the answer?" asked the young man. "Tell me. Just give me the answer."

Ten Requests a Week

I am often asked to be someone's mentor. One of the common things I notice is how few of these requests come with one of the most important words in business. And that word is *exchange*. In other words, if you are asking for something, what is that you are willing to give in exchange?

If you read *Rich Dad Poor Dad*, you may recall the story of rich dad taking away my ten cents an hour and having me work for free. As I said, for a boy of nine, working for free was a powerful lesson, one that affected my life permanently. Rich dad did not take away the ten cents an hour to be cruel. He took away the money to teach me one of the most important lessons to being rich, and that is the lesson of exchange. As rich dad said, "Money is a teaching tool." He also meant that the lack of money could be just as powerful a teaching tool.

Years after my lesson on working for free, I asked rich dad if he would have continued to teach me if I had not worked for free. His answer was, "No, absolutely not. When you asked me to teach you, I wanted to see if you were willing to give something in exchange for my lessons. If you were not willing to give something in exchange, then that was the first lesson for you to figure out—after I turned you down. People who learn to expect something for nothing usually get nothing in real life."

In *Rich Dad's Guide to Investing*, I share the story of when I asked Peter to be my mentor. When he finally agreed, the first thing he asked me to do was go to South America at my own expense to study a gold mine for him. This is another perfect example of exchange. If I had not agreed to go to South America, or asked for my expenses to be paid, I am sure that Peter would never have agreed to become my mentor. It also proved my strong commitment to wanting to learn from him.

The Lesson Behind the Lesson

While this lesson of exchange is obvious to most of you reading this book, there is another lesson, a lesson behind the lesson of exchange that rich dad taught me when he took away the ten cents an hour. It is a lesson that most people do not get, and it is a lesson that is important for anyone who wants to become rich. It is important to begin teaching your child at a young age.

Many rich people understand the lesson, especially if they earned their wealth, but many hardworking people never understand it.

Rich dad said to me, "The reason most people do not become rich is that they are taught to look for a job. It is almost impossible to become rich if you look and find a job." Rich dad went on to explain that most people come to him and say, "How much will you pay me if I do this job for you?" He went on to say, "People who think and speak such words will probably never get rich. You cannot expect to get rich if you go around looking for people to pay you for what you do."

The story after taking the ten cents an hour away from me in *Rich Dad Poor Dad* was the story of the comic books. It is in the story of the comic books that rich dad's true lesson behind the lesson of exchange came forth. After working for free, I began to see things differently. I began to look for a business or investment opportunity rather than just a job. My brain was being trained to see what most people do not see. Once I asked for the comic books that were being thrown away from rich dad's store, the store where I was working for free, I began to learn one of rich dad's greatest secrets to being rich. And that secret was *not* to work hard for money, expecting to be paid for doing a job. As rich dad said to me later, "The reason most people fail to get rich is that they have been trained to think in terms of being paid for the job they do. If you want to be rich, you need to think in terms of how many people you can serve." When I stopped working for ten cents an hour, I stopped thinking in terms of being paid for what I did for rich dad and began to look for ways to serve as many people as possible. Once I began to think that way, I began to think like my rich dad.

There Are Only So Many Hours in a Day

Most young people today go to school to learn a profession and then go looking for a job. We all know there are only so many hours in a day. If we sell our labor by the hour or in some other measurement of time, there is a finite amount of time we have in a day. And it is that finite amount of time that puts a ceiling on how much money we can earn. For example, if a person charges $50 an hour for his or her time, and puts in an eight-hour day, that person's maximum earning potential is $400 per day, $2,000 a week, for a five-day week, and $8,000 a month. The only way this person can increase that amount is to work more hours—and that is one of the reasons why, according to U.S. Government statistics, only one out of one hundred Americans become rich by age sixty-five. Most people are trained to think in terms of being paid for a job they do rather than think in terms of how many people they can serve. Rich dad often said, "The more people you serve, the richer you become."

Most people are trained to serve only one employer or a select number of clients. Rich dad would say, "The reason I became a businessman was that I wanted to serve as many people as possible." He would occasionally draw the following diagram of the CASHFLOW Quadrant to emphasize his point. (From *Rich Dad's CASHFLOW Quadrant*.)

Pointing to the left side of the Quadrant, he would say, "This side is dependent upon physical labor for success." Pointing to the right side of the Quadrant, he would say, "This side requires fiscal labor for success." He would go on to say, "There is a big difference between physical labor and fiscal labor." In other words, there is a tremendous difference between you working *physically* or your money or your system working *fiscally*. Rich dad would also say, "The less I have to physically work, the more people I can serve, and then in exchange, the more money I can make."

My primary intention for writing *Rich Dad Poor Dad* was to find a way to serve as many people as possible, knowing that if I did so, I would make more money. Prior to writing the book, I was teaching the same subject in person, or physically, and charging thousands of dollars. Although I was making money, I was serving only a few people and becoming very tired and burned out in the process. Once I realized that I needed to serve more people, I realized that I needed to write instead of talk.

Today the same lessons cost less than $20. I serve millions of people, and I make more money while working less. So that lesson of taking the ten cents an hour away from me years ago continues to pay off. It pays off because rich dad's lesson behind the lesson to getting rich was to serve as many people as possible. As he said, "Most people leave school looking for a high-paying job instead of looking for ways to serve as many people as possible."

(For those interested in learning what rich dad taught me about how to serve as many people as possible, that lesson is found in book number three, *Rich Dad's Guide to Investing*. That lesson is taught in the B-I Triangle, which is the structure that guides people on how to take their ideas and turn those ideas into multimillion-dollar businesses that serve as many people as possible. Many people have great ideas that could help make our world a better place to live; but the problem is, most people leave school without the skills necessary to turn those ideas into businesses. Instead of looking for a job, rich dad taught his son, Mike, and me to build businesses that served as many people as possible. He said, "If you build a business that truly serves millions of people, in *exchange* for your efforts, you will become a millionaire. If you serve a billion people, you become a billionaire. It's simply a matter of exchange." That is what book number three is about. It is about building a business that has the potential to serve millions, maybe billions, of people rather than one employer or just a few clients. As rich dad said, "You can get rich by marrying someone for their money; by being cheap; by being greedy; or by being a crook. But the best way to get rich is by being generous, and some of the richest people I have met have been very generous people. Instead of thinking about how much they could be paid, they thought about how many people they could serve.")

How Much Should I Pay My Child?

I am often asked questions such as the following:

- "How much allowance should I give my child?"
- "Should I stop paying my children for anything they do?"
- "I pay my child for good grades. Do you recommend that?"
- "Should I tell my child not to get a job at the mall?"

My standard answer to questions such as those is, "How you compensate your child is up to you. Every child is different, and every family is different." I simply remind you of my rich dad's lessons and ask that you remember that money is a very powerful teaching tool. If your children learn to expect money for nothing, then that *may* be how their lives wind up—a life of nothing. If your child studies only because he or she gets paid to study, then what happens when you are not there to pay your child to study? The point is to be careful about how you use money as a teaching tool. Because even though money is a powerful teaching tool, there are far more important lessons for your child to learn. It is the lessons behind the lessons that are most important. And one of those is the lesson on service.

Charity Begins at Home

My mom and dad were very generous people. But they were not generous in the same ways as my rich dad was. As the head of education for the island of Hawaii, my dad would come home, eat dinner with the kids, and go off to PTA meetings two to three times a week. I remember, as a boy, waving out the kitchen window as my dad backed his car down the driveway after dinner as he went on his way to serve as many families as possible. There were many times he would drive over one hundred miles to the meeting and return that night just to see and greet his own kids in the morning.

My mom often had us kids work with her at the church bake sales or rummage sales. She believed strongly in volunteering her time and asked her children to do the same. As a registered nurse, she also volunteered regularly for the American Red Cross. I remember during disasters such as a tidal wave or a volcano, she and my dad would be gone for days on end, serving those in need. When the opportunity to join President Kennedy's Peace Corps was offered to them, they jumped at it even though it meant a severe cut in pay.

Rich dad and his wife came from much the same point of view as did my mom and dad. His wife was active in a women's group that was constantly raising money for worthy causes. Rich dad donated money regularly to his church and various charities as well as serving on the boards of two non-profit organizations.

The lesson I learned from both sets of parents was that whether you are a socialist or a capitalist, charity begins at home. And if you want your children to be rich, teaching them to serve as many people as possible is a priceless lesson for them to learn. As my rich dad said, "The more people you serve, the richer you become."

Part III

Finding Your Child's Genius

My rich dad strongly encouraged his son and me to become rich by serving as many people as possible. He would say, "When you focus your mind on making money only for yourself, you will find it difficult to become rich. If you are dishonest, greedy, and give people less than they pay for, you will also find it difficult to become rich. You can acquire wealth in those ways, but that wealth will come at a very high price. If you focus your business first on serving as many people as possible . . . think only of making their lives a little easier, you will find tremendous wealth and happiness."

My smart dad truly believed that there was a genius in each and every child, even if the child did not do well in school. He did not believe that a genius *was someone who sat in a classroom and knew all the right answers. He did not believe that a genius was someone who was smarter than anyone else. He truly believed that each of us had a gift . . . and that a genius was simply a person who was fortunate enough to find his or her gift and then find a way of giving that gift.*

To make his lesson on genius interesting, he would tell us a story. He would say, "Before each of you were born, you were given a gift to give. The trouble is, no one told you that you were given this gift. No one told you what to do with your gift after you found it. After you were born, your job was to find your gift and give it . . . give it to everyone. If you gave your gift, your life would be filled with magic."

My smart dad also wrote the word genius *in this way:*

GENI-IN-US

Continuing with his story, he would say, "A genius is someone who finds the geni inside of him- or herself. Just as Aladdin found the geni inside the bottle, each of us is to find the geni inside of ourselves. That is where the word genius *comes from. A genius is someone who found the magical person inside of him- or herself. A genius is someone who found the gift he or she was given."*

My smart dad would then add his word of caution: "When you find your geni, your geni will grant you three wishes. Your geni will say, 'Wish number one is "Do you wish to give your gift to yourself?" Wish number two is "Do you wish to give your gift only to those you love and those close to you?" Or wish number three, "Do you wish to give your gift away?"' "

Obviously, the lesson was for us kids to choose choice number three. My smart dad's lesson always ended with him saying, "The world is filled with geniuses. Each of us is a genius. The problem is, most of us keep our genius locked tightly away in our bottle. Too many of us choose to use our genius only for ourselves or just for those we love. The geni comes out of the bottle only when we choose choice number three. The magic happens only when we choose to give our gifts away."

Both my dads believed in the magic of giving. One dad believed in building a business that served as many people as possible. The other dad believed in finding the gift we were given, finding the geni-in-us, and letting the geni's magic come out of the bottle.

Both dads' lessons worked for me as a little kid. Both stories gave me a reason to live, a reason to learn, and a reason to give. As silly as it sounded, as a nine-year-old kid, I believed in the possibility of there being a geni in me, and I believed in magic . . . and I still do. How else could a boy who flunked out of school because he could not write, write an international best-selling book?

The last part of this book is dedicated to your child's genius.

Chapter 15

How Do You Find Your Child's Natural Genius?

Most of us have been asked, "What sign are you?"

And if you are a Libra, you would say, "I'm a Libra. What are you?"

Most of us know what sign we are, just as most of us know there are four main groups of signs: earth, air, water, and fire. Most of us also know that there are twelve signs: Virgo, Scorpio, Cancer, Capricorn, Aquarius, Aries, Gemini, Taurus, Leo, Sagittarius, Pisces, and Libra. Unless we are astrological experts, most of us do not know the personality traits of all twelve signs. We are generally aware of the personality traits of our own astrological sign and maybe a few others. For example, I am an Aries, and I would say that for the most part what the charts say about Aries behavior applies to me. My wife is an Aquarius, and she also follows those general tendencies. Knowing the differences helps our relationship because we are better able to understand each other.

Few of us realize that just as there are different personality traits, there are also different learning traits. One of the reasons our current educational system is so painful for many people is that our school system is designed for only a few of the different learning traits. That would be like having a school system designed only for the fire signs and wondering why the water, air, and earth signs don't like school.

This chapter may shed further light on the different learning styles and also assist you in finding the learning styles of your children and even you, if you want to find out your unique learning style and maybe your genius.

This chapter may also explain why some people who do well in school do not do well in the real world, and vice versa.

Different Strokes for Different Folks

Most of us have heard the saying "Different strokes for different folks." And I would agree.

When I was about five years old, my family went to a popular beach with a neighboring family. Suddenly I looked up and saw my friend Willy struggling in the water. He had fallen into a hole and was drowning because he could not swim. Yelling and screaming, I finally attracted the attention of a high school boy, and he jumped in to save Willy.

After that near fatal accident, both families decided it was time all the children take formal swimming lessons. Soon I was at the public pool learning to swim, and I hated it. It was not long before I was out of the pool and hiding in the locker room, terrified of being yelled at because I could not swim properly. From that moment on I learned to hate the smell of the chlorine in a freshwater swimming pool.

Over the years I learned to swim in the ocean, because I loved spear fishing and catching lobsters. At twelve years of age I began body surfing and then surfing on surfboards, but I still could not swim the proper strokes.

Willy, on the other hand, took to swimming like a fish and was soon swimming competitively throughout Hawaii. In high school he went on to swim in the state championships. Although he did not win, the story shows how he took a near death accident and turned it into his passion. His accident caused my family to force me into swimming lessons, and I learned to hate swimming pools and never learned to swim properly.

When I went to school in New York, we were required to take a swimming test in a pool. I failed. Although I had been spear fishing, scuba diving, and surfing in very large winter surf, I failed my swimming test because I did not know the proper swimming strokes. I remember writing home and trying to explain to my friends that I was taking swimming lessons because I had failed my swim test. These were the friends I'd spent years swimming with in some of the most dangerous surf in Hawaii.

The good news is that I finally learned to swim a proper dog paddle and proper freestyle stroke in a freshwater pool. Up to then I swam with a combination breaststroke and sidestroke with a scissor kick, which was not very attractive and made no sense to the swim instructors.

The point here is that although I could not swim a proper stroke in a freshwater pool, I was very comfortable swimming in the ocean, even the very rough open ocean. I am still not a good swimmer, but I feel very much at home in the ocean. I know people who can swim perfect strokes in a pool but are terrified of rough seas, riptides, currents, undertows, and pounding waves. As the saying goes, "Different strokes for different folks."

Different Learning Styles

The point of this is not to discuss my lack of swimming ability, but to illustrate that we all learn differently and we all do things differently. Although I can now do a proper swim stroke, I find it much more practical to swim with my own strokes. I will never swim competitively like my friend Willy, and I will never get awards for my graceful style, but doing things in my own way works for me—and I think most of us are that way. We know what we should be doing, but we would rather do things the way we like to do things. Your kids are the same way about learning.

How to Find Your Child's Genius

To discover your children's genius you must first find out how they like to learn and why they will learn something. For example, I did not learn to swim because I did not want to learn to swim. I learned to swim because I wanted to surf. If not for surfing, I had no interest in learning to swim, and forcing me to learn only made me hate swimming even more. Instead of starting me in the shallow end with all the kids, I was much happier jumping in the deep end and learning to survive. The same is true with learning to read financial statements. I did not learn accounting because I wanted to be an accountant. I learned basic accounting because I wanted to be rich. If you think my swim strokes are ugly, you should see my accounting.

My smart dad realized that I was not an academic star, and that was why he encouraged me to seek my own learning style. Instead of forcing me to conform and follow the traditional ways of learning, he encouraged me to "jump in the deep end and swim for my life." He was not being cruel. He realized that my learning style was my learning style, and he wanted me to learn in the way I learn best. And just as my swim stroke is not pretty, the way I learn is not pretty.

Other people learn in more traditional ways. Many people go to school, enjoy the classroom, and enjoy following a prearranged curriculum. Many like knowing that at the end of the curriculum they will get a reward. They like the idea of knowing that they will get a passing grade or a degree for their efforts. As I said, they like the certainty of the reward at the end of the program. Just as my friend Willy did well at swimming because he loved swimming, many people do well in school because they like school.

A key to people's success in life is finding out how they learn best and ensuring that they are in an environment that allows them to continue learning in the ways they learn best. The problem is, finding out exactly how we learn and what our natural gifts are is often a hit-and-miss process. Many people never find out their gifts. Once they leave school, they get jobs, and then they cannot continue the personal discovery process owing to financial or family reasons. How to find one's learning style and one's unique genius has not been clearly defined until recently.

The Kolbe Index

I was talking to a friend of mine and explaining to her that I hated having an office. I explained to her that I have owned several office buildings, but I have never had a formal office. "I just hate being locked in a room," I said.

My friend smiled and said, "Have you taken the Kolbe index?"

"No," I replied. "What is that?"

"It is an instrument that measures your natural learning style or MO [modus operandi]. It measures your instincts, or your natural genius."

"I've never heard of that particular index, but I have done many of those types of assessments," I said. "I've found them useful, but isn't this just one more of the same type of instrument? Isn't it like finding out more about my astrological sign?"

"Well, yes, there are similarities," my friend said. "Yet there are some distinctions the Kolbe index can give you that other evaluations do not."

"Like what?" I asked.

"Well, as I said, it will point out your genius and your natural learning style. It will also tell you what you *will do* and what you *won't do* rather than what you can do or can't do," my friend replied. "The Kolbe will measure your natural instincts, not your intelligence or your personality. The Kolbe index tells you some very unique things about yourself that no other test can tell you—because it measures who you are, not who you think you are."

"Instincts," I said. "So how does that help me?" I was trying to squirm out of taking another test.

"Just take the profile and then let's talk about it. In fact, Kathy Kolbe, the creator of the index, lives right here in Phoenix. After you take it, I'll arrange a meeting between the two of you. See for yourself if her instrument does everything I say it does."

"How do I take this test?" I asked.

"Just go to the Web site and take the test. I think it costs about $50 and should only take you a few minutes to answer the thirty-six questions," she replied.

"When will I get the results?"

"Almost immediately," my friend replied. "After you take it, you can evaluate it, and I will also arrange a meeting with you and Kathy. She doesn't meet with too many people, but she is a friend of mine and I will tell her that you are my friend."

I agreed, and a few minutes later I had taken the Kolbe index. The results are on page 208.

I found the results interesting, but knowing that I was going to have lunch with the creator of the index, I decided to wait and hear what she said.

Three days later Kathy met me for lunch. Looking at my index, she said, "You're energized by taking physical risks, aren't you?"

I chuckled. Kathy has such a lovely, kind voice, and she speaks with such understanding and empathy. I could tell she knew who I was even though we had just met. "How can you tell?" I asked.

"Your strengths lie in your instincts, and this tells me your MO, or mode of operation. For you it's the Quick Start and Implementor energy that drive your actions," she said with a smile. "The lines of the graph show me that instinctively you seek out physical risks. You are naturally drawn to them. Right?"

I nodded.

"Have you ever been in grave danger?" Kathy asked.

"Yes, many times, especially when I was in Vietnam. Why do you ask?"

"Did you actually thrive in that situation?" she asked. "Were your instincts fully engaged and your energy riveted by the danger you were in?"

home   results/home
                                                    < previous
                                                 resultsChart
                                                      next >
kolbe.com   completeResults

Kolbe A™ Index Results

For: Robert Kiyosaki

MO: 2 2 9 6

Conative Strengths (Impact Factors for each Action Mode):
Simplify (FF), Adapt (FT), Improvise (QS), Renovate (IM)

Kolbe A Index Chart

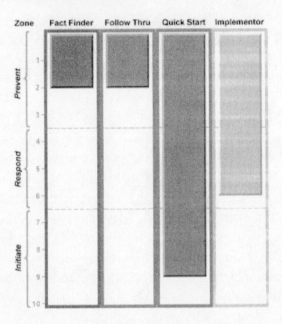

"Well, I loved flying in combat," I replied. "It was exciting as well as tragic at times. But I did love flying in combat, and I missed it once I returned to peacetime flying."

"That would make sense," she said. "Was the transition back to the ordinary military routine difficult when you returned home?" she asked. "Did that get you into trouble when you got home?"

"Yes," I said. "How did you know?"

"I know because your Follow Thru talent is for keeping lots of balls in the air at one time," she said gently. "It tells me that you do not follow procedures. Your Quick Start and Implementor results indicate that you take physical risk and thrive on a sense of urgency, so you probably did well in Vietnam. But you found the peacetime military too structured, too confining.

You need excitement. If you don't have enough excitement, you'll create it. It's called getting into trouble, often fighting with the authority figures who try to keep you in line, following the rules."

"Do you read palms also?" I asked. I then asked her if my friend had told her about me. I was becoming suspicious because Kathy knew a lot about me and we had just met.

She said, "No. I do not know anything about you. I would rather not when I interpret a person's results. I trust the accuracy of my indexes, and I would rather trust them than someone else's description of a person—or my memory of what they said." Kathy went on to say that she was meeting with me just because her friend asked her to and because she finds great joy in sharing her work with people who genuinely want to know more about it. After getting to know more about each other over lunch, Kathy began sharing with me more in depth what my Kolbe index explained about me. Pointing again to my chart, she said, "If you were in school today, you would be labeled with ADD, attention deficit disorder, and you might well be given drugs to calm you down."

"Do you agree with that type of treatment?" I asked her.

"No. Not for most kids," she said. "I think that drugging children and labeling them with this double negative is often a terrible injustice to their natural ability—and self-esteem. It robs them of their rightful pride in who they are. If you had been drugged when you were young, you might never have found your path in life. You might never have written best-selling books. You might never have found the success you have found.

"On the other hand, maybe nothing could ever hold you down," Kathy continued. "The point is, in today's school system you would be labeled a problem student, a student with a disorder. It's not that you can't learn; it's just that you won't learn in the manner our schools usually teach. You were fortunate that your dad understood this," she said. "I know you call your schoolteacher dad your 'poor dad,' but in many ways he really enriched your life. In many ways you are successful because of your poor dad. He was smart enough to let you study with your rich dad and encouraged you to learn in the way you learn best, which is, as even you admit, not very pretty."

Nodding, I said, "It definitely has not been pretty." After a moment's pause I asked, "So how do you define success?"

Kathy smiled and said, "I define success as the freedom to be yourself. And that is what your dad did for you. He respected you and granted you the freedom to be yourself.

"Many people are trapped trying to be what their parents or society wants them to be, and I don't think that is true success . . . regardless of how wealthy or powerful people become. As human beings we naturally seek the freedom to be who we are. If we don't fight against anyone or anything that forces us to act against our grain, we will lose our self-respect and deny our genius."

"Well," I said, "I would not have found success if I had followed in my dad's footsteps. In high school I was an outsider. I did not fit in with the students or the teachers."

"But I'll bet you loved kindergarten," Kathy said with a grin.

"Yes, I did," I replied. "How can you tell?"

Pointing to my chart, Kathy said, "For people with as long an Implementor line as you have, kindergarten would have been terrific. Implementors naturally touch things and build things. Your Quick Start got to experiment with a whole bunch of new things. Your Follow Thru wasn't forced into too much structure. And you weren't yet being tested on a whole bunch of facts. Suited you perfectly, didn't it?"

Nodding, I said, "Yes, it did. Today I still love building things such as new products. I love investing in real estate because I can see, touch, and feel my investments. I always say to people that I never stopped playing Monopoly. I love playing."

Kathy grinned and pointed to the Follow Thru section of the chart. "But then came the first grade to third grade; kids with a different type of Follow Thru from yours did well then."

"Why did they do well?" I asked. "Why would grades one to three be good for a person with a different Follow Thru pattern?" I was now becoming very interested in this woman's knowledge.

"Because during those years, the blocks and toys begin to disappear and order and neatness come into the curriculum, and people with long-lined Follow Thru patterns fit in well with the demand for order and neatness. And by third grade all remnants of Implementor are gone from the classroom."

"Order and neatness?" I said. "What do order and neatness have to do with education?"

Kathy again smiled and said, "I can tell by your Follow Thru pattern that following orders and being neat are not your strong suits."

"No, they are not. But would that affect my performance in school?" I asked.

"Oh, definitely," said Kathy. "I'll bet you did not thrive in first grade as much as you did in preschool and kindergarten."

"That is correct," I said. "In the first grade I began to get into fights, whereas in kindergarten I had played a lot with my toys and on the jungle gym. It was when I went to the first grade that teachers began to call me a 'problem child' because of my fighting."

"Well, that is what can happen when they take the toys and blocks away," she replied. "Boys without toys often pick on other boys."

"I would say that was true in my school," I said. "But why do people with strong Follow Thru patterns do well during this period?"

"Because at this stage of development, neatness and order are required. You now sit in straight rows instead of on the floor or in groups around a table. Instead of encouraging you to smear finger paints, the teacher begins to emphasize neat penmanship and handwriting. They now want you to begin to write between the lines instead of all over the page. Teachers like little girls who dress neatly and frilly and little boys who toe the line and don't get mussed up. I don't think you were one of the boys who dressed to impress the teacher, were you?" asked Kathy with a grin.

"No, I wasn't. It was a good thing that I lived right across the street from the school because I was often sent home covered in mud. I always found a way to slip and fall in the mud."

"Did you begin to feel different about school about that time?" Kathy asked.

"Not in the first grade, but I do remember beginning to notice some differences by the third grade," I replied. "I began to notice that there were kids who were the teachers' pets. There was one girl and one boy in my third grade class who eventually became leaders in high school. Today they are married. Everyone knew by the third grade that these two were the stars. They were good-looking, smart, well dressed, popular, and good students."

"Sounds like school was tailor-made for them. And how did they turn out?" asked Kathy. "Did they find the success they wanted?"

"I don't really know. I guess they did. They never left the town where we grew up. They are well respected in the community and are as popular as ever. So I guess they found success."

"For them, that sounds ideal. It seems they had the freedom throughout their lives, and their marriage, to be themselves," Kathy said.

"What happens after the third grade?" I asked. "Just about the magic age of nine?"

"From the fourth grade on, anyone who has a long Fact Finder line fits the mold. Our fourth- through twelfth-grade educational system was designed for Fact Finders. Some kids instinctively zero in on the name, place, and date. This Fact Finder approach is well rewarded. The classroom works well for such kids," said Kathy.

Kathy went on to explain that from the age of nine on, students are measured by a series of "blunder hunts." You take spelling tests, memorize multiplication tables, and count the number of books you read and prove it by recalling the facts in them.

I told her about Rudolph Steiner's theory of the nine-year change and how many teachers know if a child will be successful or not in the school system. I said, "By the age of nine, I knew I was not going to be a shining star in the system. They took the blocks away forever."

Kathy laughed. "Yes, a person like you with your Implementor needs would miss the blocks. With Fact Finder talent that simplifies rather than memorizes complex facts and figures, you would get frustrated. So your Quick Start would kick in and try all sorts of unique ways to get around what you would consider the stupidity of school."

"And teachers know it," I said. "That is why so many kids get labeled either smart, stupid, or troublemakers so early in their school career."

Kathy nodded sadly. "Most schoolteachers have strong Fact Finder and/or Follow Thru instincts. People tend to label others whose instincts are similar to theirs as 'smart.' Of course, intelligence has nothing to do with it. But educators have a blind spot about the value of your instincts. Their abilities work in a school environment, so they stick with it. The educational system is their natural home. They love it there.

"So the educational system continues to focus on only one learning style and continues to make finer distinctions on why kids cannot learn. This is why we may have identified so many different learning disabilities," Kathy summarized.

"That's not too intelligent," I said. "We don't have learning disabilities, we have an antiquated school system with teaching disabilities! And I hated it there," I added bitterly.

"But you love learning, don't you?" asked Kathy.

"I love learning. I attend seminars, read books, and listen to tapes constantly. I get really excited when I find something new and exciting to learn. I enjoy learning about what you have been researching," I said. "But for some reason, I just hated school. But how can you tell I love learning if I hated school?"

Kathy then pointed to my Kolbe result. "Do you see this?" she asked.

Under a section entitled "Possible Career Paths" was this list:

home

resultsHome
< previous
resultsCareerPaths
next >
completeResults

Kolbe A™ Index Results

kolbe.com

For: Robert Kiyosaki

MO: 2 2 9 6

Conative Strengths (Impact Factors for each Action Mode):
Simplify (FF), Adapt (FT), Improvise (QS), Renovate (IM)

Possible Career Paths

You create your own opportunities which you may not plan or articulate as specific goals. Because your sense of accomplishment stems from overcoming obstacles and generating against-the-odds solutions, you need to put yourself in situations that cause your creativity to kick in. You have a talent for diversity and an acute sense of the space around you — so, whatever you do, don't get boxed in mentally or physically.

"Pioneer" is not a job title, but rather a Mode of Operation (MO). It is a broad approach to how you solve problems and the talent you bring to a task. You will succeed in roles that allow you to use this Natural Advantage. The following are not necessarily recommended career paths, but are a partial listing of functions in which Kolbe Corp research has found others making good use of "Pioneer" instincts:

ACTOR	PROTOTYPE BUILDER
HANDCRAFTER OF ORIGINAL ART	PROPERTY DEVELOPER
ENVIRONMENTAL ADVOCATE	TRAUMA MEDIC
PHYSICAL SCIENTIST	INVENTOR
RESTAURATEUR	NEW PRODUCT DEVELOPER
STUNT PERSON	AV SPECIAL EFFECTS
WILDLIFE EXPLORER	TELEVISION PRODUCER
SPORTS PROMOTER	DISPLAY ADVERTISING
ALTERNATIVE EDUCATOR	TEACHER—PHYSICALLY CHALLENGED

Kathy was pointing to the career entitled "Alternative Educator." "The people I have met with this career path are generally very active learners. They just do not thrive in the structure of traditional education."

"That is true," I replied. "I attend seminars regularly. I attend seminars rather than a regular college because I do not need the degree or certificate at the completion of the course. I just want the information."

"How many of these possible career paths would you consider?" asked Kathy.

After looking over the list for a while, I said, "I'd like them all except trauma medic and restaurateur."

"Any reason why?" Kathy asked.

"I've already had too much experience in those areas. I saw enough blood and trauma in Vietnam, and my rich dad owned restaurants. But I could easily be a strong environmental advocate, and I did have an alternative education company for nearly ten years. I love teaching. Today I still build prototypes, I develop property, and I have invented and patented things. In fact, I love new product development. I really enjoy the subject of advertising and producing television ads. So I would say your list is filled with things I am interested in or have already done."

I sat silently for a while, considering all that Kathy and I had covered. I was excited because I do love learning, and I enjoyed finding out why I did not fit in school. Looking at my Kolbe index results again, I asked, "So people who do well in school after the third grade, at approximately the age of nine, are people who are strong in Fact Finder and Follow Thru?" I asked.

"Yes," Kathy said. "And that is why you began to have trouble in school, because they took the toys and blocks away and you could no longer learn by playing. You may have been physically in class, but your mind was far away, drifting out the window."

"It was," I said. "I was bored and did just enough to get by and pass. I could not wait until I graduated from school so I could get out into the real world."

"That is the Quick Start in you," said Kathy. "Because of your energy in Implementor and Quick Start, you have a knack for building tangible things very quickly, such as your games, your books, and your business. That is why manufacturing nylon wallets, as you told me, and your many other projects have led to your success. You are a natural entrepreneur with a pioneering spirit."

home

Kolbe A™ Index Results

kolbe.com

results/home
< previous
resultsChart
next >
complete/results

For: Robert Kiyosaki

MO: 2 2 9 6

Conative Strengths (Impact Factors for each Action Mode):
Simplify (FF), Adapt (FT), Improvise (QS), Renovate (IM)

Kolbe A Index Chart

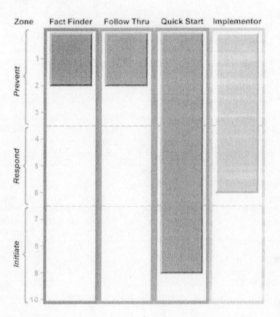

"Why do you say pioneering spirit?" I asked.

"Well, that is what your index results tell me. Your Implementor is a literal hands-on talent, and your Quick Start thrives on adventure. You are not a natural entrepreneur in the traditional sense of developing a business and products. Your drive is to be first to the frontier."

"So that is why it is often difficult to explain what I am doing, because I am often a number of years ahead of time," I added. "I'm creating products for a market that does not yet exist."

"Yes," said Kathy, pointing to the chart.* "The Quick Start's perspective is the future. The Fact Finder's perspective is the past. The Implementor is in the

Author's Note: If you study this one chart (on page 216), you begin to notice the differences among possible Kolbe index results. In her *Bottom Lines* booklet, Kathy Kolbe offers thirty pages of such charts and information that further define the differences.

Comparing the Kolbe Action Modes

Key concepts applicable to those who initiate in each Action Mode

Concept	Fact Finder	Follow Thru	Quick Start	Implementor
Time Zone	Past	Integration of Past, Present, and Future	Future	Present
Use of Time	Gauges how much time something will take through experience and expertise; puts events into a historical perspective.	Sequences events and provides continuity, paces oneself; sets a rhythm for effort and coordinates with others.	Predicts and deals with events ahead of time; focuses on future by forecasting what could be; anticipates change.	Grounded in the here and now, wanting the moment to last; creates quality products that will endure through time.
Communicate Using	Written words	Charts and graphs	Spoken words	Props, models, and demonstrations
Storing Information	By priority	Alphabetically	By color	By quality
Learning Needs	Studies books on the subject to see how it's been done in the past	Learns the theory of formula	Experiments with radical ideas and innovations	Works with models or prototypes
Goal Attainment	• Through expertise • Setting up complex plans • Comparing the options	• Integrating systems • Developing worst-case scenarios • Assuring a sense of quality	• Sense of urgency and short-term deadlines • Visionary goals • Seeking solutions that defy the probabilities	• Requiring concrete, demonstrable goals that have lasting value • Utilizing highest quality materials and technology

present, and the Follow Thru perspective is to integrate past, present, and future. You are always focused on the future and building businesses and products in the present for the future. You will always be ahead of your time."

"And that is why I often argue with people who are Fact Finders," I said. "Fact Finders want the facts and figures, and I don't have anything to show them yet because the future is not yet here."

Kathy nodded and smiled. "Yes, I would say that someone with your MO would definitely clash with someone who seeks Fact Finder details and/or Follow Thru structure. As I said, you probably had trouble in school because most teachers insist on those Fact Finder explanations and Follow Thru orderliness, both which you naturally resist."

"You know, this makes more and more sense to me. I really did respect most of my teachers, but I always knew we were not on the same page of the book," I said. "I now know we weren't even in the same book."

Kathy laughed and said, "There is a joke I heard recently at one of my classes. The question is, 'What do you call an organization filled with Fact Finders?' And the answer is, 'A university.'"

I chuckled and then added, "And what do you call an organization filled with Quick Starts and Implementors? The answer: 'A kindergarten.'"

Kathy smiled and said, "Or a dot.com company."

With that I roared with laughter. "And that is why so many dot.coms will fail," I said. "Most dot.com companies are headed by a Quick Start operating without any fundamentals, facts, profits, or real-world experience, and they have very little Follow Thru. I know because that is how I was when I first started out in the real world. That is why my first businesses failed. We had a good business, but the three of us were all Quick Start and no Follow Thru. When I built my earlier businesses, they were full of energy, went up quickly, and crashed quickly. We had no facts, figures, or Follow Thru."

"Which is why I decided to work with businesses," Kathy said. "Now that you are older and wiser, how do you feel about people who lead in Fact Finder and Follow Thru?"

"I love them," I said. "I now know that I could not survive without them."

"And that is my point," said Kathy. "We need to respect the gifts and genius each of us brings to the table and to the world. In order for any team to survive, it needs the differing perspectives in all four modes. Instead of labeling and discriminating against one or the other, we need to learn to blend our gifts and complement our geniuses. I'll bet you hated it when the teachers labeled the Fact Finder kids smart and Quick Start kids like you less smart?"

"Disliked it? I found it insulting and humiliating."

"So what did you do with that anger?" Kathy asked.

"I went out and did things my way anyway. I wanted to prove I was smart," I said. "I hated being labeled stupid and less likely to succeed. I hated when the teachers said, 'Robert has so much potential . . . but he just does not apply himself. If he would just buckle down and study.'"

"And the more they tried to buckle you down, the more determined you became to succeed?" asked Kathy. "Did you use that anger to accomplish what you wanted to accomplish with your life?"

"Well, I have done pretty well," I replied a little smugly. "I did write a best-selling book, and the kids who got an A in English still have not written one. And I do make more money than most of the kids who got the good grades." I was fairly strutting now, like the NBC peacock with its tail fanned out in an array of colors. I was venting after years of holding my anger and frustration back.

"So did you use your anger to find your own way of doing things? Did you find your own freedom to be who you are?" asked Kathy with a gentle smile.

"Yes, I did," I said, beaming. "I did it my way and I found the life I wanted and I live my life the way I want to live it. And I did not want a job, I did not want to have anyone tell me how much money I could make, and I did not want to be stuck in an office."

"Congratulations," Kathy said. "You have achieved success. You are successful because you have the freedom to be who you are."

I rocked back and let her congratulations sink in as my years of pent-up frustration from school dissipated. "I never really thought of success in those terms," I said. "I mean, I did not realize how much success my anger and frustration has brought me."

"Good," said Kathy. "And can you understand that there are other people who define success much differently from the ways you define success? Can you understand that there are people who need to research, seek job security, and thrive in a calm, stable environment? Can you understand that for some people just a simple car is enough and a simple house is enough?"

"Yes, I can," I replied. "My mom and dad were very happy with all those things. They were successful on their own terms. I just knew their way wouldn't work for me. So yes, I can understand that life is truly 'Different strokes for different folks.'"

"And now that you are older and wiser, do you appreciate the different types of people more? I mean, do you appreciate the people in your office who are strong in the Follow Thru or Fact Finder categories?"

"Now more than ever," I replied. "I love those guys. I could not do what I do without them. Without them I would not be successful."

Kathy smiled and said, "I'm glad to hear that." Pausing for a moment, she collected her thoughts, then asked cautiously, "And do you think you could get along better today with your schoolteachers, even the ones who failed you or with whom you argued?"

"Well, I don't know if I could go that far," I replied without thinking.

"You do know that it is the system of education, not the teachers, that is to blame for what happened to you?" Kathy inquired.

I nodded. "Yes, I understand it, but I still do not like it. I do realize that they were doing the best they could with what they had."

"So let me show you why you may have gotten so angry," said Kathy. "I think you got very angry because the system tried to crush your genius and force you to become a type of genius you did not want to become."

"You mean my genius in Quick Start? You mean because I was so active?"

"Well, in that area, too. But the genius I am talking about is your genius in the Fact Finder column."

"Fact Finder?" I replied with surprise. "The Fact Finder column is my weakest column. How can I have a genius in Fact Finder?"

"You have a genius hidden in every category, even Fact Finder," said Kathy, again pointing to a page out of her booklet.

Kolbe Impact Factors
Positive strengths in each Action Mode

Operating Zone	Action Mode			
	Fact Finder	Follow Thru	Quick Start	Implementor
Prevent	Simplify	Adapt	Stabilize	Imagine
Respond	Refine	Rearrange	Revise	Renovate
Initiate	Justify	Organize	Improvise	Construct

Pointing to the word *simplify* under Fact Finder, she said, "In the Fact Finder category, this is your genius. Your genius is the ability to take facts and simplify them. I think the reason your books do so well is that you took a complex subject, such as the subject of money, and you simplified it."

Beginning to understand, I said, "Well, that is the way my rich dad was. He liked to keep things simple."

Then Kathy pointed to the word *justify* under the Fact Finder mode and said, "And this is probably your smart dad's genius. Being good in school and achieving the academic environment, he had a genius for digging for the facts and figures. I would bet your smart dad was energized by collecting data, doing research, seeking specificity, and defining objectives. So his was a different kind of genius in the Fact Finder mode from yours, which explains why he did well in school and you did not."

"We all have a genius in all of the four columns," I said softly as I began to understand Kathy's work more.

Kathy nodded. "I have defined twelve different types of genius. Each of us has four different geniuses, one for each column."

"Twelve different types of genius . . . and each of us has four. That is why it is best to operate on a team, because each of you comes with a different perspective on how to solve problems. Is that what your work has found?" I asked.

Again Kathy nodded. "The more you understand these charts, the better distinctions you can make about who you are and who the people around you are. By understanding each other better, we can respect our differences and work and live more harmoniously. Working on a team can solve more problems more efficiently than if you work just on your own. That's why I love working to build more effective teams. Find joy in the differences—whether in the workplace or home environment."

"And that is your genius or your gift," I said. "You want people to work together with greater respect for each other's gifts and genius. And what categories are you strongest in?"

"I am most efficient in Quick Start and Follow Thru. That is why I explain with charts and graphs. I needed to fit the entire repertoire of human behavior into my system before I could be satisfied that it was valid. Then I needed the Fact Finders on the team to do what they did best. I greatly value their abilities, which complement my talent to simplify. Like you, I drive to the bottom line. Unlike you, I put my work into a software system with algorithms that produce the bottom lines in chart and graph formats.

It is most gratifying when I can use my natural creative talents to help other people find greater career and personal satisfaction. But I could not do all this on my own. It does take a team and all twelve geniuses to have a successful business, especially in this competitive world. I really do not know how an autocratic business leader can succeed. He or she has, at best, only four geniuses. So I do my work to make people and businesses more effective but also to insure a sense of personal dignity to everyone on the team. On a team everyone is important."

"Congratulations," I said. "You have found success in your life. You truly have found the freedom to be who you really are."

Kathy nodded and smiled. "Now let's look more closely at your genius in Quick Start."

Kolbe Impact Factors
Positive strengths in each Action Mode

Operating Zone	Action Mode			
	Fact Finder	**Follow Thru**	**Quick Start**	**Implementor**
Prevent	Simplify	Adapt	Stabilize	Imagine
Respond	Refine	Rearrange	Revise	Renovate
Initiate	Justify	Organize	Improvise	Construct

"In Quick Start, your genius is found in the word *improvise*. That means your instinct is to take risks, initiate change, promote experimentation, seek challenges, seek innovation, defy the odds, ad-lib, act on intuition."

I winced when I heard Kathy describe many of my tendencies. "You call that my genius? I always thought it was my insanity."

"Never underestimate this ability. A team—or any organization, for that matter—needs your genius. You get things started quickly when other people sit around and talk for hours, forming committees and doing nothing. So being a person who gets things moving, takes risks, and defies the odds is an important part of your genius."

"I wish you could tell my schoolteachers that," I said quietly. "They did not see it as genius. They called it something else."

Kathy chuckled and continued. "And your smart dad was probably a person who would not go off half-cocked. He had to know the facts first. He apparently was not impulsive like you, and he was not ambiguous. He gathered the facts. He would not create chaos and would not operate in a crisis environment. He would calculate the odds and then not go against them."

"That sounds like him," I said. "And that is why he did well in school and eventually became head of the entire state school system."

Kathy nodded. "So your genius is that you get an idea and, as Nike says, 'Just do it.' Your Quick Start and Implementor can take an idea and turn it into a product, company, or money pretty quickly. You have the touch of the alchemist. I'll bet you can make money from nothing. Of course, a long Quick Start line can make rags to riches a round trip."

I nodded. "That I can do. I can take an idea and go to action pretty quickly. Yet I do go off half-cocked many times, but that is how I learn. I jump in the deep end and drown for a while. But after I survive, I am a lot smarter because I have learned physically. I learn in exactly the same manner we all learn to ride a bicycle. And since I learn physically, when people ask me how I did what I did, I can't tell them. I can't tell them because I learned it with my body rather than my mind. It would be like you trying to tell someone how to ride a bicycle without letting him or her ride it. I have found that people who need the facts and are afraid of taking risks often do not get much done because they fail to learn physically. They spend their time just studying it rather than just doing it."

"And someone like your dad, a man who leads in Fact Finder, might get bogged down in what we commonly call 'analysis paralysis,'" said Kathy. "You would go to a strange city and wander around for days, while your dad would buy a map and read a travel book on the city first. Can you understand how different you are?"

"Yes, I can. My smart dad needed to research the facts forever before he did anything. I don't like to do research, so I just jump in and after I get into trouble, then I start doing the research I should have done."

"And that is how you learn. That is how you get smart, and your dad was smart enough to recognize this."

"He and I played golf together only a few times because of this," I said. "My dad would measure every shot. He would take forever calculating the wind and the distance to the cup. He would measure the slopes of the green and even the direction the grass was bent. I would just walk up and hit the ball and then figure out what I did wrong after I hit the ball."

"So you prefer team sports?" Kathy asked.

"Yes. How did you know? I love rugby, and I captained my rowing team at the academy. But I don't like sports where I have to do everything on my own."

"I can tell, because for you to be successful, you need a team around you. That is a desire or preference that reflects your respect for diverse talents. Sometimes people with a long line in both Fact Finder and Quick Start actually believe that they can do it all. (See the diagram on page 224.) They set the appropriate priorities and then jump in and try to pull it off. They are good at the start-up but require more explanation to recognize as readily as you do that they need more than that over the long term."

"Oh, that makes sense," I replied. "Many of my friends who are successful think they have the ability to be pretty self-contained. So they would have longer Quick Start and Fact Finder. I create a team to give me a hand."

"And that's a great part of your wisdom. It is also why you prefer a team sport to playing golf," Kathy continued. "Recognizing your need for a team around you has helped you build a larger business than someone who tries to be more self-contained. Also, a person who adds Quick Start with Fact Finder would tend to take more calculated risks, while you tend to make more physical risks. Which doesn't place you inside your office very often."

"That makes sense," I said. "I am hopeless on my own. I like having a lot of people helping me do things."

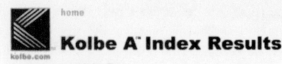

home

results/home
< previous
resultsChart
next >
completeResults

Kolbe A™ Index Results

kolbe.com

For: John Doe

MO: 8 2 7 4

Conative Strengths (Impact Factors for each Action Mode):
Justify (FF), Adapt (FT), Improvise (QS), Renovate (IM)

Kolbe A Index Chart

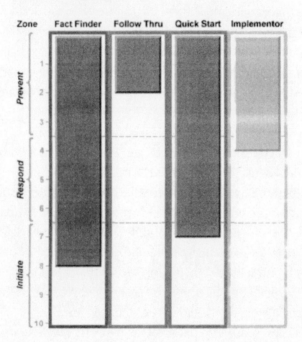

"And that may be why you did not do well on tests in school. You needed the team for brainstorming the answers—but the teachers would call that cheating."

Laughing, I asked, "Are you sure you weren't sitting behind me in class?"

"I didn't have to. My classes were filled with people like you. You may not have done well in the classroom, but you did well in team sports or anything that required a team to get things done. You make sure you don't take the tests of life on your own."

"That is why I always sat next to the smart kids in school and why I still want them on my team when I work. My rich dad always said, 'Business is a team sport.' And that is why he always had a team of very smart people around him to help him with his finances."

"You are just as smart, but their smarts were in Fact Finding. When that is added to your talent, you cover more of the bases, you help each other complete the puzzle. The twelve geniuses working together will always come out on top," she said. "Of course, it also helps to have the right genius in the right place to solve a particular problem."

"So my dad struggled financially because he operated on his own, while my rich dad operated on a team. My dad did what he learned in school, which was to take tests on his own, and my rich dad took his financial tests with his team. And that made a world of difference in the real world."

Kathy just nodded. "With the right combination of instincts, you will win, and no one person covers them all." Our time for lunch was up, and we agreed to meet again, this time with the entire company. As we parted I asked her:

"Do you have the Kolbe index for children?"

Beaming, she said, "I'm glad you asked. Yes, we do have instruments for children starting at a fifth-grade reading level. In fact, I have a youth index similar to the Index A you took, as well as other products I call Think-ercises. They help kids learn to trust their instincts and use their genius."

"It would be great for children to know what their learning strengths are and find out where their geniuses lie," I said. "And the sooner the better. It would save years of trying to find out by trial and error."

"That is why I do this work," said Kathy as she climbed into her car and waved good-bye.

WHO KATHY KOLBE IS

In 1985 Kathy Kolbe was selected by *Time* magazine as one of seven American "new pioneers . . . with imagination, boldness, energy, and an iron determination" representative of the "Man of the Year." She has also been honored as one of the outstanding Small Business People of America and chosen by the White House as one of the fifty Americans with the "can do" spirit. She conducts seminars and lectures worldwide. Her best-selling books include *Conative Connection* and *Pure Instinct.* Kathy was greatly influenced by her father, E. F. Wonderlic, creator of the Wonderlic Personnel Test. She speaks of him lovingly but found that her contribution was to learn how she had to do things differently from him. He was the founder of personnel testing, with his cognitive instrument. She never believed this IQ-type approach got at true genius or natural ability. With his encouragement, she used the expertise in test development she had learned from him to search for the next generation in testing.

If you would like to find out more about Kathy Kolbe and her products, go to www.richdad.com/kolbe and find out more information. Kathy's organization is a joy to deal with. Personally I feel I have met a kindred spirit in this work, the work of bringing more dignity and respect for the student, to the world of education. She is one of the few people who agree with me that each of us has gifts and geniuses often not recognized by the educational system. In today's Information Age, her information is refreshing and enlightening.

We have included the Kolbe index for adults as well as for children on our Web site at www.richdad.com/kolbe if you would like to take the profile or have your children take her youth profile. The youth index is called the "Kolbe Y index." As part of the children's profile, it will analyze the following three areas:

How You Can Do Your Best School Work
How You Can Do Your Best Recreationally
How You Can Communicate Better

I found great validation in who I am instinctively when I reviewed my Kolbe results. It immediately showed me why I was labeled a misfit or stupid by my teachers in school. If I had taken the Kolbe index at a young age, I might have been able to avoid, or at least better understand, many of the problems I encountered in school. I hope that you will find the same validation.

AUDIO DOWNLOAD

In each of our books we like to provide an audio interview as a bonus with additional insights. As a thank-you to you for reading this book, you may go to the Web site www.richdad.com/richkid and download an audio of my discussion with Kathy Kolbe called "Find Out How Your Child Learns Best . . . Because All Children Learn Differently."

Thank you for your interest in your child's financial education.

Chapter 16

Success Is the Freedom to Be Who You Are

When I was a kid, my teachers often said, "You need a good education so you can get a good job."

My rich dad, on the other hand, would draw the CASHFLOW Quadrant. Instead of telling me to get a job, which would have limited me to the E, employee quadrant, he offered me a choice of quadrants.

When I was having trouble in school, my smart dad offered me the choice of finding my own learning style.

More Choices Give You More Opportunities to Succeed

The point of this chapter is that in today's world we have more choices. Each time we add a new industry, such as the airline industry or computer industry, we expand our choices of careers and interests. One of the problems with raising kids today results from having too many choices, aka distractions. Nonetheless, the more choices we have, the greater chance we have for success.

If parents begin to take choices away from their children, it can create discord in the home. If, as a parent, you say, "Don't do this," or, "Don't do that," the chances are your children will do what you don't want them to do, or they may have already done it.

One of the things that worked for me as a child was that my parents did not limit my choices but instead simply offered me more choices. It does not mean I was not disciplined when I stepped out of line, but one of the things both my dads did was to offer me choices rather than limit me to what I could or could not do.

So the hope of this chapter is to give parents more choices to offer their children so that the children will ultimately find their own way of becoming successful. And as Kathy Kolbe says, "Success is the freedom to be who you are."

What Do You Want to Be When You Grow Up?

Instead of simply telling me, "Go to school to get a job," my rich dad offered me these choices. It is the CASHFLOW Quadrant, which book number two in this series is about.

For those who may not have read the book:

The E stands for employee.
The S stands for self-employed or small business.
The B stands for business owner.
The I stands for investor.

By being offered a choice, I felt I had more control over my destiny and what I wanted to study. Along the way I also found out that the tax laws were different for each of the Quadrants, and that fact also helped me chart my path into the future. As most of us know as adults, taxes are our single largest lifetime expense. And unfortunately, it is the E and S Quadrants that pay more than their fair share of taxes.

When talking to your child, you may want to offer a choice of Quadrants rather than simply say, "Go to school so you can get a job."

By having a choice, I knew that the course of study that best suited me was the course of study that would lead to the B and I Quadrants. I knew that was what I wanted to be when I grew up. Today, whether we are in the E, S, or B Quadrant, we all need to be investors, or in the I Quadrant. Hopefully you no longer expect the government or your employer's company to be responsible for you after retirement.

Choices and Consequences

A tremendous financial head start that my rich dad gave me was the understanding of the choices and consequences found on a financial statement.

When you look at the entire financial statement, you can understand how this education can be important.

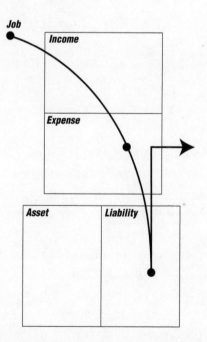

By doing our financial homework, Mike and I soon realized that with each dollar we received we had a choice, and that choice was found in the expense column. We soon realized that each time we earned or spent a dollar there was a ripple effect, or a consequence to that action. By taking a dollar and buying a liability like a car, we knew that the long-term consequence was that we became poorer, not richer.

By making spending decisions, or choices that looked like the following, the long-term consequences were different.

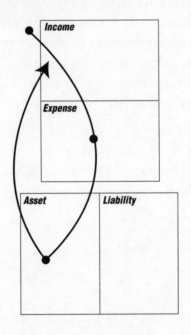

As little boys we could see that making a spending *choice* to invest in assets had this long-term *consequence*. Both Mike and I knew by the age of nine that only we had the power over our financial destiny, not anyone else. We knew if we made lifelong financial choices that looked like the second financial statement, we would be rich whether or not we had a good job or good education. We knew that our financial success was not a function of our academic success.

In his latest book, *The Millionaire Mind*, Thomas Stanley, author of *The Millionaire Next Door*, discusses the point that his research finds no correlation between financial success and academic success. The two are not related. And that is easy to understand. All we need to review is what was discussed earlier, which is the fact that our school system focuses primarily on academic skills and professional skills. What is missing from our school system is the instruction of the skills my rich dad taught me, which are financial skills.

As stated at the beginning of this book, "In the Information Age, education is more important than ever before. And to best prepare your child for the future, sound financial skills are vitally important."

By teaching your children the fundamentals of financial education, which is the financial statement, you give them the power to take control over their financial destiny. They will have that power regardless of what career they choose, how much money they make, or how well they did in school. As my rich dad often said, "Money does not necessarily make you rich. The biggest mistake that most people make is that they think that making more money will make them richer. In most cases, when people make more money, they get deeper in debt. That is why money alone does not make you rich." And that was why he taught Mike and me that with each dollar we spent, we had a choice, and with each choice, there was a long-term consequence.

The Power of Four

Most of us have heard the saying "No man is an island." Or "Two minds are better than one."

While I personally agree with these statements, our educational system tends to disagree with some of the wisdom found behind them. In *Rich Dad's Guide to Investing* I discussed the power of a tetrahedron. The following is a tetrahedron, aka a pyramid:

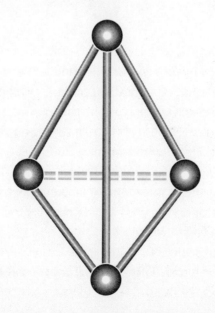

In my study of solid geometry, I found out that the tetrahedron is the minimum solid structure and the most stable of all structures, which is why the pyramids have lasted so long. The key is the magic found in the number 4.

When you look at astrology, you see that there are four main signs: earth, air, water, and fire. If you were to put the four basic groups into a shape, it would look like the tetrahedron:

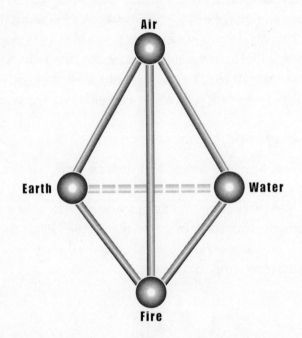

The four basic elements make up the world we know.

Looking at the world of money and business, we find the CASHFLOW Quadrant. Again, the magic number is 4. The four sides are (E) employee, (S) self-employed or small-business owner, (B) big-business owner, and (I) investor. And again, a tetrahedron could be made.

The ancient Greek physician Hippocrates (460–377 B.C.), often called the father of medicine, also used four different personality types to describe different people. He used the terms *choleric, sanguine, phlegmatic,* and *melancholy.*

In the twentieth century Dr. Carl Jung also categorized the four personality types, using the terms *thinker, feeler, intuitor,* and *sensor*.

In the 1950s, Isabel Myers and her mother developed the Myers-Briggs type indicator (MBTI). The MBTI defines sixteen different types of people, which, interestingly enough, is then narrowed down to four main categories: D for dominance; I for influence; S for support; and C for compliance.

Today, many of these personality-type instruments are available, and many companies use these instruments to insure that they place the right person in the right type of job. The point I want to make is the importance of the number 4.

There are several things I found interesting with Kathy Kolbe's work that add further distinctions to this search to discover more about ourselves and what makes us unique. One of the things that Kathy's work distinguishes is why certain children do well in school and why some do not. When you look at the tetrahedron, it is easy to see why so many young people have trouble in school.

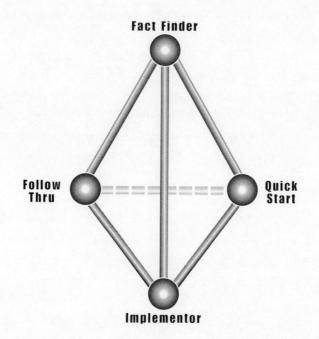

It is easy to see that the current system of education is designed primarily for students who are strong in Fact Finder. The other three categories often struggle through the process. In other words, the world is made up of four different learning types, but the school system recognizes only one.

And the Power of Twelve

Most of us know that there are twelve months in a year and twelve signs of
the zodiac. Throughout humanity's development, the numbers 4 and 12
have reappeared constantly as numbers of significance. When you study
solid geometry, you can understand why this relationship would occur repeatedly. It is unfortunate that our current educational system recognizes
only one learning style and one type of genius. The point being made by this
book is how important it is for parents to be aware of the four learning styles
and the possibility of twelve different geniuses in their child. In other words,
you now have more choices in raising your child and ways of developing
your child's genius. As stated earlier in this book, the word *intelligence*
means the ability to make finer distinctions, and the word *education* is de-
rived from the same root as the word *educe,* which means "to draw out," not
"to put in."

When you look in your young child's eyes, always remember that in your
child there lives a little "geni." It may not be the same one that the school
system looks for, but your child's genius is there nonetheless. And although
the school system may not look for it, it is important for you the parent or
the teacher to look for it. For whenever you look inside a child's eyes and see
his or her genius, this child's genius is there to remind us all that we too have
a geni-in-us. It is this geni in all of us that brings the magic of life to life.

The Most Important Job in the World

My smart dad used to say, "There are two kinds of kids. There are kids who succeed by following the path, and there are kids who hate following the path and feel they must blaze their own trail. Inside each of us lives these two kids."

Don't Touch the Stove

That was my smart dad's way of letting me know that it was okay for me to seek my own path in life as long as I was honorable and used integrity in my search. And there were times I was off the path for a long time. Regardless of how long I was off the path, however, my dad kept the light on and always welcomed me home.

He often did not approve of what I did, and he let me know that he did not approve, but he did not stop me from doing things. He would say, "The only way a child knows what the words *hot stove* mean is by touching a hot stove."

I remember watching him address a PTA meeting one evening, telling his hot stove story. There were about 150 parents in the audience as he said, "The only way we as adults know what a hot stove is, is because we have all touched the stove. We all touched the stove even though we were told not to touch it. And if any of you haven't touched a hot stove yet, I advise you to touch one soon. You haven't lived till you've touched one."

The parents and teachers laughed with that remark. A parent then raised his hand and asked, "Are you saying that we should not discipline our children?"

"No. I did not say that. I am saying that your child will learn by life's experiences. I am saying that the only way a child will know what the words *hot stove* mean is by touching one. If we tell them to not touch the stove, we are being ridiculous. The kid is going to touch the stove. That is how God designed the child to learn. The child learns by doing, making mistakes, and then learning. We as adults, in our attempt to educate our children, tell them not to make mistakes and then punish them for making mistakes. That is a mistake."

I was only about fourteen years old, but I could tell many of the parents and teachers did not like my dad's message. For many of them, avoiding mistakes was a way of life. Another parent raised her hand and said, "So you're trying to say that making mistakes is natural. That making mistakes is how we learn."

"That is what I am saying," my dad said.

"But the school system punishes our children for making mistakes," said the same parent, who had remained standing.

"And that is why I am here tonight," my dad said. "I am here because we as teachers have gotten away from correcting, and we have been too focused on looking for and punishing students for making mistakes. I am afraid the more we punish mistakes rather than teach our kids to correct and learn from their mistakes, the more we miss the point of education. Instead of punishing kids for making mistakes, we need to encourage them to make more. The more mistakes they make and learn from, the smarter they become."

"But you teachers punish as well as fail students who make too many mistakes," said the parent.

"Yes, we do. And that is a flaw in our system, and I am part of that system, and that is why I am here tonight."

My dad went on to explain that a child's natural curiosity is what drives a child to learn. But just as curiosity can kill a cat, so can too much curiosity be destructive to a child. My dad's message that night was that the job of a parent and a teacher was to correct without damaging the child's natural curiosity.

He was then asked, "How do you correct without damaging the child's natural curiosity?"

My dad replied, "I don't have the answer. I believe it is an art as well as a situation-by-situation process, so there may be no one answer." He went on, saying, "I am just here to remind you as parents that we all learned what a hot stove was by touching one. We touched it even though we were told not to touch it. We touched it because we were curious and we wanted to learn something new. I am here representing your child's natural curiosity and desire to learn. All children are born curious, and our job is to protect that curiosity, at the same time doing our best to protect the child. It is important to protect that curiosity because that is how we learn. Destroy that curiosity and we destroy the child's future."

Another parent raised her hand and said, "I am a single parent. My child is out of control right now. He stays out late and refuses to listen to me. He is running with the wrong crowd. What do I do? Do I encourage his curiosity or do I wait for him to go to jail?"

My dad then asked, "How old is your boy?"

"He just turned sixteen," the single mother replied.

My dad shook his head. "As I said, I don't have *the* answer. When it comes to raising children, there is no 'one answer fits all.'" Gently he said, "Maybe the police will have the answer your son is looking for. For your son's sake, I hope they don't."

My dad then went on to tell his story about the two types of kids, the one kid who follows the straight-and-narrow path and the other who needs to create his or her own path. My dad went on to say that all a parent can do is keep the light on and hope the child comes back to the path. He also reminded the parents that many of them had themselves gone off the path. He reminded them that inside each of us is a person who sometimes just wants to find his or her own way. He explained further, saying, "We all believe there is a right way and a wrong way. But sometimes, our own way is the best way for a while." He ended by saying, "And sometimes our path is not our child's path."

Not satisfied with the answer, the young mother again came to her feet and said, "But what if he wanders off in the darkness and never comes back? What do I do then?"

My dad paused and, with eyes that said he understood her concern, quietly said, "Just keep the light on." He then collected his notes and stepped off the stage. Stopping before exiting the silent room, my dad turned and said, "A parent's and teacher's job is to keep the light on. It is the most important job in the world."

You cannot teach a person anything, you can only
help him find it within himself.

— GALILEO

Appendix A
Allowance or No Allowance:
The Age-Old Battle
by Sharon Lechter, Mom

To pay an allowance or not to pay an allowance, the never-ending question. What is a parent to do? There just doesn't seem to be a definitive answer.

Many parents get so lost in determining the "allowance" issue, they forget to teach their children what to do with the money they receive. Whether it is money from an allowance or payment for specific tasks, your children need to learn fiscal responsibility.

Whether or not your child receives an allowance is *not* the magic formula for his or her future financial success. Whether or not your child learns fiscal responsibility *is* the magic formula to his or her future financial success. As we describe in chapter 14, rich dad taught Robert that the right side of the CASHFLOW Quadrant is where fiscal responsibility is found. Great business owners and successful investors have mastered fiscal responsibility and demonstrate it with their continued success.

Allowance
The definition of allowance is "a sum regularly provided for personal or household expenses." While an allowance may be appropriate in many cases, how it is determined and communicated to the children is vitally important. Will the children view the allowance as an "entitlement" or earned compensation for completion of agreed-upon tasks or responsibilities? In a world where the entitlement mentality is an ever-increasing problem with adults, we believe it is very important that parents not train their children to think they are entitled to a certain amount of allowance every week. For instance, consider the difference between these two statements:

"John, since you are twelve now, you are old enough for an allowance. Every Friday I will give you an allowance of $10 to spend however you would like."

"John, you are busy with homework and sports activities every night, and we want to acknowledge your efforts and encourage you with those activities. While you are busy with these activities, you will receive an allowance of $10 per week for spending money."

Pay for Specific Tasks

The debate of paying an allowance versus paying for specific jobs has many facets. We do not want to dictate parenting philosophy but hope to provide alternatives that parents may choose from to fit their own personal parenting style. While paying an allowance can develop the "entitlement" mind-set, "paying for specific jobs" can also have a negative inference in that it creates an employee mentality. "You do this and I will pay you $10." While earning compensation for completion of specific jobs or tasks is an important issue, it is only a component of teaching overall fiscal responsibility.

When All Else Fails, Resort to Bribery

Children need to understand that they need to contribute to the greater good of their family or social group without the expectation of financial reward. Too often parents resort to "bribery" in an attempt to get their children to perform tasks that should be performed by the children for no financial reward at all. I can speak about this with great personal knowledge. When you find yourself resorting to bribery, hear it as a wake-up call. You are giving control over to your child when you try to bribe him or her. You are transferring your parental power into the hands of your child. Many parents whitewash this "bribery" form of parenting by calling it a "reward" system.

A Parental Strategy

Without dictating parenting philosophy, we have developed a parental strategy that may be helpful to you in determining the allowance policy for your family. We suggest that you develop a four-phase program with your children. Most important, we recommend that you communicate this policy openly and consistently with your children.

Phase 1, Personal Responsibility—determine certain duties or tasks that your children need to perform for their own personal health and development. (For example brushing their teeth every morning and night should be expected and communicated as a personal responsibility. Some parents may include making the bed or taking the dinner plate to the sink after dinner.) There should be *no* financial reward for personal responsibility.

Phase 2, Family or Social Responsibility—determine certain duties or tasks that contribute to the family or social environment that do *not* result in financial reward. These are acts that contribute to the greater good of your child's environment. (Setting the table for dinner, reading to a younger sibling, or helping an elderly woman with her groceries are examples of family or social responsibility.) There should be *no* financial reward for family or social responsibility.

Phase 3, Establishing an Allowance or Payment for Specific Tasks—optional, based on a parent's individual beliefs. Determine guidelines that include what general tasks or duties are expected that will result in the "earning" of the allowance.

Endeavor to prevent an "entitlement" attitude from developing in your children. Have the children participate in the determination of tasks expected. You may want your children to "bill" you for their allowance, thus making them more accountable for the underlying expectations. (Washing and cleaning the car once a week could be an expectation that is outside phase 2 for some parents and could be part of a consideration for an allowance each week.) Some children are so busy with athletics and schoolwork that their parents provide them with an allowance to acknowledge their efforts. The important issue here is to openly communicate your expectation of your child's responsibility.

Phase 4, Encouraging Your Child's Entrepreneurial Spirit—encouraging your child to think of ways to earn money. Have them suggest tasks or share stories of how other children have earned money to open their minds to opportunities that present themselves. Encourage them to identify specific "tasks" that need to be done, and establish a set payment for completion of each task. Have them bill you for their work upon completion.

This is where rich dad's philosophy of your job versus your business needs to be communicated. The amount of pay determined for each task is the definition of your child's "job." What your children do with their money is their "business." The earlier in life your children understand the difference between working for others and working for themselves, the better their chances for financial success. Explain to them that what you do during the day (eight to five) is your profession, or your job, but what you do with the money (your paycheck) is your business.

Fiscal Responsibility

Many parents get so lost in determining the "allowance" issue, they forget to teach their children what to do with the money after they receive it. Whether it is money from an allowance, gifts, or payment for specific tasks, your children need to learn fiscal responsibility. Fiscal responsibility is developed only after your child understands financial literacy. Furthermore, we need to battle today's entitlement trend by educating our children about delayed gratification and credit card debt.

Financial Literacy

Teach your children the concepts of assets versus liabilities; the difference between earned, passive, and portfolio income; the importance of passive and portfolio income; and the definition of doodads. Refer to the simple drawings in *Rich Kid Smart Kid* and *Rich Dad Poor Dad* and use them to teach your children. Armed with this type of financial education, your children will be better prepared to develop sound fiscal responsibility.

Delayed Gratification

Fiscal responsibility demonstrates financial literacy as well as an understanding of "delayed gratification," which is discussed in greater detail in *Rich Dad Poor Dad*. One of the benefits of establishing a savings program for your children is that it teaches them the power of this concept of delayed gratification. By setting financial goals with your children and helping them determine a financial plan to achieve those goals, you instill the formula for success. The self-esteem that is built when they achieve those goals is priceless. In today's world of instant gratification, we are robbing our children of the powerful feeling of success that results from achieving a goal. How? By being given something instead of earning it on their own.

For example, your child wants a new bike. Start with the philosophy introduced in *Rich Dad Poor Dad*, where poor dad said, "I can't afford it," but rich dad said, "How can I afford it?" Teach your child to say, "How can I?" instead of, "I can't." Help him or her develop a plan on how to earn the money to buy the bike. Encourage your child to think of ways to earn money. Help assess his or her progress along the way, and make adjustments to the goal as needed. Have your child purchase the bike as the ultimate reward for completion of the plan. Acknowledge your child's effort and ultimate success.

Debt and Credit Cards

Credit cards today are the tools of instant gratification. Unfortunately the end result is delayed trauma, when the bills arrive. A much better message is delivered with a financial goal-setting and delayed gratification exercise similar to the bike story just described.

No matter how we feel about credit cards, they are ever-present in our society today. Our children are bombarded with "Just charge it" messages every day through television, radio, or peers. Parents need to complete the picture for their children by exposing them to the other side of credit cards. Have them watch you pay bills. Explain the multiplying impact of the interest charged on the balance due on the credit cards. Show them that credit limits do exist for each card.

Explain that there are also benefits from using credit cards. Credit cards can greatly assist in record keeping and tracking how you are spending your money. Many people use credit cards wisely, paying off the balance each month so no interest charges are incurred.

Many parents have difficulty with their own credit card debt and are concerned about creating fear in their children if they share too much of their financial situation. The realities of "real life" credit card debt may also be beyond your child's level of comprehension. We have created CASHFLOW for Kids, a patented financial board game, to help parents teach their children financial literacy. The game deals specifically with the "pay cash or charge it" decision-making process. Your children will learn both sides of the credit card world (instant gratification and delayed trauma when the bills arrive) while having fun and using play money. They will be much better prepared to face, and avoid, the perils of credit cards when they become adults.

Part-Time Jobs

Once your child is old enough, it is important for him or her to learn about the responsibility of a job. Let your children take on part-time jobs, if their schoolwork and sports activities allow it. Review their first paycheck with them so they understand that the government takes out its share of income taxes before they get their check.

When I was in high school, my parents required me to save or invest 50 percent of everything I made at my part-time job. It became a habit to immediately deposit 50 percent of my paycheck. I was allowed to spend the other 50 percent any way I pleased. This instilled in me the "pay yourself first" concept at a very early age. By the time I graduated from college I had accumulated over $20,000 in investment assets just from saving 50 percent of my income from part-time jobs as a student.

As a parent I used the same rule with my children when they started part-time jobs. They saw the "pay yourself first" concept in action and came to recognize the long-term benefit it can create. Unfortunately, my oldest son was bombarded by credit cards when he went to college. Unbeknownst to his father and me, he was in deep credit card debt before he knew it.

This is where you see hindsight is twenty-twenty. I felt that the best way to teach my children was through example. My husband and I have several credit cards, which we use regularly, including ones that count toward frequent flyer mileage. Our credit cards serve as great bookkeeping tools for us and help us track where we spend our money. We pay the total amount due each month so we never have to pay any interest on the credit card. Our son, however, was swayed by the lure of low monthly payments. He got instant gratification but found delayed trauma when his credit limit was hit. It took him four years to clean up his credit from that mistake, but he learned a very valuable lesson in the process. Today he pays off his credit cards on a monthly basis. Today he has also learned to pay himself first. Today he is fiscally responsible.

Financial Success

In summary, the age-old question of whether or not to pay your child an allowance can be decided only by you. But ask yourself what the policy you establish related to the allowance is teaching your child. Are you training your child to have:

- an entitlement mind-set?
- an employee mind-set?
- an entrepreneur's mind-set?

Fiscal responsibility combined with entrepreneurial spirit can be a mighty powerful force. Help your children develop both and then sit back and watch them achieve one financial success after another.

Robert's Comment

I agree with Sharon and would like to add one subtle distinction that may further clarify the lesson.

My poor dad focused on how much money he made. That was why he always said, "Get a good education so you can get a high-paying job."

My rich dad focused *not* on how much money he made. Instead he focused on how much money he kept. That was why he said, "How much money you keep is much more important than how much money you make." He also said, "People who focus only on how much money they make *always* work for people who focus on how much money they keep."

Regarding the subject of allowance, it's more important to teach your child to focus on *keeping* money than *making* money. My rich dad would say that each dollar in his asset column was like an employee of his: It worked for him. Once a dollar was in the asset column, it never left the asset column. If he sold an asset, he would use the proceeds to buy another asset. The assets he bought can now be handed down to the next generation.

By developing this philosophy and teaching it to your children, you can help them learn the path to financial independence.

Appendix B

Financial Field Trips: Money Exercises for Parents to Do with Their Children

Sharon Lechter, C.P.A. and Mom

These exercises may assist you in teaching your children about money. By using real-life experiences in teaching your children, you automatically show the practical application of the lessons. For instance, we have an exercise called "Financial Field Trip to a Bank." After completing that field trip, your child will remember the lessons learned during the visit every time he or she passes the bank. It is often referred to as "experiential learning," and it can be a powerful tool in teaching your children about money.

The financial field trips were developed as dialogues or scripts for you to use to teach basic financial concepts. There are no right or wrong answers. These are simple exercises and observations intended to help you create a dialogue with your child about specific financial issues and broaden your child's awareness of the financial world we live in. But it is also an opportunity to have fun with your children.

Financial Field Trip to the Dining Room Table

A. PAY YOUR MONTHLY BILLS

Have your children sit with you while you pay your monthly bills. Let them look at each bill and explain what each covers. This will give them a better understanding of life. You do not need to provide total disclosure of your finances to your children, but start with a simple awareness of the basics.

1. Pay Yourself First

Start by paying yourself first, even if it is only a few dollars. After watching you pay yourself first over and over, your child will most likely follow your example when he or she starts receiving money.

2. Pay Household Expenses

Explain the utilities bills and let your child review the bills. It will give your child a better appreciation of how your money is spent. Understanding that you pay separately for lights, water, gas, trash pickup, and other household maintenance expenses will open your child's mind to the idea of how many businesses are needed to support your lifestyle. (You may discover an additional benefit from this exercise—we have heard from parents that their children actually start turning off lights more often and taking shorter showers after this lesson.)

3. Pay Your Mortgage Payment

Explain your mortgage payment to your child in very simple terms. Explain how the bank helps you buy your house by loaning you most of the money and then you agree to pay the bank back over time. In order to be able to do this, you agree to pay the bank a certain fee, or interest, until the total amount is paid back to the bank. Show your child your mortgage payment and how each payment includes payment for interest and payment against the principal amount due on your home.

4. Pay Your Credit Card Bills

Explain your credit card bill to your child. This may be a difficult exercise for you if you have a large amount of credit card debt. Nevertheless, it is important for your child to understand the negative as well as the positive side of credit card use. Here are some simple definitions.

Credit Cards—"Credit cards are issued by banks or other financial institutions or stores to you so you can buy goods or services. You receive the goods or services immediately, and the bank or store pays for the goods or services for you."

Statement—"Each month they will send you a statement that shows how much you spent that month (how much they paid for you) and the date you must pay the total amount due in order to avoid interest charges and late payment fees."

Interest on Credit Cards—"If the amount due on your statement is not paid by the due date, interest will be charged on the outstanding balance, and at a much higher rate than other types of borrowing."

Minimum Payment Due—Many banks and stores allow you to pay a "minimum payment" instead of the total amount due. Interest is then charged on the balance still due. In fact, they discourage you from paying off your entire bank card bill at once. They feel that since they went to all the trouble to establish this credit for you, you should stretch out your payments so they can earn a lot more interest.

Important: It is this single feature of credit cards that has created the tremendous debt many people face today. How does this happen?

- One month you are a little short of cash, so you pay the minimum payment due on your credit card. The card balance continues to grow as you continue to charge new items.
- Paying the minimum payment was so easy that you do it again the next month and the next. But you also keep charging.
- Since you are paying the minimum payments, your credit rating is still good, and other companies send you new credit cards. Soon you have five different credit cards in your wallet (according to CardWeb most households in America have between five and six different bank credit cards).
- You continue to pay the minimum payments on the five cards, therefore keeping a good credit rating, but now you have a total balance due on all the cards that is staggering.
- One day you realize that you are paying out a lot of money in minimum payments but your total balance due keeps increasing every month.
- It is only when you find you cannot make even the minimum monthly payments that your credit rating suffers.
- Then you find that you have spent the maximum on the credit limits of your cards, you cannot get any new cards because your credit is not so good anymore since you have missed a few payments, and you can still barely pay the minimums due on your current cards.

This is unfortunately the vicious circle many people find themselves in today. While this may sound depressing and *not* something you want to burden your child with, it is best to start understanding this issue at an early age. How can you explain this complex subject to children? We have developed the game CASHFLOW for Kids and included this very issue in the game. Your children will learn they have a choice—pay cash or charge it— and that each choice has a consequence. Initially they usually choose to charge an item, since that is what they are accustomed to hearing at home. The consequence of charging is that they must increase the expenses they have to pay each and every payday. They soon learn that it is better to pay a little more cash up front than to increase their expenses indefinitely.

In our book *Rich Dad's CASHFLOW Quadrant* we include a section on how to get out of debt. It shares a formula for paying off debt in five to seven years.

5. Encourage Your Child's Curiosity
Encourage your child to ask questions, and answer the questions as honestly as you can. If your child asks a question that you cannot answer, seek someone who can answer the question, and learn with your child.

6. Record Keeping
Have your child help you file your bills after they are paid. Good record keeping is a learned habit.

B. DEVELOP A BUDGET FOR A WEEK OF MEALS
Now that your child has a better understanding of paying the bills, it is time to introduce the concept of budgeting. Rather than disclosing your full financial picture to your child, start small. For the sake of this exercise, let's say that you have your child plan your menus for a week. The task will be to feed your family for a week within a set budget. Your child needs to make the family happy as well as meet the financial budget. It is important that you allow your child to develop the menu as well as purchase the food. You may assist in the preparation, since cooking is not part of the lesson.

1. Set a Budget
Determine how much you usually spend for a week of food for the family. For convenience, you may want to include only breakfast and dinner. For the purposes of this exercise, we will use $200 for a family of four for seven breakfasts and seven dinners.

2. Have Your Children Plan the Meals on a Chart
For each meal have your children record what the menu will be. You may want to visit the grocery store to help them understand the costs of certain items.

3. Have Your Children Prepare a Shopping List

After they have completed the menus for the week, have your children prepare a shopping list so that they will know what food needs to be purchased.

4. Have Your Child Shop for the Food

At the grocery store watch your children as they review items for purchase. You may want to suggest that they take a calculator along to keep a total of the amount that is being spent. It is important that they keep within the budget set.

5. Have Your Children Record What They Spent for Each Meal on the Chart

You may want your children to record the amounts on the chart as they shop. But they also need to fill in the chart at home from the receipt, as there may be taxes that need to be included in the meal costs.

6. Prepare the Meals

Depending on your children, you may need to assist in the preparation of the meals.

7. Analyze Results

First, check to make sure that the family was satisfied with their meals. This is a very important part of the exercise, as feedback comes with everything you do in life.

Next, have your children compare their budgeted amounts to the actual amounts spent for each meal. For each meal determine the amount spent over- or underbudget, then determine the total over- or underbudget spent for the entire week.

8. Review the Process

This is the most important part of the exercise. Allow your children to share their experiences with you. What did they learn? Listen to their observations. You may find a growing appreciation from your children for the role you play as a parent.

9. Apply the Process

Now discuss with your children how you need to budget for all expenses. If you prefer not to disclose your specific financial information, create a sample budget. Discuss the need to budget what income is coming into the household and how it will be spent for all the expenses that need to be paid.

If they have completed the "Pay Your Bills" exercise, your children will have a greater understanding of what items need to be planned for.

Just as they had to plan the menus within a budget, you must learn to plan your life within a budget.

INCOME
   Paychecks
   Rent from rental properties
   Interest or dividends
   Other income

Less

INVESTMENTS
Budget a regular amount to be invested. This is the "pay yourself first" category.

Less

EXPENSES
   Taxes
   Mortgage payment or rent
   Food
   Clothing
   Insurance
   Gas
   Utilities
   Entertainment
   Interest on credit cards or other debt

AMOUNT LEFT AFTER ALL INVESTMENTS AND EXPENSES

Now, calculate the percentage of your income that you invest (keep as assets) and the percentage of your income that you spend. Are there ways for you to increase the percentage of income that you invest (keep as assets) and reduce the percentage of income that you spend?

If you can increase your assets and therefore increase your income from assets, more of your money will work for you. Your paycheck represents you working for money.

10. Follow-Up

After a week or so has gone by, discuss the exercise with your children again. What do they remember from the experience? Would they like to repeat the exercise? Do they understand the long-term impact of investing, buying assets, or paying yourself first?

Financial Field Trip to the Bank

Initial exercise: Take your child to the bank. Point out the tellers and the customer assistance people sitting at the desks. If the bank is not busy, ask the teller and customer assistance people to explain what they do. Have your child ask how much interest the bank pays on money deposited in the bank. Include savings accounts, certificates of deposit, and other bank instruments available through the bank. Have your child take notes.

Then have your child ask how much interest the bank would charge for a car loan, house loan, or consumer credit loan. If the bank issues its own credit card, have your child ask for the interest rate on the card's outstanding balances.

Then leave the bank and go somewhere quiet to complete the following table:

Bank pays interest to you at:		You pay interest to the bank at:	
Savings Account	____ %	Car Loan	____ %
Money Market Account	____ %	Consumer Loan	____ %
CD	____ %	Credit Card	____ %
_____	____ %	Mortgage	____ %
_____	____ %	_____	____ %

Ask your child to review the table and then ask the following questions:

1. Which column shows the higher rates?   _____
2. Complete the following sentence:

"So the bank pays me interest of __(savings account rate)__ on my savings account, but when I want to borrow money for a car I will have to pay the bank __(car loan rate)__ for the money I borrow. I will be paying __(car loan rate minus savings account rate)__ more than I am receiving."

3. Now review chapter 10, "Why Savers Are Losers," with your child. Explain that it is always wise to have some money in a savings account and that is how we start learning good money habits. In fact, it is recommended that people keep enough cash in an account to cover from three to twelve months' worth of expenses in case of an emergency. We are not recommending that you rush out and withdraw the money you have in savings accounts. We are saying that savings accounts are not good investment vehicles.

4. In summary, ask your child, "If you had the following situation, would you be making money or losing money?"

You have $10,000 in a savings account earning 4% interest.

How much interest would you be earning per year?

$$(\$10,000 \times 4\%) \qquad = \qquad \underline{\hspace{2cm}} \text{ (A)}$$

and

You have a $10,000 consumer loan on which you make only interest payments for the first year at a rate of 9%.

How much interest would you be paying?

$$(\$10,000 \times 9\%) \qquad = \qquad \underline{\hspace{2cm}} \text{ (B)}$$

now

After one year, are you making money or losing money?

$$(A) \text{ minus } (B) \qquad = \qquad \underline{\hspace{2cm}} \text{ (C)}$$

After ten years, how much money have you made or lost?

$$(C) \times 10 \text{ years} \qquad = \qquad \underline{\hspace{2cm}} \text{ (D)}$$

ANSWER KEY:

A = $400; the bank will have paid you $400 interest on your savings.

B = $900; you will have paid the bank $900 interest on your loan.

C = losing $500 (or −$500), you will have lost $500.

D = losing $5,000; after ten years you will have lost $5,000. You will still have $10,000 in savings and you will still have a consumer loan of $10,000, but you will have paid $5,000 more in interest than you received over the ten years.

ADVANCED EXERCISE

Review the facts above, but let's add the impact of income taxes to the situation. The government taxes you on interest income but does not allow you a deduction for the interest you pay.

Start with the net amount you calculated for (C) above; remember, it may be a negative number.

(C)   =   _____

Take the amount of your interest earnings from (A)

(A)   =   _____

Multiply it by an income tax of 50% (tax rate will vary based on your total income).

(A) × 50%   =   _____ (E)

Now subtract (E) from (C) to determine the amount of money you made or lost after taxes.

(C) minus (E)   =   _____ (F)

After ten years, how much money have you made or lost?

(F) × 10 years   =   _____ (G)

ANSWER KEY:

E = $200; you will pay $200 in income tax on the interest you earned from the bank, assuming a tax rate of 50%.

F = losing $700 (or −$700); after the income tax effect, you will be losing $700 per year, or paying $700 more in interest on your consumer loan than you receive on your savings, after taxes.

G = losing $7,000; after ten years you will have lost $7,000. You will still have $10,000 in savings and you will still have a consumer loan of $10,000, but you will have paid $7,000 more in interest and taxes than you received over the ten years in interest on your savings.

IN REVIEW:

A quick review would show that the example above would *not* be a wise investment plan. Unfortunately, many people follow this exact plan without realizing it. Here are some ideas to improve this investment plan.

Easy. Use your $10,000 savings to pay off your $10,000 consumer loan. This way you won't lose any more money. You will earn no interest and pay no interest.

Average. Find an asset to buy with the $10,000 in your savings account that will generate enough cash flow to pay for your consumer loan. You will need to find an investment that generates a cash flow of $900 per year. Another way to look at this is that your cash ($900) on cash ($10,000) return is 9 percent ($900 divided by $10,000). Understanding cash on cash return is essential for any investor. This way your asset pays for your liability, the consumer loan. (The impact of income taxes is not included in this example since the income tax applicable to the asset you buy may vary.)

Complex. Buy the asset with the cash on cash return of at least 9 percent. Then determine how you can convert the $10,000 consumer loan into a business loan. This would make the $900 of interest paid on the loan deductible for income tax purposes. This idea is covered in more depth in *Rich Dad's Guide to Investing.*

   Please remember that this exercise is intended to demonstrate the difference between saving and borrowing as well as the difference between saving and investing. Additional components have been added to introduce higher levels of complexity. Start explaining the initial example to your child and continue only if your child is interested and shows a true understanding of the initial concepts.

Financial Field Trip to the Grocery Store

The best way for your children to learn is through experience. From a very early age, you can start talking to your children about money. This exercise can be done prior to the budgeting exercise to assist your children in their shopping efforts when planning their family's meals for a week.

   When you go to the grocery store, you are constantly making decisions related to quality and pricing. Instead of talking to yourself silently, talk to your kids about the process. I often see people shove a toy or electronic game in their children's faces to keep them quiet. Engage them in the process. Show them how the stores provide price per unit comparisons, and let them tell you which can of beans is the better bargain.

It may be equally important for you to explain why even though one can is less expensive you choose to buy a more expensive can. The quality of the beans may justify the difference in price. You may want to buy both cans so you can show the difference to your child at home.

Let your children pay and count out the money and the change they receive. The concept of value and exchange is very important for your children to learn.

Financial Field Trip to the Car or Appliance Dealer

If you are going to buy a car or major appliance, take your child with you.

Discuss the decision of paying cash or financing the purchase. If you finance the purchase, make sure you tell your child that you must now include the new payment in your monthly budget.

By sitting through the financing process, your child can learn about borrowing and the need for good credit at an early age. Have the loan officer explain to your child what good credit is and how important it is. Generally the loan officer will be happy to share stories about potential customers who have failed to qualify for credit as well as other customers who have had stellar credit ratings.

It is through this process that your child will start to understand how your personal financial statement and good credit are your report cards in real life.

This can be a brief visit, but just the exposure to the situation broadens your child's mind and awareness about money and borrowing.

Financial Field Trip to a Stockbrokerage Firm

After you have visited the bank, take your child to a stockbrokerage firm. Ask the stockbroker to explain his or her job to your child. (You may want to prearrange this visit so that you find a willing broker.)

If your child is a teenager, you may want to open an account at the firm. Have your child assist in the paperwork process. With your and the stockbroker's assistance, allow your child to select the investments to fund his or her account.

Have the broker explain the different types of investments and their relative rates of return to your child. Most adults do not understand the differences among corporate stocks or how mutual funds operate. Your child will have a terrific financial head start by understanding the basics of these investment tools.

Unless your child is grasping every concept the stockbroker is presenting, it may be premature to discuss concepts like P/E ratios and other aspects of fundamental and technical analysis. Further discussion on these topics can be found in *Rich Dad's Guide to Investing.*

Some parents have opened accounts for their children with the on-line trading firms. The choice is yours. In the earlier stages, however, it may be beneficial to have a stockbroker your child can meet with face-to-face. Your child will establish a relationship and be more at ease asking questions about what he or she may not understand.

Teach your child how to read the financial pages of your local paper. If you are not comfortable with this either, have the stockbroker teach both of you.

Always start small. Do not allow your child to have investing authority over large amounts of money. This process is suggested for educating your child about the world of money and the power of money. Access to too much money could allow the power of money to take control of your child and create a monster. It is better to start small and learn by doing. It is much easier to recover from a small mistake than a big one when it involves money.

Financial Field Trip to McDonald's
It shouldn't be too difficult to take your child to McDonald's. This time, however, plan enough time to include the following exercise:

As you drive up to McDonald's, point out the following to your child:

- "Someone owns the land underneath the McDonald's, and they get paid rent for letting the McDonald's be on their land. The owner of the land doesn't even need to be here. They just get paid rent every month."
- "The same person may also own the building and get paid rent for it."
- "Someone owns the company that makes the golden arches for McDonald's. Can you imagine a factory filled with golden arches? Maybe that's how McDonald's knows that all the arches will be the same color and look the same."

After you order your food and have eaten, point out the following to your child:

- "See the clerk behind the counter? She is an employee of McDonald's. She gets paid so much per hour to show up and do that job. As long as she shows up when she is supposed to and does the job she is trained for, she will get paid. When she gets her paycheck, she will be paid only for the time she has physically been here working."
- **Then ask:** "What other employees do you see?"
- **Then summarize:** "So it takes quite a few employees to make this McDonald's operate so it can serve its customers well."

Look around the restaurant and point out some of the following observations:

- "See the cups they use and the paper they wrap the hamburgers in? Those are made specifically for McDonald's by other companies. Those companies have to make sure the cups and papers look exactly how McDonald's ordered them, or they may not get paid for them. Someone, also an employee, probably at a corporate office for McDonald's located somewhere else, is responsible for ordering those items and making sure they are delivered to each McDonald's before they run out of their current supplies."
- **Then ask:** "What other items do you see that might be made for McDonald's by other companies?"
- **Then summarize:** "So it takes a lot of different companies with different areas of manufacturing expertise to supply products to McDonald's to make sure it operates efficiently."

- "See the man working on the soda machine (or fixing the lights, or washing the windows)? He is probably self-employed or owns his own small business. The manager of this McDonald's hires him to do a specific task, like fix the machine or wash the windows. It would be too expensive for the store manager to hire an employee with those skills full-time, since he needs his help only when something breaks or the windows get dirty."
- **Then ask:** "What other jobs or tasks do you see that the manager might hire an outside company to do instead of hiring an employee?"
- **Then summarize:** "So it takes a lot of different types of services from outside companies to make sure this restaurant operates efficiently. It

is an opportunity for small businesses and self-employed people with particular areas of expertise to work for McDonald's and help it support its operations."

- "Have you ever noticed that every McDonald's is similar? The food is always the same. The employees are different but usually say the same things. The ketchup is always the same. The reason this happens is that McDonald's has developed something called 'systems.' Every store has policies and procedures that it must follow if it wants to continue being a McDonald's. These policies and procedures describe the systems that must be followed. They have systems that cover all aspects of their operations. There is a system for how they fill or clean the milk shake machine or the French fry fryer."
- **Then ask:** "What other systems can you identify?"
- **Then summarize:** "The systems in place in this McDonald's and every other McDonald's in the world are what make it such a successful franchise. Wouldn't it be great to own these systems or help create systems for your own business that could be this successful?"

- "Have you noticed that I have never talked about the owner of McDonald's being here? The owner has hired a manager. The manager is responsible for the day-to-day operations of the restaurant. The manager hires and fires the employees, makes sure sufficient supplies have been ordered, makes sure the customers are happy, and makes sure everything is running smoothly. The manager contacts the owner only to report the restaurant's progress on a regular basis, maybe on a weekly phone call or at a monthly meeting (held at the owner's office or home). The owner wants these phone calls or meetings so he or she will know how much money the McDonald's is making for him or her. The McDonald's is an asset owned by the owner. He or she owns the systems that make the restaurant work. In fact, the owner could be over on that golf course right now, playing golf."
- **Then ask:** "How much time do you think the owner spends at this McDonald's?"
- **Then summarize:** "So the owner has his or her asset working for him or her instead of the owner working for money! Because this as-

set is generating cash flow for the owner, the owner is free to spend his or her time on building more assets, or on the golf course."

Financial Field Trip to an Apartment Building

Find an apartment house near where you live, preferably one that your child will recognize or may see often in your travels. Park your car in front of the apartment building and make the following observations:

- "This is an apartment building. The people who live here are called 'tenants,' and they pay something called 'rent.' The rent allows them to live in one of the apartments, but they don't own the apartment. It is as if they are paying to borrow the apartment. Usually their rent also allows them to use the common areas like the pool, laundry room, or front yard."
- **Then ask:** "How many units do you think there are in this complex?"
- **Then summarize:** "So all of these tenants are paying rent to use these apartments to the owner of the apartment building."

- "So the owner of the apartment building owns all of the units. Usually the owner has also borrowed money, called a 'mortgage,' to buy the building and has to pay the bank each month an amount of interest and an amount of the borrowed money."
- **Then ask:** "If there are __ units and each tenant is paying $1,000 rent per month, then the owner of the apartment building is making a lot of money from these units."
- **Then summarize:** "So if the owner collects more rent each month than the amount he has to pay to the bank, he will have a positive cash flow."

- "But there are other expenses, like yardwork, maintaining the pool, or painting the building, that the owner also has to pay to keep the apartments in good shape for the tenants."
- **Then ask:** "Can you think of some other expenses the owner might have to pay?"
- **Then summarize:** "So the owner needs to collect enough rent each month to make sure the income (rent) from the apartments is more than the expenses to own the building and keep it maintained."

- "In most cases the owner of the apartment building does not live in one of the apartments in the building. So the owner needs a system of how to charge and collect rent, and also a system to notify the tenants of any changes to the property."
- **Then ask:** "What other systems do you think the owner needs to make the apartments successful?" (For example, a way for the tenants to notify the owner of problems with their apartments and a way to deposit money and pay the bills related to the apartment.)
- **Then summarize:** "So this is similar to McDonald's in that it needs systems to make it run efficiently and successfully. This apartment complex is really just another business."

- "You may not ever see the owner of the apartment building around here since he or she does not live here. There may be a property manager who handles all the rent, maintenance, and tenant issues. Sometimes the property manager may live on the property, but not all the time."
- **Then ask:** "So if the owner is never around and the property owner coordinates everything, is this similar to the owner of McDonald's?"
- **Then summarize:** "Once again, the owner of the apartment building owns an asset. He or she also owns the system, usually coordinated by the property manager, who makes sure the apartments are run efficiently and smoothly. The property manager reports to the owner on a regular basis so the owner knows how much money the asset is putting into his or her pocket. The owner has his or her asset working for him or her, rather than the owner working for money."

In summary, your child will see the apartment building in an entirely new light after this visit. Also, if you have chosen an apartment building near your home, every time your child passes it, he or she will be reminded of the business of owning an apartment complex.

You can also explain that there are many people who own rental single-family homes and office buildings as investments to which this analysis can also apply. The apartment complex example was used because of its simplicity and familiarity to children. The important concept to be learned is the power of money. You want your money working for you instead of you working for money.

About the Authors

Robert T. Kiyosaki

Born and raised in Hawaii, Robert Kiyosaki is a fourth-generation Japanese-American. After graduating from college in New York, Robert joined the Marine Corps and went to Vietnam as an officer and helicopter gunship pilot.

Returning from war, Robert went to work for the Xerox Corporation and in 1977 started a company that brought the first nylon Velcro surfer wallets to market. In 1985 he founded an international education company that taught business and investing to tens of thousands of students throughout the world.

In 1994 Robert sold his business and retired at the age of 47. During his short-lived retirement, Robert wrote *Rich Dad Poor Dad.* Soon afterward he wrote *Rich Dad's Cashflow Quadrant* and *Rich Dad's Guide to Investing.* All three books are currently on the best-seller lists of the *Wall Street Journal, Business Week, New York Times, E-Trade.com,* and other distinguished lists. Robert also created his educational board game CASHFLOW to teach individuals the same financial strategies his rich dad spent years teaching him . . . the same financial strategies that allowed Robert to retire at the age of 47.

Robert is often heard saying, "We go to school to learn to work hard for money. I write books and create products that teach people how to have money work hard for them . . . so they can enjoy the luxuries of this great world we live in."

Sharon L. Lechter

Wife and mother of three, C.P.A. and business owner, Sharon Lechter has dedicated her professional efforts to the field of education.

She graduated with honors from Florida State University with a degree in accounting. She joined the ranks of what was then one of the big eight accounting firms and went on to hold management positions with companies in the computer, insurance, and publishing industries, all while maintaining her professional credentials as a C.P.A.

As her own children grew, she was keenly involved in their education. She became a vocal activist in the areas of mathematics, computers, reading, and writing education.

So she was delighted to join forces with the inventor of the first electronic "talking book" and help expand the electronic book industry to a multimillion-dollar international market. Today she remains a pioneer in developing new technologies to bring education back into children's lives.

"Our current educational system has not been able to keep pace with the global and technological changes in the world today. We must teach our young people the skills, both scholastic and financial, that they will need to not only survive but to flourish in the world they face."

How To Give Your Child A Financial Head Start In Life For Less Than $100.00

I recently received this letter from a fellow accountant. It best states why I think our educational game is important for your child's future.

Sharon Lechter, C.P.A. and Mom

"I don't want my child to make the same mistakes I've made. I want my child to learn to responsibly manage his money early in life...before he develops the bad habits I developed...even though I am an accountant. I don't want my child to be 40 years old and deeply in debt. I want my child to be financially literate before he enters high school. I want him to know the differences between assets and liabilities before financially unsophisticated salespeople try to teach him what they think assets and liabilities are. That is why I love your CASHFLOW for Kids game. My son loves the game so we play it regularly. We have fun and my son is getting a financial head start in life. Thank you for developing such a fabulous teaching tool. Every parent should know about CASHFLOW for Kids."

Chuck Kinsley
Tax Accountant
Scottsdale, AZ

To order your own CASHFLOW for Kids game, or for more information, visit our Web site at www.richdad.com. For less than $100, you can give your child a priceless financial head start in life. Of course if you are not satisfied or your child does not find the game fun to play, there is a 90-day money back guarantee.

RichDad.com

CASHFLOW® TECHNOLOGIES, INC.
480.998.6971 • 800.308.3585 • f : 480.348.1349
4330 N. CIVIC CENTER PLAZA, SUITE 101 • SCOTTSDALE, ARIZONA • USA 85251

From an Expert

As a mathematics professor in the College of Education at Arizona State University West and as the principal investigator for a $2 million grant from the National Science Foundation to promote mathematics learning in the primary grades, I send this letter in support of the game CASHFLOW for Kids.

This game was beneficial for my children because I could immediately see an improvement in their mathematics knowledge and their understanding of money. The game is self-rewarding and my children (brothers) wanted to play it again after they finished playing the very first time. In their second game they made their decisions faster and their decisions were more strategically planned than in the first round.

As a parent, I was pleased to observe the money attitudes of my children as they played the game. They learned from the choices they made, accelerating their understanding in future games. CASHFLOW for Kids is a great learning tool for all children.

I thank you for a game that simplifies the complex subjects of mathematics and money so that all children can participate in the game and grow in knowledge as they play.

— Yolanda De La Cruz
Ph.D., University of California at Berkeley
Professor of Mathematics, College of Education
Arizona State University West

As an educational psychologist with over 3 decades of experience in teaching, and researching methods of effective teaching and learning, I have become increasingly alarmed at the failure of our public schools. I share Robert Kiyosaki's and Sharon Lechter's concerns about the new demands that the Information Age places on all of us, especially our children. Because schools cannot teach our children everything, it becomes even more important for the family and community to be aware of meaningful and beneficial methods that encourage our children to learn.

The ideas presented in this book and the game CASHFLOW for Kids are based on tried-and-true principles of learning that have been shown to accelerate and stimulate children's learning. CASHFLOW for Kids teaches not only vital financial skills but also vital human interaction skills.

—Ann Nevin
Ph.D. in Educational Psychology

Hello, my name is Tim. I am 15 years old and I am a great fan of Robert. I play CASHFLOW 101 every day. (I have gotten to the point where I can get out of the rat race before I go around the board.) I have read *Rich Dad Poor Dad, CASHFLOW Quadrant,* and am in the middle of *Rich Dad's Guide to Investing.* All of my friends think I am wasting my time, but I believe these years of my life will be the turning point of my life. I used to be into drugs, and getting in trouble with the law, and I was just a bad kid, until I met my uncle. He introduced me to Robert's books and in 5 months I am now helping him start his business and buying houses for him to invest in real estate. I am no longer into anything illegal and I am passing school now. I owe it all to Robert. So let him know he has helped me when no one else could—he gave me a will to live and made me believe I can be something in life. May be hard to understand, but it's true. Thank you.

—Tim, age 15

CASHFLOW for Kids has allowed us to sit around the table with our children and discuss money matters and teach them lessons they can use for the rest of their lives.

—Stacy and Michelle Tetschner

Please visit our Web site,
www.richdad.com
to review:

- Additional Information About Our Financial Education Products
- Frequently Asked Questions (FAQs) About Our Products
- Cashflow Technologies, Inc.'s Events and Robert Kiyosaki's Appearances and Interviews

Thank You

To Order Books Visit: www.twbookmark.com

North America/South America/Europe/Africa:
CASHFLOW™ Technologies, Inc.
4330 N. Civic Center Plaza, Suite 101
Scottsdale, Arizona 85251
USA
(800) 308-3585 or (480) 998-6971
Fax: (480) 348-1349
e-mail: info@richdad.com

Australia/New Zealand:
CASHFLOW™ Education Australia
Reply Paid AAA401 *(no stamp required)*
PO Box 1126
Crows Nest, NSW 1585, Australia
Tel: 1 (800) 308 358 or (61) 2 9923 1699
Fax: 1 (800) 676 992 or (61) 2 9923 1799
e-mail: info@cashfloweducation.com.au

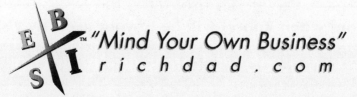

"Mind Your Own Business"
richdad.com

Let Robert Kiyosaki teach you how to profit in both good times and bad.

- Robert Kiyosaki Live! 2001 -

"My rich dad taught me the secrets to investing so that no matter what the market and economic cycles did, I would profit.

"I would like to teach you these fundamentals of investing at my upcoming seminar tour."

—Robert Kiyosaki, best-selling author, *Rich Dad Poor Dad*

Now you can experience Robert Kiyosaki live during his 2001 seminar tours across North America.

At these events Robert will share the secrets that his rich dad taught him about the fundamentals of investing.

Robert Kiyosaki's message is clear: Take responsibility for your finances or take orders all your life. You're either a master of money or a slave to it.

Find out when Robert will be in your area, by visiting:

www.robert-kiyosaki-live.com